PRA

THE VALUE FLYWHEEL EFFECT

"*The Value Flywheel Effect* is a timely and hugely valuable book providing a set of principles and ways of working to navigate and exploit the fast-changing technology and business landscape. Without sense-making capabilities, organizations are increasingly struggling to act effectively in the modern disruptive technology context, so much so that the ideas in *The Value Flywheel Effect* amount to a kind of 'survival handbook' for the next decade or two. *The Value Flywheel Effect* is essential reading for any leader or practitioner who wants to help their organization to survive and thrive."

—**Matthew Skelton**, Co-Author of *Team Topologies: Organizing Business and Technology Teams for Fast Flow*

"I'm delighted to see that David, Mark, and Michael have taken the time and considerable trouble to explain how they architected and delivered serverless innovation at Liberty Mutual. Why? Because change is the only constant, and the pace of technology innovation is accelerating this change. As Jon F. Kennedy said 'those that look only to the past or the present are certain to miss the future'. This book is required reading if you want to leverage serverless technology."

—**Dr. Jacqui Taylor**, CEO and Co-Founder, FlyingBinary, and #15 Most Influential UK Technologist

"The future for company creation and innovation relies on speed, scalability, and sustainability. To nurture thriving products, organizations, and cultures, you need to understand the landscape you're competing in, along with the path to choose to succeed. Packed with real-world examples, case studies, and practical tools applied to complex domains, *The Value Flywheel Effect* is required reading to plot your future and the business you want to be."

—**Barry O'Reilly**, Co-Founder Nobody Studios, Author of *Unlearn* and *Lean Enterprise*

"Required reading for every level of an organization adopting modern cloud, and grounded in unparalleled lived experience of transformation. I'm sure I'll be referencing this for years."

—**Ben Ellerby**, Founder, Aleios, and AWS Serverless Hero

"The journey to the cloud is one of leadership and change management rather than purely a technical pathway. *The Value Flywheel Effect* is a great foundation for any organization on a modern cloud journey. Based on how it's applied in the real world, to real problems, there are great insights into how to navigate waves of change."

—**Seamus Cushley**, VP Product Development, Bazaarvoice

"Serverless architecture combined with clarity of purpose is a lethal combination for winning in today's competitive landscape. *The Value Flywheel Effect* provides powerful insights on how you can leverage these modern practices to navigate an enterprise cloud transformation and accelerate the delivery of value."

—**Drew Firment**, SVP, A Cloud Guru

"*The Value Flywheel Effect* shares a surprising collection of leadership and transformation practices that are sure to help you stir up the right kind of trouble, no matter where you are in the organization. Also an excellent reference for your Wardley Mapping practice, with helpful guidance, plenty of examples, and new things to try as well!"

—**Ben Mosior**, LearnWardleyMapping.com

the Value Flywheel Effect

POWER THE FUTURE AND
ACCELERATE YOUR ORGANIZATION
TO THE MODERN CLOUD

the Value Flywheel Effect

DAVID ANDERSON
with Mark McCann & Michael O'Reilly

Forewords by Adrian Cockcroft *and* Simon Wardley

IT Revolution
Portland, Oregon

25 NW 23rd Pl, Suite 6314
Portland, OR 97210

First Edition

Printed in the United States of America
27 26 25 24 23 22   1 2 3 4 5 6 7 8 9 10

Cover and book design by Devon Smith/D. Smith Creative, LLC

Library of Congress Control Number: 2022939507

ISBN: 9781950508570
eBook ISBN: 9781950508587
Web PDF ISBN: 9781950508594
Audio: 9781950508600

For information about special discounts for bulk purchases or for information on booking authors for an event, please visit our website at ITRevolution.com.

THE VALUE FLYWHEEL EFFECT

MIX
Paper from
responsible sources
FSC® C011935

To my partner, Treasa, my children, Sarah & Thomas, and all my family for all the love and support. Thanks to all the engineers for taking the time to "see what you think."
—**Dave**

To Mairead, Aoife, and my immediate family for the love and support, and my inspirational colleagues from whom I am always learning. I am eternally grateful.
—**Michael**

To my amazing wife, Gillian, and my awesome kids, Isabella and Lucy. Thanks for all the love, support, and inspiration.
—**Mark**

CONTENTS

PART IV: PHASE THREE: NEXT BEST ACTION

PART V: PHASE FOUR: LONG-TERM VALUE

LIST OF TABLES & FIGURES

FOREWORD
BY ADRIAN COCKCROFT

Back in 2010, I gave my first public presentation trying to explain what Netflix was doing, how we were moving to the cloud using open source, the distributed architecture later known as microservices, chaos testing, and how developers were on-call operating the service, which became one of the flavors of DevOps. The reaction was a mixture of bafflement, a general opinion that we were a weird "unicorn" that no one else could copy, and that we would soon be back in our datacenter running enterprise licensed products when we gave up trying to make it work.

However, there were a few people who were more curious and excited, and there were a lot of discussions on Twitter with a group known as the #clouderati. I met Simon Wardley in that group and explained in detail to him, as part of his research, what we were doing. In return, he explained his mapping techniques to me. These maps helped me understand that even though Netflix wasn't using maps, it did have excellent situational awareness, an appropriate use of doctrine, a systems-thinking approach, and was well aligned with many of the best practices that Simon described.

In the last twelve years, as the ideas moved from crazy to mainstream, a big part of my job has been to try to explain and apply the ideas developed at Netflix and Amazon to other organizations and applications, big and small. This book is the best distillation of how to do that that I've encountered. This book uses Wardley Mapping to take today's best ideas and make sense of when to use what doctrine or technique in which situation.

The ideas we developed at Netflix were synthesized from what came before. Many of us had decades of experience to draw from and were familiar with Frederick Brooks's *The Mythical Man-Month* and Conway's Law. We also absorbed Werner Vogels's "Run What You Wrote" *ACM Queue* story from 2006[1] and were inspired by open-source development practices. The Netflix team brought ideas we'd developed at Sun Microsystems, Xerox PARC, and the early days of eBay, Google, and Yahoo. Netflix CEO Reed Hastings deeply understands software, and he encouraged us to start afresh and build an architecture that would scale and support innovation.

Some attempts to copy the ideas we developed at Netflix missed that they are artifacts of a dynamic underlying system, where the parts reinforce each other using principles and doctrine to organize in a fluid way, rather than rules and best-practice patterns that are more rigid and evolve slowly. This often led to "architecture theater" and failed attempts by organizations trying to copy Netflix's success.

Many of these organizations also struggled with the question of how to get "The Business" to let the technology organization work more like Netflix or Amazon. One CIO told me that they couldn't copy Netflix because they didn't have the super talented engineers we did. I responded that we had just hired someone from his organization.

Talent isn't the problem. The problem is the very idea of having a separate business organization. No one at Netflix or Amazon ever talks about "The Business." When I worked there, Netflix was organized as a single-product organization. Everyone in product management and development reported to the chief product officer. There wasn't a CIO or CTO in charge. Amazon is organized into a huge number of independent service teams—none of them report to the CIO or CTO.

At the end of 2014, AWS Lambda was launched. I thought it was interesting then, but at the end of 2016, I joined AWS and was judging a one-day AWS re:Invent hackathon. I was surprised to see every team choosing to build serverless architectures using Lambda, and I was also amazed to see what they were able to build from scratch in one day. I started to tell this story in my microservices workshops and found some audience members responded with similar stories of huge amounts of functionality being developed by tiny teams in very little time and with very low operating costs.

This was eye opening, but the problem was that serverless seemed like a fairytale. When it worked, the results were better by an order of magnitude or more—a ludicrous improvement that most people discounted as fantasy or something that only "unicorns" could use.

Like with the ideas I expressed in my initial Netflix talks in 2010, most people remained baffled or dismissive, but a few latched onto the idea of serverless. Simon Wardley was also paying attention, mapped the evolution of the cloud, and declared that serverless was the future. Meanwhile, AWS was systematically removing every objection that customers raised as to why they couldn't do serverless, and I started giving talks titled "Serverless-First," which expressed my opinion that organizations should try to build everything using serverless as their first attempt and only then fall back on containers and specialized instance types when they really have to.

I was talking to lots of AWS customers at that time, and at some point, I connected to Liberty Mutual and discovered David Anderson and his team. We clicked immediately and set up a regular meeting that we continued over several years. The systematic approach David and his team were taking at Liberty Mutual put together the latest best practices, including serverless, and used Wardley Maps to make sense of how to apply these practices.

The amazing thing was that this old insurance company had built one of the most innovative and fast-moving development organizations I was aware of. They were going so fast and at such a low cost that product teams stopped looking at competing technology platforms until they had tried serverless-first. When some people talked about using Kubernetes by default to avoid lock-in, the response was, "Why should I spend ten times as much in time and money? If we need to make it portable later for some reason, we will spend the time and money then." They also told me that the bottleneck for delivering products had moved to the product managers, as ideas were being built faster than new ideas were being figured out. They explained the advantages of serverless-first all the way up the management chain as a core advantage for the company.

I recently retired, left Amazon, and don't have to explain what we did at Netflix or Amazon as my day job anymore. I'm happy to pass that baton to David, Mark, and Michael, who via this excellent book, will spend the next few years explaining what they did at Liberty Mutual to the next generation of baffled and curious audiences.

—**Adrian Cockcroft**
2022

FOREWORD
BY SIMON WARDLEY

All entities strive for success in the game of life. But success assumes there exists some form of competition, either with the environment or other entities or both. Competition (the act of seeking together) comes in many forms—conflict, cooperation, and collaboration. The way we undertake these forms are governed by the age we live in. Competition today is not the same as competition yesterday. It is instead sculptured by the technology and practices available to us and the age in which we live.

This book explores the practices and technology of the modern age and the beginning of what many have dubbed the Fourth Industrial Revolution. It examines how the business and technology can communicate seamlessly together, the importance of technology changes (such as serverless), and why situational awareness of our landscape matters.

Competition in the past was often some form of conflict over territory described through a map of the physical landscape. Those ideas of conflict often extended within the organization, with departments jostling for control. Today's competition is over the supply chains that underpin our technological marvels. This book explains how to map that new territory, the landscape of components that make our businesses, and how to achieve this through collaboration that does not conflict between business and technology.

This book also examines these practices, not from the standpoint of theory or some consultancy's favorite "PowerPoint strategy deck," but from the very act of practice itself, covering the different journeys of a traditional $40 billion revenue, one-hundred-plus-years-old insurance company to a modern software start-up that sold for almost $2 billion. This diversity of experience matters because there are no copycat lists or "one and done" exercises for success; instead, there are sets of practices that need to be applied to your context. The business of insurance is not the same as the business of training, but there are practices that can be applied across both.

At the heart of this is a concept known as the Value Flywheel Effect (the title of this book), derived from a paper napkin sketch by Jeff Bezos, founder of Amazon, which itself was an adaptation from the work of Jim Collins. If you wish to survive and thrive in this Fourth Industrial Age, if you wish to understand the landscapes you are competing in, if you wish to understand how modern practices will change your organization, then I would recommend that you read and study this book carefully.

I'm certain Laura and Clive would agree.

—**Simon Wardley**
2022

INTRODUCTION

After twenty-five years in the technology industry, I can now look back and empathize with all the people I drove crazy—mostly IT managers. Let's face it, software engineers are usually hired to build things quickly, not fix the sociotechnical issues of the larger organization. And yet, that is what I have found myself drawn to time and time again. After all, I have always believed that if you fix the system, then everyone can build quicker, and the business can deliver value sooner. The power of the group is always greater than the power of one.

Whether I was working on improving security, introducing Agile working methods, creating good engineering principles, improving enterprise architecture, building a machine learning (ML) capability, modernizing systems, designing cloud platforms, fixing the developer experience—you name it—I always believed that improving the larger system would improve everything else.

Over the years, I've lost count of the number of times a manager has asked me, "Why are you doing *that* task? I need you to write more code!" I would always be polite and point out that writing code is important, but improving the system is more important. Of course, plenty of code was written, but code is a liability. When we eliminate the burden of something like infrastructure concerns for software developers, it creates room for focus elsewhere, such as developing software assets.

I have been writing code since I was nine; therefore, you could say I've always been a coder. But being a *software engineer** is different. A software engineer should be hired to solve problems and create value for the business. Most software engineers code as a pastime, not as a job. Code written "on the job" should be part of a larger value creation effort, not an effort to write X lines of code in X hours.

---

* Mathematician Margaret Hamilton was the first programmer hired by MIT to work on the NASA Apollo missions and coined the job title "software engineer." She had been tasked with designing software programs for the guidance computers on Apollo. To legitimize the importance of her work, she immediately changed her title from programmer to software engineer, as she felt she was "just as much an engineer as the men who were building the spacecraft."[1]

Unfortunately, too many people in IT write code, build systems, and perform tasks without any idea why. They obsess over function and forget about purpose.* And too many people from the business see software developers and engineers as nothing more than programmers who should just make the system do what the business says it should.

In my experience, I've taken huge risks by focusing on these larger sociotechnical systems. I've had to deal with a lot of push back from middle management for not doing what I was supposed to (i.e., write more code). But I always had the conviction to push on. It was like I was in a poker game and sitting on a hand that would pay big. When you see that kind of opportunity, you must take it. Taking that risk, playing that hand, ended up paying off big.

Serverless Transformation at Liberty Mutual

In 2013, Liberty Mutual Insurance, the sixth-largest property and casualty insurance company, started to move its services to the cloud, and I was lucky enough to find myself part of the transformation.

I had joined the company back in 2007, spending a few years designing and building a large eCommerce platform with co-authors Mark McCann and Michael O'Reilly as well as many other talented engineers and leaders.

I was impressed with the quality of individual engineers at Liberty Mutual, but I could see there was still a significant opportunity to create value. I could see that the connection between the business and technology needed work. And (most importantly) I could see that the engineers were crying out for change. But, like many legacy enterprises, Liberty Mutual was like a big oil tanker—any attempt to steer it in a new direction was going to be difficult and very slow.

By 2013, I moved into a CTO position in Belfast, Ireland. I had built a small team of architects and a solid technical leadership community. Liberty Mutual had begun exploring solutions for security and test data in the cloud using AWS. This was a significant opportunity. I quickly realized that the cloud was not just another datacenter; it could offer a transformational way of working. I just didn't quite know what that was yet. I decided that my team and I would try and figure out a way to build better software in the cloud. The cloud was new to many of us, and "application development" was our area of expertise. I could sense a paradigm shift and knew it was time to start exploring.

---

* Simon Sinek elaborates on this eloquently in his depiction of the golden circle and in his book *Start with Why*.[2]

I wondered, "What does cloud application architecture look like in this brave new world?" I knew it would take a few years for the foundational capabilities (security, governance, infrastructure, processes) to be ready at scale, but I was certain which direction we should take. We had a window of opportunity. I just needed a way to map a path, even if that map would change along the way.

Mark and I had begun following the work of Simon Wardley. We were enjoying his technique, called Wardley Mapping, which is a method for building situational awareness to map out a potential business strategy. We didn't fully understand it yet, but it felt exciting and described the evolution we knew was coming. Mapping allowed us to ask questions about how things could evolve; it let us peek into the future and turn hunches into strategies that we could then either test or look for early signs. We decided to attempt to map out what we thought could happen with Liberty Mutual's shift to the cloud.

We asked ourselves hard questions:

- Will we still write thousands of lines of code in this new place?
- Will infrastructure as code happen? What will it look like?
- What happens when continuous delivery is in place?
- How will the cloud providers like AWS evolve?
- What things do we do now that we won't do in the future?
- What will be valuable for our business when all of this is complete?

We spent many hours writing lots of rubbish on dry-erase boards. The architect team grew, and we experimented and worked with peers across the organization to try and better understand the cloud landscape. We didn't know it then, but we were building situational awareness and informing our maps.

Eventually, the team could sit in a small room and discuss the entire technology landscape of a Fortune 100 company and use Wardley Mapping to predict what might happen in the next year, five years, etc. We had become a sensemaking machine. This, fortuitously, coincided with the launch of AWS Lambda.

AWS Lambda was a significant innovation in cloud technology and provided the opportunity for a huge mindset shift for developers. Previously, organizations moving to the cloud still had to manage the infrastructure (costing hours and hours of developer time). But with Lambda, there was now the option to leave the infrastructure management to the cloud vendor! This could move the cloud from a product to a commodity the business consumed like electricity. This would give our teams more time to focus on creativity and innovation, including operational constraints, performance constraints, the total cost of the solution, and user experience, instead of just keeping the lights on. Teams could start to write systems rather than simply applications. And there were clear cost savings for the business as well.

This was the beginning of what came to be known as serverless computing, where companies no longer managed their cloud operations themselves but gave that toil over to the cloud vendors. With this model, an organization could run an application when needed, shut it down when needed, and pay only when it was being used.

But we had a problem: How could we use the cloud to create business value? The answer had presented itself: serverless. The technology was very raw, but we could see the potential. My team and I believed we had a map for the future of technology. We could see the trends that would disappear. We could see the capabilities that would be critical in the future, and we could guess how the cloud providers might evolve. We had that winning poker hand that I alluded to earlier. We decided to take the plunge and experiment in this new serverless world. Our experiments quickly accelerated our engineering team's ability to focus on things other than infrastructure management. And the more we experimented in this space, the more we started to see a flywheel effect, small wins accumulating over time to drive momentum. We were delivering more value into the hands of our business partners faster. And we started to see that the cloud was more than just another datacenter. It provided a transformational way of working.

We tried to map out what we were experiencing. First, we had a clear purpose (Phase 1). Next, we had the right environment in which to thrive (Phase 2). And serverless-first architecture provided us with the next best action (Phase 3) we could take to create long-term value (Phase 4) for our organization.

We deployed this same pattern many times, spinning the flywheel again and again, creating more and more momentum and less and less inertia, and the success was evident. Engineers were moving faster, creating lower-cost solutions and more innovative approaches with a better connection between technology and the business.

As was reported by *TechRepublic*, a single web application at Liberty Mutual was rewritten as serverless and resulted in reduced maintenance costs of 99.98%, from $50,000 a year to $10 a year.[3] That small savings is hugely powerful when you have hundreds or thousands of similar applications running at the same time. I've seen this type of successful pattern repeated at Liberty Mutual and across different industries.

Thanks to serverless and our flywheel, we were also able to release applications quicker, which meant getting feedback from users and customers sooner. This in turn gave us an advantage in the market to more rapidly respond to customer demands and changes. Serverless also opened new possibilities that seemed too costly or difficult before, such as integration with AI and data services or event streaming services.

This new mindset shifted our perspective of code as well. Instead of an asset, we began to see that more code was a liability. The less code we wrote, the better. And the code we did write must have demonstrable business value. Surprisingly, our software engineers loved this shift to writing less code. Many didn't want to go back to "the old ways" of doing things.

We started to adopt what came to be known as *serverless-first architecture.* In other words, a team's first implementation choice should be serverless, and if that's not a good fit, then you work backward (i.e., introduce more infrastructure, like containers).

By 2019–2020, things on the cloud front had progressed significantly. At one point, I had four AWS Heroes (individuals recognized as AWS community experts and who enjoy legendary status!) in my extended team, which was unheard of at the time. Many of the engineers on my team were giving talks and keynotes about our successes at major AWS and technology conferences. And the business metrics delivered became simply unbelievable: 95%+ runtime cost-savings, new functionality delivered months ahead of schedule, global roll out in weeks instead of years, and innovative features leading the market and deploying multiple times a day.

Also, we created a software accelerator using the AWS Cloud Development Kit (AWS CDK), an open-source software development framework in which engineers can use familiar programming languages to define cloud application resources, to help deploy new applications quickly. These acted like code templates that could be used by software engineers to rapidly build projects rather than writing the code from scratch.

I was frequently challenged at external events, as these metrics seemed farfetched (for example, cost savings of 99.5% and similar). Amazon CTO Werner Vogels even started to praise Liberty Mutual and our serverless-first architecture, calling it organizational nirvana.[4] Our "Serverless-First Enterprise" concept was starting to take hold.

In a global organization with thousands of people, the sociotechnical element of driving a paradigm shift like this is significant; moving to the cloud and embracing a new way to write software might only happen once in your career. It's not enough to have some cool tech. Winning hearts and minds is the real challenge.

By this time, we had been evolving our methods and practices for ten years, so we decided to encapsulate them in a set of principles we referred to as the "Serverless-First Organization Strategy." The running joke I had with the tech leads was that it was impossible to measure if the principle was true, but blindingly obvious when it was not! We tried to paint a picture of our ideal software development team in a set of principles as follows:

A high-performing, serverless-first team will:

1. chase a business outcome (KPI)
2. be secure by design
3. keep high throughput of work
4. reliably run a high-stability system
5. rent/reuse, with build as the final option
6. continuously optimize the total cost
7. build event-driven via strong APIs
8. build solutions that fit in their heads

We knew from experience that a successful team needed to know what they were doing and should be able to recite the business metrics from memory (principle #1).

We knew that security and threat modeling were table stakes; it's everyone's job (principle #2).

DORA's metrics for high-performing teams (as illustrated in the book *Accelerate* by Dr. Nicole Forsgren, Jez Humble, and Gene Kim),[5] provided clear standards for code quality (principles #3 and #4).

We worked to spread the attitude of the evolution of technology and the idea that code is a liability (principle #5).

Trying to encourage builders that you don't always need to build is a significant challenge. The great cloud principle and mindset change needed is cost and OpEx. Teams need to be aware of the cost, not to save the company money, but to think frugally and efficiently (principle #6).

We set the bar high for integration patterns and encouraged clean design (principle #7).

And finally, borrowed from our friend and mentor Dan North, we held that software should fit in your head.[6] It shouldn't be overcomplicated (principle #8).

We often joke that it took ten years to write these eight bullet points, but each represents a lesson learned. The principles landed well, and after considerable risk, many engineers learned in this environment, contributed, and succeeded. Even today, serverless is still not widely accepted. Learning a brand-new way of writing code could set an engineer's career back considerably, especially if the technology doesn't "win." It's always a leap of faith when moving to a new technology.

The Value Flywheel Effect Materializes

Of course, lockdown changed everything, and we all retired to our home offices and conference calls in early 2020. The "Serverless-First Organization Strategy" still stood up. It gave the engineering teams a clear focus, which was build well for engineering value. The collaboration continued, if in a different way. But it was clear that the flywheel we had discovered (having a clarity of purpose, the right environment, a clear next best action, and creating long-term value) was fully in effect now. Not even a pandemic could stop the flywheel from spinning.

As I made sense of this "Value Flywheel Effect" approach that we had worked out, I knew I needed to stress test the thinking with true industry thought leaders—people I respected and who I had followed for years. Life is full of gambles, but I figured that in lockdown, people might have more time on their hands. I (honestly) had only two names on my list—Simon Wardley, who had created Wardley Mapping, and Adrian Cockcroft, VP of Cloud Architecture at AWS (at that time).

I had been listening to and reading the work of both leaders for over ten years, but I didn't have a personal relationship with either of them. After a bit of effort, I tracked them down and asked for their feedback.

My question was simple: I think this idea of the Value Flywheel Effect is good, but why is no one else doing this? What am I missing? Both (who I later learned are friends) separately told me: "No, you're not mad. This is good stuff. Let's talk more."

That positive response and the invitation to collaborate had not been on my map. I sat in Belfast deciding what to do next. Two of my heroes had just told me I'd hit proverbial gold. Well, this book is the result.

In this book, I've distilled this set of practices (what I've termed the Value Flywheel Effect) learned from people "not doing what they were supposed to." The practices are all real. They are derived from real experiences, real scars, real success. This is not a book about technology (even if there's a healthy dose in it). And it's not a book about job functions. This is a book for all the business leaders, at any level, who aren't afraid of not doing what they're supposed to. This is a book for leaders of the future who will forage a clearer alliance between the business and technology to navigate the unknown waters ahead of us.

But before we go any further, I must ask you to forget everything you know about the IT departments and technology teams you've worked in or with in the past. To succeed on our journey, we must get away from the mental and physical image of IT as a separate entity or department. Instead, we must create a shared, ambitious goal for technology and the business, as they are increasingly the same. Today, every leader is a technology leader.

The inherent need for IT and the business to unite has been accelerating at breakneck speed for more than a decade, fueled by advances in technology and drastic changes in the way people work. In fact, many have dubbed this the Fourth Industrial Revolution. Unlike the Third Industrial Revolution, which used electronics and information technology to automate production, this new revolution is characterized "by a fusion of technologies that is blurring the lines between the physical, digital, and biological spheres."[7]

In fact, it's becoming increasingly clear from the "velocity, scope, and systems impact"[8] of technologies today that we're in a wholly different era. According to the World Economic Forum, "the speed of current breakthroughs has no historical precedent . . . evolving at an exponential rather than a linear pace. Moreover, it is disrupting almost every industry in every country. And the breadth and depth of these changes herald the transformation of entire systems of production, management, and governance."[9]

It should come as no surprise, then, to anyone reading this book that the technological advances of today have a significant impact on businesses. My own story of exploring serverless technologies at Liberty Mutual is but one example. Global leaders and business executives say that "the acceleration of innovation and the velocity of disruption are hard to comprehend or anticipate and that these drivers constitute a source of constant surprise, even for the best connected and most well informed."[10]

This digital revolution is

significantly disrupt[ing] existing industry value chains . . . [and] flowing from agile, innovative competitors who, thanks to access to [global talent and] global digital platforms for research, development, marketing, sales, and distribution, can oust well-established incumbents faster than ever by improving the quality, speed, or price at which value is delivered. . . . Overall, the inexorable shift from simple digitization (the Third Industrial Revolution) to innovation based on combinations of technologies (the Fourth Industrial Revolution) is forcing companies to reexamine the way they do business."[11]

As we enter this new era of business and technology, it is irresponsible for modern organizations to ignore or waste the potential that effective technology brings to the business and the power and potential of serverless and the modern cloud—both represent software in its purest form, without hardware. Executives must learn to harness today's technology to drive innovation and power change. They must challenge their own assumptions, continuously innovate, and adapt to their changing environment.

But even with this evidence, some leaders continue to ask if technology is genuinely driving their business forward. Honestly? I imagine if you asked Jeff Bezos or Elon Musk that question, they'd probably reply, "Yes, but we could be doing better." If digital-native unicorns like Amazon and Tesla think they can do even better, what hope is there for the rest of us?

The question every business leader must ask themselves is this: Is technology really driving your business? There is a significant culture change required to truly achieve this. Just lifting and shifting into the cloud will only give you a nicer datacenter. Simply writing more code only increases your organization's liability; it doesn't guarantee you'll win in the marketplace. You won't really be benefiting from what these technologies have to offer your business unless you embrace a deeper mindset shift.

The organizations of today and tomorrow need a mechanism to accelerate the business and technology evolution. They must move away from the siloization of IT from the business, which creates an inherent lack of focus. IT departments are valuable parts of the company and have huge potential to create value. They are not costs to be squeezed. Integration of the departments—technology with the rest of the business—is fundamental to the success of the whole organization.

The organizations that recognize this will create a space for innovation. Small successes will breed larger success and spread through the organization like wildfire. This power and momentum will increase, and the path forward will become smoother. This is the Value Flywheel Effect, when the business and technology strategies power and drive each other, turning the organization into a sensemaking machine with the ability to easily pivot to the challenges of today and to whatever the next great transformation will be.

Organizations that achieve true alignment between the business and technology will find themselves riding a wave of continuous momentum thanks to the Value Flywheel Effect. To achieve continuous momentum means to be in the lead, to break new boundaries. In the mechanical world, when a power source is inconsistent, a flywheel is used to absorb energy and evenly distribute it so the machine runs smoothly. I believe that both business and technology drivers must merge in this same way to ensure smooth progress forward.

As business technology leaders, the next wave of technology will not worry about servers, instances, and traditional models—it will be serverless. When we free ourselves of the operational burden of managing infrastructure and think about capability more abstractly, the organization can move more quickly. When we let go of the constraints from yesteryear and forget about IaaS, PaaS, and FaaS,* we

---

* Infrastructure as a Service, Platform as a Service, Function as a Service.

accelerate. We know we need to consume capabilities and assemble systems that will drive our business forward.

The Value Flywheel Effect exists in every organization, but it will turn very slowly if you lock all your engineers in the basement and demand that they crank out code. There is a better way. I have seen it, experienced it, and now I am sharing it with all of you.

I hope you enjoy it and learn from it. Mark, Michael, and I have worked very hard to learn these lessons and distill them into this book. We are so pleased that you are taking the time read it, challenge it, and (hopefully) evolve it.

How to Read This Book

We have broken this book down based on the elements of the four phases of the Value Flywheel Effect.

- Part I focuses on an introduction to the Value Flywheel Effect, including the use of the Value Flywheel and Wardley Mapping.
- Part II focuses on Phase 1 of the Value Flywheel Effect: Clarity of Purpose and Vision. We start with a clarity of purpose or a north star, which helps measure key metrics. Time to value (as a version of lead time) is essential to capture here. To flesh out the purpose, a competitive map of the market is beneficial. What are your differentiators?
- Part III focuses on Phase 2 of the Value Flywheel Effect: Challenge and Landscape. An early assessment of psychological safety is crucial for understanding your organization's "sociotechnical" elements. An important question regarding the way of working is, "Does challenge exist in your organization, *challenge* being a healthy inquiry and debate of critical components?" Mapping the capability of your organization is essential. Do you have the people and capability to do what you need to do?
- Part IV focuses on Phase 3 of the Value Flywheel Effect: Next Best Action. At this stage, there is a purpose and situational awareness. A robust technical strategy is required to start improving your time to value. A frictionless developer experience is an excellent place to start, and we recommend a serverless-first approach. After all, code is a liability! We must start as we mean to go on, so we must create the correct mindset here. What's the next best action we can take to make progress? A popular map here is "mapping the tech stack." What's good or bad about the

tech stack? You may find that your engineers waste vast amounts of time on a flawed process or an outdated solution.

- Part V focuses on Phase 4 of the Value Flywheel Effect: Long-Term Value. As the Value Flywheel starts to turn, the longer-term value becomes essential. Well-architected systems and sustainability combine nicely to create a culture of problem prevention. Companies can use any of the three maps discussed throughout the book (market, capability, or tech stack) to troubleshoot issues, communicate, or discuss options. Mapping should be a constant and quick exercise through which we build competency.

This book contains plans, case studies, and advice for creating and accelerating your Value Flywheel Effect, helping you build confidence in the fast-changing eco-system that is the modern cloud. We discuss twelve tenets of the Value Flywheel that provide further guidance on the four phases, depending on your specific role in the organization.

Remember, the Value Flywheel Effect is a cycle (identify a purpose, challenge existing procedures, act to improve time to value, and sustain your efforts), so you won't accomplish everything on the first pass. Once you get into a cadence of identify, challenge, act, and sustain, meaningful change will happen quickly.

This book is not just about technology or moving faster; it's about generating value for your organization. Used correctly, going serverless (using the modern cloud) will deliver more value than you have ever imagined, but you must behave like a next-generation company to unlock it. When the modern cloud is used appropriately, it will tighten up your bottom line, but the real benefit is driving the growth of the top line of your business.

Technology changes and market opportunities are coming thick and fast. Your organization needs to have the capability, agility, and cohesion to leverage the transformation opportunity. The "Great Digital Transformation" was not a one-off event. The iPhone 1 from Apple in 2007 was not the end of the mobile revolution from the previous fifteen years; it simply marked an acceleration that started the next fifteen years of evolution, and not every company could keep up.

We tend to think of technological advancements as events that have discrete starts and ends. But technology moves forward due to rapid progress and fast iterations. There is an essential question here before you start your journey: Are you happy to *consume* the event or use your Value Flywheel Effect to *create* the event? If you're one of the ones looking to *create* the event, then read on. The Value Flywheel Effect will help you get there.

I

Starting the Expedition

CHAPTER 1
THE VALUE FLYWHEEL EFFECT

M omentum is a strange thing. It's difficult to imagine what it will feel like and takes a great deal of effort to achieve.

When we learn to ride a bicycle, for example, it feels clunky and awkward at first. It's hard to get the wheels turning in the beginning, and our frustration is often evident. But our teacher assures us that it will pass. When we finally start to build momentum, the exhilaration takes our breath away. Every push of the pedal gets easier and takes less effort. Suddenly we can focus on the larger experience of gliding through a beautiful forest or tree-lined street. The value of our hard work is evident, and we can now continue to reap the benefits with less and less toil.

However, just as the work becomes second nature, new challenges present themselves—namely, turning, shifting, and, importantly, stopping.

This cycle of nerves, uncertainty, confidence, drive, and then back to nerves is repeated by everyone, from five-year-olds learning to ride for the first time to Olympic cyclists racing in their hundredth or thousandth race. When it comes to riding a bike or any similar task, we know this cycle exists. We overlook the initial challenges of getting started because we know the value we will reap in the end. We have seen others do it, so we steel ourselves for the journey, not just the start.

It should be no different in business, especially in a world where we are constantly and with increasing speed being thrown new and more difficult challenges. And yet, too many organizations are frozen in the initial phases of nerves and uncertainty, content to remain still instead of pushing to move forward.

The Value Flywheel Effect can help organizations escape this state of stagnation and fear in the face of new challenges. For example, one of the most ubiquitous challenges organizations face today is when, if, and how to start a cloud transformation. The modern cloud (serverless) promises speed, low friction, and reduced costs, but most organizations don't realize that achieving these results requires more than just lifting and shifting their existing architecture into the cloud.

For Liberty Mutual, as was illustrated in the Introduction, it took focusing on a clarity of purpose, creating an environment for success, and experimenting with the next best action we could envision (serverless) to finally realize the long-term value that was promised. Then, using one small win (one pump of the wheel) we were able to experiment again and achieve another success (another spin of the wheel). With each success (each spin of the flywheel), the effort and work it took to earn another success was reduced. We built the momentum that eventually shot us into the forefront of technological innovation and excellence and drove huge business growth.

It can be challenging to start turning the flywheel. There are nerves and uncertainty, and it requires significant effort. Technology and product drivers are necessary, and the flywheel needs to absorb both. But as the flywheel starts to turn, it releases energy that will drive your organization forward. It achieves momentum. The systemic forces are now hard to stop but easier to guide.

Unlike many frameworks, the Value Flywheel Effect is not a "one and done" exercise. The entire idea of a *project* conjures up the image of a start and an end, point A to point Z. The fast iteration of a flywheel, however, is more akin to *Atomic Habits*, the seminal book by James Clear.[1] By breaking larger actions down into smaller efforts and moving through the four phases of the Value Flywheel, progress may seem insurmountable, but it will be faster.

Origin of the Value Flywheel Effect

The inspiration for the Value Flywheel Effect comes from three sources: Amazon's Virtuous Cycle, James Collins's flywheel concept from *Good to Great*, and from our own experiences.

In *The Everything Store: Jeff Bezos and the Age of Amazon*, journalist Brad Stone explains that the "flywheel effect" in the company's early stages worked like this:

> Lower prices led to more customer visits. More customers increased the volume of sales and attracted more commission-paying third-party sellers to the site. That allowed Amazon to get more out of fixed costs like the fulfillment centers and the servers needed to run the website. This greater efficiency then enabled it to lower prices further. Feed any part of this flywheel, they reasoned, and it should accelerate the loop.[2]

The flywheel story described is also known as the Amazon Virtuous Cycle and, as you would expect, focuses on the customer (see Figure 1.1).

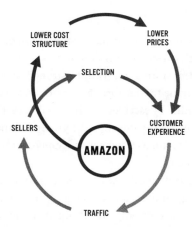

Figure 1.1: The Amazon Flywheel (also known as the Amazon Virtuous Cycle)
Source: The Everything Store: Jeff Bezos and the Age of Amazon *by Brad Stone.*

Bezos's Virtuous Cycle is itself an adaptation of Jim Collins's flywheel from the book *Good to Great* (see Figure 1.2). As Collins describes it,

No matter how dramatic the result, good-to-great transformations never happen in one fell swoop. In building a great company or social sector enterprise, there is no single defining action, no grand program, no one killer innovation, no solitary lucky break, no miracle moment. Rather, the process resembles relentlessly pushing a giant, heavy flywheel, turn upon turn, building momentum until a point of breakthrough, and beyond.[3]

Collins's model drives organizational change and is primarily focused on leading change in the organization.

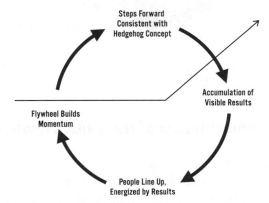

Figure 1.2: The Flywheel Concept from Jim Collins
Source: Good to Great: Why Some Companies Make the Leap and Others Don't *by Jim Collins.*

Bezos's flywheel tells us how a new business can energize the customer as a virtuous force for change. Collins's flywheel shows how to use a small, successful organizational change to foment a larger transformation within a struggling business. But how do we build momentum and continue to transform an already successful company?

The Value Flywheel Effect described in this book (see Figure 1.3) is the third iteration of the concept of the organizational flywheel, combining elements from Bezos's Virtuous Cycle and Collins's flywheel and applying much of our own technical leadership lessons learned.

This Value Flywheel Effect reveals the rapid acceleration and transformation that is possible when technology and business strategies intertwine. If the focus is only on the customer (as with Bezos) or only on the organization (as with Collins), organizations will continue to struggle to bring technology and business together. They will struggle to improve how long it takes them to realize value. In the modern digital age, technology and the business must become one. As we evolve the works of Collins and Bezos, this Value Flywheel Effect will be the catalyst for all our future endeavors.

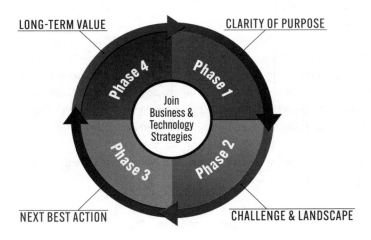

Figure 1.3: The Value Flywheel Effect

The Four Phases of the Value Flywheel

The Value Flywheel has four phases, starting with *clarity of purpose*. A clear and definitive purpose is often hard to achieve (like starting a mechanical flywheel), but it's a critical starting point. As Simon Sinek points out with his "Golden Circle" concept, we have to "start with why" (from his book of the same name). Once you have clarity on your why (your purpose), only then can the flywheel start turning. As you saw in the introduction to this book, Liberty Mutual first had to align to three main areas of digital transformation: customer centricity, agility, and cloud-native development. This became the north star we used to direct all our future efforts.

Once a purpose is selected, this will inevitably lead to challenges (the second phase of the Value Flywheel). How are we going to achieve this? What actions do we need to take to reach our goal? Challenge is good. It helps an organization question its business-as-usual attitudes. It helps lead them out of stagnation. Only through embracing and confronting challenges can an organization hope to grow and meet the demands of an ever-changing market.

In today's landscape, solutions to challenges need to be executed quickly. Instead of waiting for the perfect solution, the goal should be to quickly identify and implement the next best action (the third phase of the Value Flywheel). There is no need to over-plan or stall. Instead, the organization must ask itself, "What's the next most useful thing we can do to provide some value?" and then act accordingly. Overcoming challenges demands speed, so this is not the time for over-engineering or deep analysis.

This next best action must have the goal of turning small wins into lasting, long-term value (the fourth phase of the Value Flywheel) to ensure that your organization creates a sustainable practice early instead of building quickly but badly, creating further complications down the line.

But the journey is not over. Once the wheel has spun, it is essential to return to clarity of purpose (the first phase of the Value Flywheel). A fast experiment should have supplied some valuable feedback so that the whole iteration (a turn of the flywheel) can start again. And again. And again. The faster your organization moves through these iterations (turns of the flywheel), the more you will learn, the more value you will deliver, and the more opportunities that will present themselves. The business strategy never stands still. There will be new ideas, new opportunities, and new developments. There will also be improvements to the technology stack and to the teams themselves. The Value Flywheel works as it absorbs changes from the business and technology (both never stop evolving).

The Value Flywheel Effect always intends to move and absorb challenges, energized through pragmatic decision-making. It's crucial to maintain momentum—to never slow down or stop. Note that the Value Flywheel Effect is neither a hybrid strategy nor operational efficiency. It's about creating a true bias for action, aligned with the pragmatic and proven ways of working that we've seen work in our own experiences.

The Value Flywheel is designed to spin many times, so don't feel that you need to do everything in phase two before moving on to phase three. Momentum and bias for action are more important than anything else. The flywheel gets its energy through feedback and ideas from both product and technology, so getting moving is critical. The flywheel then levels out these requests and maintains a steady flow of power throughout the organization.

The Value Flywheel Effect in Action

Let's look at the Value Flywheel in action. The first phase of the Value Flywheel is *clarity of purpose* when a new requirement emerges. Can we line it up to a north star? Are the benefits of this ask clear? What is the value proposition that this ask will deliver, and is the time to value clear? A well-thought-out ask will quickly move you through this phase.

Next is the *challenge*. An ask will always require specific capabilities. Is there a safe environment to challenge and explore this ask? Can we pick at it and get behind it? Is the opportunity cost of doing this over another thing clear? Are the teams well-positioned to do this work? From a sociotechnical perspective, is our system set up for success, or could this ask be a breaking change?

Once we have confidence that the ask aligns with our capability, we move on to the third phase, finding and acting upon the *next best action*. This is one of the most critical stages of the Value Flywheel. Most organizations that are moving to serverless will eventually use public cloud providers as their platform. Cloud platforms exist to enable and provide acceleration. The smart organizations that leverage the cloud properly will see the benefit of acting quickly. If the engineers have a frictionless developer experience and execute against a serverless-first strategy, they will build well and fast.

Finally, *long-term value* is our check and balance against technical debt, which slows the flywheel down. This phase benefits from seeds planted at the start and aims to prevent longer-term issues. A problem-prevention mindset is often forgotten when we go to market quickly, and we rarely come back to clean up the mess. Facilitating and investing in well-architected and sustainable engineering/product development will ensure that we think ahead and keep the flywheel turning smoothly.

If the ask moves through these four phases smoothly, we have ensured that our flywheel will output value and is ready to turn again. The momentum generated in the organization by building this way is invaluable.

Key Tenets of the Value Flywheel

The Value Flywheel Effect, enabled by cloud adoption, will accelerate your business. Each phase of the Value Flywheel is anchored by three key tenets (twelve in total), as detailed below and in Figure 1.4. These tenets will help guide you through each of the phases of the Value Flywheel (and the remaining Parts II through V of this book are organized according to these tenets).

That said, it's essential to understand that we are constantly evolving—these tenets may not hold in a few years. For that reason, we will also illustrate them using Wardley Maps. You should map your context and adapt these principles to work in your environment.

We've also broken these tenets down based on personas, or the role in an organization that would be most concerned with each phase of the Value Flywheel. The persona listed for each section is not the sole owner of these tenets, but the individual who would sleep easy if their three tenets were followed.

Figure 1.4: The Value Flywheel Effect & Key Tenets

Phase 1: Clarity of Purpose (Persona: CEO)

1. Clarity of purpose: A data-informed north star.
2. Obsess over your time to value: Innovation is a lagging metric.
3. Map the market: Can you differentiate in the market?

Phase 2: Challenge & Landscape (Persona: Engineers)

4. Psychological safety: Team-first environments always win.
5. The system is the asset: A sociotechnical systems view.
6. Map the org for enablement: Enable empowered engineers.

Phase 3: Next Best Action (Persona: Product Leaders)
7. Code is a liability: A serverless-first mindset delivers value.
8. Frictionless developer experience: An easy path to production.
9. Map your solution: Align on how you will serve customers.

Phase 4: Long-Term Value (Persona: CTO)
10. A problem-prevention culture: Well-architected and engineered systems.
11. Keep a low carbon footprint: Sustainability.
12. Map the emerging value: Next-generation companies can see ahead.

Let's discuss the key tenets in relation to the four phases of the Value Flywheel in more detail.

Phase 1: Clarity of Purpose

From a company perspective, the CEO is the individual we can use as the persona most concerned with the first three tenets. Though these tenets affect everyone in the organization, the CEO has the interest of the company at heart and can ensure these three tenets are met.

Clarity of purpose is the number one job of the CEO. The company must have a vision and not just a few words written on the wall. Clarity of purpose can be tested by creating a north star–model using the North Star Framework from Amplitude (more on this in Chapter 5). Ideally, the north star is a lagging metric (one that takes a long time to measure), and you should be able to identify the leading metrics (actions that lead to an outcome) and the effort that will drive its success.

Many CEOs *demand* innovation, which often leads to innovation theater and little actual innovation. If the CEO tracks time to value instead—which means reducing the time taken from "idea conception" to "value in the hands of customers"—then innovation will happen. Innovation is a lagging metric. Rather than focusing on the nebulous idea of innovation, improve the leading metrics that you can control. (We'll explore this in Chapter 6.)

Related to the clarity of purpose is the intellectual property of the organization. Is there clarity regarding the market you are operating in? Performing a Wardley Map on your value chain will help distinguish your differentiators and your enablers. (We'll explore this more in Chapter 7.)

Phase 2: Challenge & Landscape

The software engineer in an organization is focused on a different set of tenets than the CEO. The engineer's responsibility is to build well, so there are specific tenets that will help set them on the right path.

Psychological safety is critical here, as it is the foundation for an environment that fosters success. Engineering requires collaboration, challenge, vulnerability, calculated risk-taking, and skill. A highly charged political environment will negatively impact the team's success. Alternatively, a team-first environment, like in many sports, will lead to better results and engagement all around. (More on this in Chapter 9.)

Often, engineers will obsess with the code while non-engineers will consider the people. But the key contributors to any software system are the people that interact with technology. It is this combination and interrelationship between the socio (the people) and the technology that is of vital importance. If the sociotechnical system is valued and understood, then engineers can make huge impacts. If it is not, inertia will slow down your flywheel. (We'll explore more on sociotechnical systems in Chapter 10.)

The top issue for engineering teams is often friction. Decision-makers in a business often try to govern and ensure compliance by restricting teams. If we Wardley Map the engineering environment, it should be clear that certain functions are stuck in the wrong phase. This map can be a valuable source of continuous improvement that will enable instead of frustrate engineering teams. (We'll explore this map in Chapter 11.)

Phase 3: Next Best Action

There are many flavors of business or product roles, but they should all represent customer value. For the third phase of the Value Flywheel Effect, the product leader, who represents the customer, is the driver. They ask the question: How can we optimize for maximum customer value? It's important to recognize the depth of the product discipline and the many important techniques available. In *The Value Flywheel Effect*, we'll focus on speed—deciding what to build is a whole other set of books!

One of the biggest misunderstandings in the world of software is the value of code. But code is a liability, as we'll say repeatedly in this book. The more code we write, the more complexity and risk we generate for ourselves. In the modern cloud, it's important to offload as many capabilities to the provider as possible. Less code allows teams to move faster. Taking advantage of serverless is the clearest next best action for many modern organizations. (We'll explore the benefits of a serverless-first mindset more in Chapter 13.)

When teams do release new features, it's critical that there is a frictionless developer experience. Organizations must make it easy for the engineers to make changes quickly and in a safe, secure manner to deliver value for the business and keep the flywheel moving. Automation is a key enabler in reducing developer friction. (We'll explore this more in Chapter 14.)

To embrace a serverless-first mindset (offloading infrastructure management to the cloud) it's a valuable exercise to Wardley Map the existing technology stack with engineers. With this map, it will quickly become clear which components either slow the team down, generate little value, or are easily replaced by a cloud service. (We'll explore this mapping technique more in Chapter 15.)

Phase 4: Long-Term Value

The final persona driving the Value Flywheel Effect is the CTO (chief technology officer or similar), who represents the architecture of the system. Often misunderstood, the architecture of the system should support future changes, reduce risk, and meet the business need. Like security, good architecture often results in bad things not happening, which is often difficult to measure. And good architecture leads to sustainable, long-term value versus short-term gains.

Many organizations reward teams for fixing problems. An alternative model should be to create a culture of *preventing* problems: reward the teams that use well-architected and strong engineering practices to prevent issues from *ever* occurring and lead to more reliable systems in the long term. (We'll explore problem-prevention culture in Chapter 17.)

Good architecture is often hard to define and measure; therefore, efficiency can be a strong measure here. And efficiency can also be represented as sustainability. Cloud providers are starting to measure the amount of carbon burned in a specific workload or system. Quite simply, if a team can reduce their carbon burn, they are providing a benefit to the customer, the company, and the environment. (We'll explore this more in Chapter 18.)

A key role of architecture is looking ahead and anticipating change. One thing in technology that is certain is there will be an evolution of capability. Wardley Mapping provides the perfect mechanism to map how key capabilities in your value chain will evolve and what emerging capabilities or needs will surface in the future. Once mapped, you start preparing for evolution today instead of waiting for the future to hit you in the face. (We'll explore this map more in Chapter 19.)

Avoiding Inertia with Your Value Flywheel

There's a very good reason why the mechanism we present throughout this book is a flywheel: to succeed, inertia must be avoided at all costs. Inertia is the resistance of matter to change. This includes changes to speed and direction. Organizations today cannot afford to suffer this inertia. They must have the ability to increase their speed (improve time to value) and change direction (adapt).

With sequential change, there is always inertia that will either slow or misdirect effort. It's very hard to avoid. The Value Flywheel Effect provides a tight feedback loop, making it possible to smash inertia before it becomes an issue. The inertia of a flywheel opposes and moderates fluctuations in the speed of an engine, or in this case an organization, and then stores that excess energy for intermittent use. An organization can draw upon this stored energy in times of great change without having to exert more effort.

Change is difficult, but the Value Flywheel Effect will keep things moving. Sometimes a simple motto like "code is a liability" or "improve time to value" will keep engineers moving more effectively than a fifty-five-minute town hall with the same presentation that was delivered in some boring meeting last week.

At an executive level, there is often the need to gradually cascade strategy. You do not need to do this here. Once the high-level strategy is in place, you can let the teams advance at their own pace. To prevent inertia from slowing down your flywheel, give your engineers permission to move quickly. The flywheel nearly removes the need for executive oversight. In fact, command and control is the biggest creator of inertia in this approach.

With cohesive feedback loops, progress is transparent. Transparency can help leadership craft the right language and drive the Value Flywheel Effect. The more your teams understand this feedback loop—what worked and what didn't work—the quicker your progress will be.

Takeaways

The concept of the flywheel is not new; it has been used to describe company change and customer interaction for decades. Now we're showing organizations how to use the Value Flywheel Effect to inform impactful strategy as the business and technology combine. With the current technology picture, this flywheel has never been so central or needed to turn so fast—and it's not slowing down. It's time to find that flywheel in your organization and recognize the four phases: Clarity of Purpose, Challenge and Landscape, Next Best Action, and Long-Term Value.

To help you on your journey, we've provided twelve key tenets based on personas in your organization to help you see areas of improvement and build situational awareness.

Some of the traditional models for creating and analyzing strategies may not work in today's fast-paced environment. The Value Flywheel Effect helps to seamlessly distribute power throughout the organization, turning technology and product needs into momentum and value.

But power without direction will leave any organization spinning in circles. Wardley Mapping—creating a visual representation of who you serve, what they need, and how you fulfill that need—helps the organization navigate the rough waters ahead and find direction. In the next chapters, we'll explore the method of Wardley Mapping in more detail to help you practice it in your own organization and build necessary situational awareness.

CHAPTER 2
WARDLEY MAPPING

Now that we have our flywheel turning, how do we ensure we are moving in the right direction? The flywheel provides and distributes the power, but applying Wardley Mapping throughout all four phases of the Value Flywheel Effect provides direction and prevents derailment. Wardley Mapping encourages organizations to make constant micro adjustments to maintain direction and move at pace.

After all, any change effort, or even the process of building something, requires a cadence—a synchronization point to ensure a group of people is on the same page. In the early days of software, a build was seen as "one and done." We build the house, and then we're finished. Software is more like creating a botanical garden. It's an iterative process. It requires thought about the grand design, the detail requires attention, and there is as much maintenance as there are new additions. Thankfully, the Agile Manifesto has changed the mindset of linear builds versus iterative builds, but there are still many ways to approach this.

Applying Mapping to the Value Flywheel Effect

One of the most challenging things to achieve in software is a shared understanding. The process of developing software involves layers upon layers of abstraction: we take code and hide it behind a single call or button, and then we build again on top of that. The code is an abstraction, the architecture is an abstraction, and the deployed system (especially on the cloud) is an abstraction.

In a group of more than three or four people, team dynamics start to take effect, and responsibilities require clarification (never mind teams with several hundred people). The software serves a market, which is usually represented abstractly too. Finally, there's leadership, who need to understand all this context, shape a compelling purpose, and work it into a plan to reach an outcome.

Laced through these layers of abstraction is a sense of urgency. Few will admit it, but many companies or executives do not have a strategy—short-term thinking prevails ("Let's hit our numbers this quarter." rather than "Let's pivot to address new customer needs."). Of the companies that do have a strategy, there are two issues. First is the planning off-site—a day or two at the start of every year or quarter to "do strategy." Despite the best intentions, the planning off-site won't result in lasting change; usually, this point-in-time conversation is more about alignment than strategy. Second is the fact that many of the strategic tools used are static—they don't factor in movement.

Within each phase of the Value Flywheel Effect, it is essential to use mapping to help direct your path and course-correct along the way. Let's look at the four phases of the Value Flywheel Effect in more detail as they relate to mapping.

Phase 1—Purpose and Vision: The critical activity here is to clarify a purpose or "north star" and measure some key metrics. Time to value (as a version of lead time) is essential to capture here. How long does it take to build a feature and get it into the customer's hands? We'll use a map to flesh out the purpose. Often a map of the competitive market will help identify gaps your business can address. What are your differentiators? Do you understand what customer needs you are solving?

Phase 2—Challenge and Landscape: An assessment of psychological safety is crucial to understand your organization's "sociotechnical" elements—that is, how your people interact with your technology. Can you see the system of technology and people that your company is built from, or is it a big ball of mud? Question your organization's "way of working." Does challenge exist in your organization? Do healthy inquiry and debate of critical components exist in practice? The ability to map the capability of your organization is timely here. Do you have the people or capability to do what you need to do? How can you grow your people?

Phase 3—Next Best Action: We now have a purpose and situational awareness. Next, you'll need a robust technical strategy to start improving your time to value. A frictionless developer experience is an excellent place to start, and we recommend a serverless-first approach. Remember, code is a liability! Start as you mean to go on, so create the correct mindset now. Here, it's helpful to map the tech stack. What is good and bad about your organization's tech stack? You may find that your engineers are wasting vast amounts of time on a flawed process.

Phase 4—Long-Term Value: As the flywheel starts to turn, longer-term value is essential. Well-architected systems and sustainability combine to create a culture of problem prevention. Teams can use any of the three maps discussed in the next chapter (stack, org, or market) to troubleshoot issues, communicate, or discuss options. Mapping should be a constant and quick exercise as the team starts to move through the Value Flywheel.

Why Do We Need Mapping?

Let's be honest here: most companies are not performing effective software engineering, and they are wasting money. Why? Because aligning software engineering to business strategy is very difficult. To illustrate why we need something like mapping, let's look at the competition. How would a group of people (let's say cross-functional leaders) align on a strategy?

> **SWOT:** SWOT (or strengths, weakness, opportunities, and threats) is a simplistic exercise. It might be okay to use when we need to simplify strategy, but it's too easy to game SWOT and too hard to paint an accurate picture with it, as it often fails due to the ambiguity of language. A real challenge with SWOT analysis is that situational awareness and movement are not clearly shown. You can't draw a value chain from a SWOT analysis alone.

> **Business Model Canvas:** The Business Model Canvas (and several other similar canvas templates) is a powerful method of mapping out the commercial drivers and "nuts and bolts" of the business. That said, it's challenging to apply it to a team or department within a company, let alone apply it to software. Funnily enough, Business Model Canvases can often lead to teams deciding to create a "pay-per-use" service as a product. It is always an exciting conversation, but it's usually a waste of time when you're not a SaaS company, and you are unlikely to serve your customer.

> **Mission Statement:** When JFK gave his famous "We choose to go to the moon" speech in 1962, it was the original mission statement, the original moon shot. The Apollo program had already been running for two years, and the space race was five years old. The mission statement is usually the starter's flag—it's the signal to go! Mission statements are incredibly important to align everyone, but they must be built on an extensive body of work. Put it this way: if anyone "makes up" a mission statement without

extensive research and analysis, then ask them to leave your company. A cosmetic mission statement is highly damaging to a business's image.

OKRs: Objectives and key results, as an organizational objective, must include some metrics to aim for, and these metrics should be a stretch. They also need to be big, not incremental. They do not help you hit them, they don't give guidance on how to hit them, and they are tough to write. There have been lots of articles and books written on the many traps of writing OKRs. As a mechanism for communicating a goal? Fantastic. To make sense of things and figure out what to do? Nearly useless.

The Strategy Deck: The ease and ubiquity of PowerPoint has made many leaders over-reliant on thirty-year-old software to communicate strategy. Many leaders obsess with the look and feel of the slide, the speaking notes, and the distribution of such documents. The ability to create a "great deck" is scarce, and it takes a long time—but a slideshow is a point-in-time document. Strangely, we find it hard to reuse software, but we excel in reuse when it comes to PowerPoint. Obsessive tweaking of text and graphics is usually a sign that the "message must be controlled," which isn't a collaborative discussion. A big challenge with PowerPoint is often the creator's sense of ownership over the slides. Requesting change is often a direct challenge against the author, and it's a lot of work to create the deck. PowerPoint has contributed to an extraordinary and uncollaborative environment in many meetings. The strategy deck is important, but it can be misrepresented, and it's hard to change it.

The Six-Pager: Partly to challenge the proliferation of PowerPoint, Jeff Bezos from Amazon did a wonderful thing by introducing the six-pager, a memo that describes a proposal in detail, with lots of numbers, facts, and data. There is also a culture of continuous challenge and refinement until the document is correct. The six-pager is great, but it's time-consuming and requires skill to write and a particular type of culture comfortable with challenges. Unfortunately, many leaders don't have time, don't have the writing skill, and are uncomfortable with challenges.

The Backlog: With a sizable Agile team or organization, why not just put a story on the backlog and let the engineers figure it out? This may be a good way to drive throughput, but it lacks situational awareness. The team may move fast but ultimately end up at a dead end.

The Story: An executive narrative is very effective at creating a shared understanding, very compelling to listen to and brilliant for morale, but like the mission statement, it needs to be backed up by data and analysis.

Objectives: Often leaders compete to add a goal to everyone's objectives. This is not a strategy; it's execution, and it's often very weak.

What the Value Flywheel Effect shows us is that, unlike the aforementioned techniques, the habit of mapping must be developed and constantly in use. We may map as a team for alignment, communication, and challenge, but that map is then carried into the work, and the common language developed is used as the work unfolds. All these techniques do have a place as change is rolled out—we're not saying you can't ever use them. But mapping is essential as an early activity for several reasons.

- **Maps track movement:** It's possible to create a value chain and predict what will happen when certain bits evolve due to, for example, technology advancements.
- **Maps can provide focus by anchoring them to a specific user:** This ability to "scope a map" can keep everyone focused.
- **Maps allow for sensemaking:** How well do we understand certain areas? A knowledge gap will appear very quickly when mapping. The activity is quick, and it can be an iterative process. It's easy to answer a few questions and then reconvene.
- **Maps help us visualize the how:** A decent map should provide a narrative. This is the current state, then these changes may happen, which will result in this, and we then need to act.
- **When a map is created by a team, team members challenge the map, not the individual:** A map is an abstract representation, so it's never 100% correct. Feedback and insight are always helpful in building a better picture. The collaborative and incremental way that we map is almost the opposite of creating a PowerPoint (even collaboration in PowerPoint often ends up in assigning out slides individually).
- **Maps are quick when you get over the initial phases:** A map can be drawn on a dry-erase board with a marker in two minutes, and the value conversation starts instantly. Online tools also make this just as easy in remote or hybrid work environments.
- **Maps visualize inertia, incoming disruption, or potential problems:** Thanks to group situational awareness, it's possible to map out a scenario and come to the "we need to avoid that" conclusion quickly.

- **Maps and stories go hand in hand:** Some concepts in mapping predate the technique and are well established in a strategy. Using a common language and painting a compelling narrative is made more accessible with mapping. It helps prevent "smoke and mirrors" storytelling.
- **It's possible to track progress via mapping:** You can come back to a team months later and ask them to map again. Often, the team will show where they have made progress and moved things and what inertia has appeared and slowed them down. This makes it easy to assess how the team is moving forward and performing as a group.

Mapping is challenging, largely because defining and refining a purpose is challenging. It's tough to draw a map if you're unclear about where you're going. Remember, the organizational purpose is different from individual goals. You may have an individual goal to become a great mechanic, but your company might want to lead the market in low-cost automobiles. Company and individual goals should complement each other, but they are different. Mapping helps surface individual and company goals into a format that can be openly discussed and probed.

Why Wardley Mapping?

The constraints and language that Wardley Mapping provides are compelling for aligning your teams or peers. When mapping any scenario or problem, the first questions are the most potent: Who is the customer, and what do they need? Wardley Mapping starts by asking you to give the customer a name and understand who they are. Now, let's talk about what they *need*, not what they *want*.

Let's look at an example of Wardley Mapping. As cloud adoption started to grow in the late '00s, Simon Wardley surprised many people by describing the future before it happened. Using a technique he created, called Wardley Mapping, Wardley was able to create situational awareness and show how the future evolution of specific components in the value chain would change behaviors (see Figure 2.1). What was so impressive about using this technique in a deeply technical environment was the fact that many technologists spend a lot of time dissecting the details, and Wardley Mapping provides a common language to lift everyone at the same time.

Just at the time when containers and containerization were looking like the big strategic play for the cloud, Wardley declared that containers had won the battle, but serverless had won the cloud war. And sure enough, he was right. This ability to inject situational awareness and "look ahead" is critical in today's business environment and essential to realizing the full benefit of Wardley Mapping.

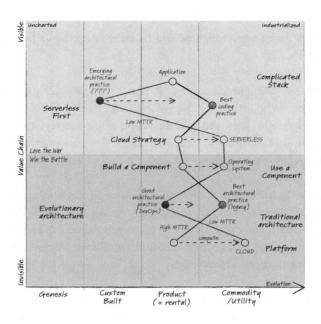

Figure 2.1: Serverless Won the War: Simon Wardley's Map Prediction of the Future
Source: Based on the famous map from Simon Wardley: https://twitter.com/swardley/status/10699651
23962527745?s=20&t=4NNhqXmcJXzFVZyZM5Vinw. Used with Permission of Simon Wardley.

Principles of Wardley Mapping

The first principle of mapping is to admit you are unsure of the way forward. It's worth exploring this principle and others deeper before we dive into the syntax of mapping. Mapping is not an easy skill to master, and it's worth understanding these key principles first.

Courage: Admit we are unsure of what to do next. Embrace the unknown by admitting the way forward is unclear. We need to explore and map out the territory, and then we'll be better informed when we decide to act.

Collaboration: Mapping is a collaborative exercise; debate is essential. Mapping in the open reduces tension and creates alignment. Creating a map individually and showing it to the team as "the plan" is not a good strategy. Using the elements of mapping as a "common language" helps the team connect, even outside the mapping session. Simple observations like "that's a commodity," "this feels like custom build," or "that's an inertia point" carry much more weight when the team understands the impact of those statements.

Empathy: The user's needs come first. Every mapping session starts with the question, "Who is the user and what do they need?" This gives the session an "outside-in" lens and sets the scope of the conversation. It's also important to discuss what we need to do for the customer, not how we make things easy for ourselves.

Perspective: Either dive down into the weeds or go big. Set the scope at the start of the conversation and try to stick to it. It's one of the most challenging things and may require a "parking lot" for submaps you'll draw later. It also reduces complexity: "This component represents data; we can deep dive on the data landscape in a separate map."

Narrative: Find the story. Ultimately, many maps will create a narrative. Part of the joy of mapping is that it's difficult to predict what that story will be. Once found, it's easy to describe the map using that story. This is also an excellent way for people new to mapping to understand it.

Focus: Don't map the world. It's very tempting to put everything down as a component. Once you have more than twenty elements (or components) on your map, it's gone too big—break it down.

Dialogue: The conversation is more important than the map. Mapping is not a formal notation; the point is not to create the perfect diagram, put it in a document, and send it to everyone. The map is merely a stepping stone to key observations. Treat the drawing as a throwaway and make sure meaningful conversation is captured on the map.

Challenge: Challenge the map, not the individual. The hidden magic of mapping is the facilitation of challenge. Compare these two statements: "I think that component should be more to the right," versus "I think this slide is incorrect." The first statement is straightforward, as the effort needed to move a component is tiny. The second statement is a popcorn moment. Just sit back, start snacking, and wait for the fireworks. But a single slide could be days or weeks of work. Maps facilitate the challenge of ideas by focusing on the map, not the person who suggests the idea.

Antipatterns of Mapping

Just as there are things you should do during mapping exercises, there are things you shouldn't do. We outline a few antipatterns to avoid below.

Gaming the system: Don't preempt or influence what the map will look like. It's a collaborative exercise, not a tool to influence others. Use the map to explore, to discover new information, and come to a shared understanding.

Mapping by yourself: If you bring a map into a team, then it's your map—not the team's map. The act of cocreation is one of the superpowers of mapping—remember, the conversation is more important than the map. A map represents a conversation and a line of thinking. Mapping by yourself is a good way to flesh out a thought process, but it's *your* thought process, not your team's. There are some things you can do to save time with the team, but don't do all the work up front.

Recreating an architectural diagram: Don't draw an architectural diagram and try to squeeze it into a map. Architectural diagrams are complex and important. Maps don't need the detail, and the relationships in maps are dependencies, not calls. Architectural diagrams rarely include the customer, apart from a token stick person. Maps revolve around the user's needs.

Over complicating: A map should simplify. It's okay to leave things out. There's a rule that the less experience you have in mapping, the simpler your map should be. Expert mappers: use no more than fifty elements in a map. Intermediates: no more than thirty elements. Beginners: don't use more than fifteen elements.

Endlessly asking, "What is a component?" Maps aren't formal notation; focus on finding the flow of users and needs. Identifying a component is an art form, not a science. You'll eventually find a "right size" for your map. It's sometimes helpful to think of a component as a service or capability. Think about what the thing does, not what it is (e.g., disposes garbage, not sanitary worker).

Making everything a map: If you're excited by the technique, don't overuse it. You'll drive your coworkers crazy! Yes, it's useful when thinking about value chains, user need, and the evolution of components. But mapping takes time to fully comprehend, so forcing mapping on people who have not been on your journey may not have instant success.

Showing the map to new people: Start with the conversion and observations. Some people will not care about the map. Every map has a narrative, and that narrative starts with an observation. Many people will only care about the observation and never need to see the map, while others will be interested in the narrative that led you to the observation. The narrative is not the order you drew the map in, it's the value chain narrative, starting from the anchor.

Working in a top-down environment: If a bad environment exists in the room, collaboration will suffer. It's not productive to force people to map. There are many techniques for creating psychological safety, and often preparation is required to get people into the room with the correct attitude. Facilitation is still required and critical for successful mapping sessions.

Getting Started

Starting a map is often the most challenging part. First, two things are required: One, you must have the expertise to examine it. Either you are the source of that expertise or have access to expertise (perhaps a book, person, or website). And two, you must have an approach to prevent analysis paralysis, or "failure to start." It's important not to over complicate the mapping process.

For a quick guide, especially when mapping a large area like your market competition, the Wardley Mapping Canvas (see Figure 2.2) contains a nice sequence of steps.[*]
The canvas has six main steps.

1. **Purpose:** This is straightforward. What is the purpose of the industry or market you are mapping? Capture a sentence (avoid jargon) about what your goal is. This helps frame the exercise. For example, "Electric automobiles provide transport without the combustion engine."

---

[*] The canvas is free to use, thanks to Creative Commons, and was created by Ben Mosior. The LearnWardleyMapping.com site that Ben created is one of the best places to learn to map, and Ben is an excellent teacher. He has many videos that are great primers.

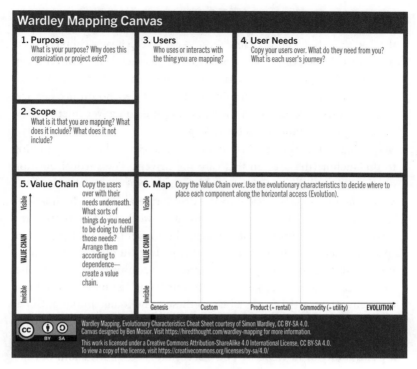

Figure 2.2: Wardley Mapping Canvas

2. **Scope:** How can you narrow the scope? It's very important to narrow up front, as the temptation to "map the world" will be frustrating and endless. For example, "We'll focus on the consumer within electric automobiles, only cars (not vans or bikes) and not infrastructure or support services."

3. **Users:** Let's be very specific about the user. This is the map's starting point and will anchor the entire exercise. If there are two or three user types, you may have one big map or several specific maps. At this point, decide on one user type to start with. For example, "Our user is the driver of our electric automobile."

4. **User Needs:** Keep it very simple and start listing what your user needs in this market. Describe the needs as a capability. There's no need to be extensive. Try and generalize. For example, "Our electric automobile driver needs a comfortable, electric-powered car with smart technology and low running costs." There are many more variations, but let's keep it simple to start.

5. **Value Chain:** The value chain is the activities or capabilities that support the user's needs. It's good to link these. Again, keep it very simple. This is not a formal notation, so you don't need to be precise. The conversation and overall shape of the map are more important than minor levels of detail. For example, "Low running costs might depend on tax, service, and fuel costs. Taking one of those, tax depends on government policy, which depends on the transport strategy."

6. **Map:** Finally, the value chains can be taken across to the map by linking to the anchor (the user, in this case the driver). The vertical position of the chain will be in the same order, the lowest point (closest to the x-axis) being the least visible to the driver (the anchor). The horizontal positioning of the point is more intricate work. Start by putting the whole chain in the Product phase. Keep the anchor (user) in the Product space and move to the first user need (e.g., low running cost). Now it's time to start talking and guessing. Is the low running cost in phase one, two, three, or four of evolution, with four being the most evolved and one being the least? We put labels to these to help our thinking: Genesis (1), Custom Built (2), Product (3), and Commodity (4). Usually, a process of elimination works. For example, "low running cost" is not a Commodity or in Genesis. The discussion is around Custom Built or Product. "It depends." Have the debate, challenge each other, and make a call. If you're wrong, you can come back and change it.

Higher-Level Mapping

The ability to think about and evaluate organizational capability is critical. Some confuse the issue with individual skills, even using the word "capability" to mean "skills." While a focus on the individual is essential, to move the company forward it's vital to be aware of the full organizational capabilities that currently exist and those that are needed. Once we have this vision, we can assess its effectiveness.

Ideally, you would map organizational capability directly with the CEO, which saves a lot of wasted time and effort trying to guess at their priorities and perspective. But you might also map organizational capability with other managers. Middle management often has two separate agendas at play. First, a manager needs to move the company forward, and second, the manager needs to make sure their team is protected. Often the second objective will kill the first.

It can be difficult to bring the audience, particularly managers, in as a partner in a mapping exercise, but hopefully, we can teach you some techniques in this book. First, ask yourself some of these key questions before starting your mapping session:

- What tool will work best to build your map with this audience? Are you remote or in the same office?
- What is the audience expecting?
- Do I give the audience a primer on Wardley Mapping beforehand?
- Do I send a preread? How detailed should I get?
- How detailed should I go in the session? Should we map a basic value chain or attempt to map the world?
- How fast or slow should I go?

Let's examine two scenarios of "mapping in the wild."

Mapping with the CEO

The first scenario involves a CEO and a group of leaders representing portions of the business. The CEO has a specific ask about removing a constraint. The task at hand is to present a technology strategy. The risk here is clear: the leaders in the room are hungry for the technology strategy and are eager to dissect, challenge, and engage. This is healthy, as their departments will drive this forward, committed. The CEO doesn't need to know the exact details of the tech strategy and may become frustrated if the original ask is forgotten when we drop into the weeds.

- What if we create a Wardley Map that shows the key value chain, the key organizational capabilities, and the key forces that will likely advance organizational capability? *That might work but there are sure to be some challenges.*
- What tool will work best? *It can't be very technical—maybe use Power-Point to create the map.*
- What is the audience expecting? *It's doubtful the leaders will agree to do a Wardley Map ahead of time, so let's not risk mentioning it.*
- Do I give the audience a primer on Wardley Mapping? *As per the previous question, no primer.*
- Do I send a preread? How detailed should I get? *No—just describe a basic value chain and a simple evolutionary axis.*
- How detailed should I go? Should we map a basic value chain or attempt to map the world? *Stick to a single value chain. Try to map anything larger than that and the group will lose focus.*

- How fast or slow should I go? *Let the conversation dictate the pace. Don't be afraid to pause and be comfortable in the silent contemplation of the room.*

The stage is set. There are sixty minutes scheduled, and the activity will start with a straightforward value chain in a slide. Start by explaining the value chain and the evolutionary axis (the *x*-axis). For the axis, label the four phases differently: instead of Genesis, Custom Built, Product, Commodity (labeled via activities), use Novel, Emerging, Good, Best (labeled via practices).

Start the value chain with "time to market" and flow several needs underneath. After a brief explanation, start the conversation in the room. Gesturing to the bottom of the map, ask: How does everyone feel the company does at achieving a good time to market—novel, emerging, good, best?

Slowly, the people in the room start to offer opinions. One says, "I think it's emerging; some do this well, but others don't. We know how to do this, but we don't have consistency yet." To provoke a response, move that element on the map left or right and ask for responses (audience participation is always a good icebreaker). Repeat for other elements and let the conversation (and the map) grow organically.

The CEO instantly understands the shape of the graph but doesn't lead the discussion, letting the other audience members share their views. The team finishes the exercise, and there is a frank assessment of the map: the organization looks healthy, but there are some prominent areas of opportunity. Some organizational capabilities need to be improved more than others.

Now you have an "as-is" map. The next step is to move some elements around, so the audience agrees on the "to-be" picture and includes ideas to drive that movement.

The CEO and team have just created a Wardley Map and agreed on what they'll do to evolve the organization. The end of the meeting discusses which actions should be prioritized to drive that movement.

Looking back, you note that the CEO immediately understood the shape of the map, despite not being aware of Wardley Mapping. A value chain is easy to understand, and the effectiveness of practices (evolutionary axis) is also straightforward. With the context set, the group can now start tracking plans, execution, and results. While the leaders in the room enjoyed the exercise and gave a frank assessment, they wanted to see a more detailed version of the plan. That's normal, as they'll be the ones to implement the new strategies.

Mapping with the Experts

The second scenario involves a group of experts performing their first Wardley Mapping session. They're all technical leaders, so they're seasoned strategic thinkers and not afraid of new syntax to help the discussion. The ask is to assess organizational capability and make a buy versus build decision. Can we cocreate a Wardley Map (or maps) of a large area and derive insights and observations from it?

Let's look at the same set of questions as before:

- What tool will work best? *Cocreation is critical, so an online whiteboard will give team members a way to provide input and time to think.*
- What is the audience expecting? *The team is willing to try a mapping session, so we have put aside time.*
- Do I give the audience a primer on Wardley Mapping? *Yes, this group is prepared and willing to learn. Send them a link to Ben Mosior from Hired Thought's site (LearnWardleyMapping.com) and encourage them to play around with maps.*
- Do I send a preread? How detailed should I get? *Yes, but resist the temptation to overload. Send a basic Wardley Map and explain its shape.*
- How detailed should I go? Should we map a basic value chain or attempt to map the world? *The scope will be broad, so don't introduce advanced techniques like pipelines or flow. Stick to value chains and movement.*
- How fast or slow should I go? *Create a time allocation and a goal. Give lots of time for collaboration and maybe split the time into two or three sessions (sixty to ninety minutes is a good block for one session).*

Share the preread and kick off the session a couple of days later. First off, don't assume the preread has been read. The team is mapping out a large area, so they have things they want to say and ideas they don't want to lose. These are climatic patterns, and the team captures significant insights, events, or risks on the map.

This provides an excellent basis for identifying as many value chains as are needed. Straight away, different concerns take shape, so three different anchors (or personas) are created to split the value chains. Some of the value chains apply to two or three personas, but that's okay. There are three or four example value chains created (a user need with a few dependent capabilities); this is enough to start the team off.

Even though the team has expertise in this topic, this is the first time they've stepped back and created simple value chains for their users and the fundamental user needs. Customer-centric analysis sounds like a straightforward approach, and many designers will see it as a self-evident approach, but it's not as prevalent as it should be.

The team spends a considerable amount of time creating, discussing, and tweaking value chains. This is a relatively easy activity. The challenge in Wardley Mapping often comes with positioning components on the evolutionary axis (*x*-axis), so sometimes it is best not to start with evolution. When the value chains are complete, the facilitators add them into a Wardley Map to further discuss effectiveness, importance, movement, and buy versus build.

Remember, even very technical individuals will struggle with Wardley Mapping, but starting with value chains always results in a fruitful conversation. Adding the value chain into a map might take some effort and help from a mapping expert, though.

In discussions after the exercise, team members shared two overriding feelings: First, "I love this technique. It made me think completely differently about our problem." And second, "I can now understand a map, but I don't think I could draw one yet."

While mapping provides a view of an organization's needs and underlying structures, they're hard to draw, and no map is perfect or correct. The best advice is to try it, enjoy it, and never regret a session.

Takeaways

One of the most common problems in business is the phrase "but I didn't know"—in other words, the biggest problem in business is lacking situational awareness. Mapping is a superpower for building situational awareness, discussing it in a group, and sharing insights.

A word of caution: Wardley Mapping is a difficult skill to learn and even harder to master. Practice by reading maps, drawing simple maps, and discussing the evolution of components and value chains with peers. There are some basic first steps, but don't go all in too early. Be good to yourself. Give yourself the permission and the space to learn. But here are a few more tips to help you on your journey.

- **Don't be too formal with mapping.** The best maps are the ones that cut through the leadership and organizational blockers.
- **Don't be afraid to practice.** Grab a pencil and paper and draw a quick map. It's okay if it's not perfect. The map isn't wrong, it's just not right. In fact, they are never "right," but they don't have to be. Their purpose is to provide insight and raise questions.
- **Every map has at least one story in it.** Your job is to find that story, and hopefully, it may have an ending that you hadn't noticed or considered.
- **Bring other people in.** The conversation is always valuable when drawing a map. Start with the user need and see what happens. Remember, when you're part of a group that's working on a map, it's important to challenge the map, not the mapper.

- **Good situational awareness is a superpower.** Use Wardley Maps to find yours.

Next, we'll dive into how to draw Wardley Maps in more detail. (If you're already quite familiar with Wardley Mapping, you can choose to skip or skim this next chapter.)

CHAPTER 3
HOW TO WARDLEY MAP

The practice of mapping is difficult. Anyone who claims they are an expert mapper should be immediately discounted. In this chapter, we'll break down a little of what you need to know to get started. But keep in mind that mapping, like any skill, takes practice. And the more you practice, the better you get.

If you're already experienced at Wardley Mapping, you might choose to skim over this chapter. But as we said, mapping takes practice, and we can all use more practice from time to time. So, we encourage even experienced mappers to review this chapter before moving on in the book.

Anatomy of a Map

The Axes

In Wardley Maps, the *y*-axis (vertical) represents visibility to the user. Like a traditional value chain, the higher the component, the more the user can see it. For example, a web page might be at the top, while a database or a server might be near the bottom.

The *x*-axis (horizontal) is more complex and contains the four stages of evolution—I, II, III, and IV. They are usually labeled as Genesis, Custom Built, Product, and Commodity (see a blank Wardley Map in Figure 3.1). It's okay to change the labels, but the progression should be similar. Let's break them down further.

I—Genesis: The object is rare, poorly understood, and uncertain. There is the potential to have high future worth. The object is described with wonder, and it's different from anything else in the market in this context. It should be a competitive advantage and experimentation is rife.

II—Custom Built: More people are starting to consume and understand the object. The market is forming, and there is potential ROI. As understanding increases, users start to find its value, but inconsistently. The key focus is learning.

III—Product/Rental: Consumption is rapidly increasing as the market grows. The object is profitable, new features can differentiate it, and there is a refinement of needs. Things are starting to get competitive, and the profit margins mean it's a crowded market.

IV—Commodity/Utility: The object is widespread and stabilizing. It's a mature and ordered market. The high volume has decreased margins. Operational efficiency is king, and failure is not tolerated in the market. This is the cost of doing business (like electricity).

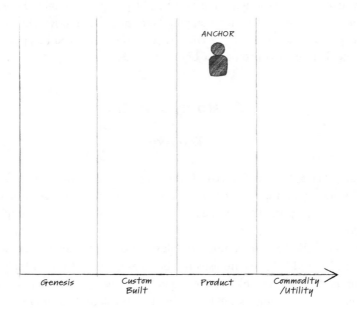

Figure 3.1: A Blank Wardley Map

The labels on these four stages can change, as we stated above, but it's more important to place components in the correct stage. It's not a precise act; it should *feel* about right. Sometimes an easy way to start is to place the least common elements to the left on the *x*-axis (Genesis) and the more common elements to the right (Commodity).

The User and Components

Most maps will have one or two users at the top; this is the anchor component and forms the top of the value chain. It's often helpful to discuss the user in detail, almost like a user persona. The user will have needs (which are components), and those components will have dependencies. The full link from user, to needs, to dependencies equals your value chain.

A simple example for a café would be:

- The customer needs a hot drink (cup of tea).
- The cup of tea needs a cup, some tea, and hot water.
- Hot water needs a kettle and water.
- The kettle needs power or heat.

The dependencies between components are often shown as lines or arrows—both are fine. Some people add a label to the dependency to add extra context, but this is not necessary. Don't add too much additional information and overload the map unnecessarily. There are several types of components, but describing components is a more advanced notation. For example, is the component built, rented, or bought? There are many other aspects you could mention, but when starting to map, it's best to keep it simple. Figure 3.2 shows an example map of a café.

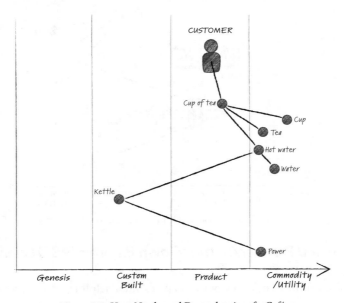

Figure 3.2: User, Needs, and Dependencies of a Café

Movement and Inertia

Once a value chain has been mapped out, arrows can be added to show a component moving to the right along the *x*-axis. This denotes a future evolution as a product becomes more commoditized. Compute is a famous example—it took forty years for computing to move from Genesis (a new differentiator in a business) to Commodity (something you rent from any cloud provider).

It's also essential to show inertia in your maps, where components are being blocked from moving to the right on the *x*-axis. Inertia blocks are usually things like regulation, company culture, cost, immature technology, etc. Inertia is represented by placing a block to the right of a component.

Inertia can be caused by any number of reasons. Sometimes it's helpful to write the reason on the map. In Figure 3.3, the staff would like to upgrade the kettle, which would speed up service. The inertia point is the café owner doesn't see the benefit and is prevented the staff from making the upgrade.

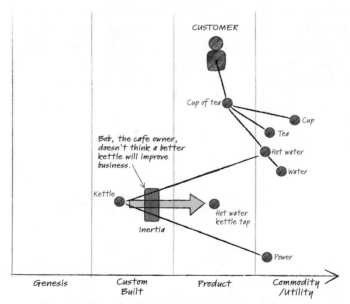

Figure 3.3: Example of a Block (Inertia Point) along the *x*-Axis

Team and Pioneer/Settler/Town Planner (PST) Overlay

When you've got the basic shape of the map, it's often helpful to overlay two separate views (either one of them or both) onto the map. The team overlay denotes that team

A works here, team B works there, and so on. Seeing which team does what can help you assess if the technical ownership responsibilities are correct. If everyone owns everything, you've got a problem (likewise if there's no ownership).

In the "cup of tea" scenario, the map in Figure 3.4 shows two different groups: "front of house" and "kitchen." This is quite a clean grouping. In your map, you might see teams that either overlap or are all over the map. This suggests that teams might be doing the wrong work or that they are spread too thin.

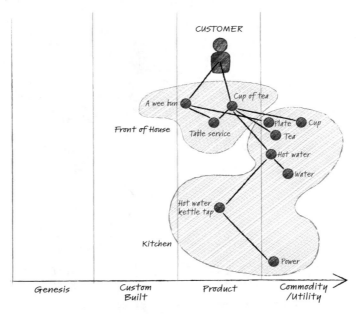

Figure 3.4: Team Overlay

The second overlay is pioneer/settler/town planner (PST). This will be discussed more as we move on, but in short: Pioneers love uncertainty and thrive in building the new. They're likely to create "the first-ever X." Settlers can scale; they will refine, harden, and understand the concept. Settlers love to learn and share their learnings. They listen to customers and build things they love, and they're likely to create "that fantastic product." Town planners build well-defined things well. They industrialize well-understood concepts and create the building blocks for pioneering teams. They are likely to make things that are fast, cheap, and failure-proof.

All three groups are equally important, skilled, and critical. When the PST overlay is combined with the team overlay, you might find that a pioneering team is working on a commodity, or a town planner team is working on a custom build. These mismatches may be the source of some of your pain.

In Figure 3.5, we extend the "cup of tea" scenario map to include some artisan ingredients. A pioneer/settler/town planner lens has also been added. The buyer is very much living in uncertainty, trying to find novel new ingredients, and is thus a pioneer. The "front of house" is very customer-centric and learning as they go about what works and what doesn't work—typical settlers. The kitchen represents the town planners: focused on efficiency, little failure, and established processes. All three groups are critical to the success of the café but in different ways.

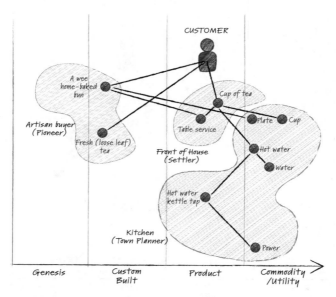

Figure 3.5: Pioneers/Settlers/Town Planners Overlay

Pipeline

Another useful mapping element is the pipeline. A pipeline shows the continuous evolution of a component, usually when there is a clear path of evolution, not just a shift.

In Figure 3.6, we can see the tea component represented as a pipeline. On the left, fresh tea (or loose leaf tea) is novel and evolves from a nice pyramid tea bag to a regular tea bag. Cost is likely high on the left and lower on the right.

The right-hand side of the pipeline includes more mass-market tea and represents a more evolved state. You can think of a pipeline as a slider from which you can select one component, fresh tea (loose leaf) or a tea bag, not both together. When reading the map, we select one component from the pipeline to use in our example (Figure 3.6).

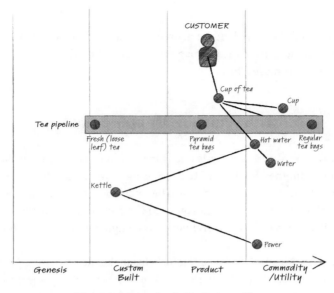

Figure 3.6: Example of a Pipeline on a Map

Submaps

When a map becomes complex, you might need to make a submap. In Figure 3.7, we've replaced the components of the kitchen with an annotation for a submap.

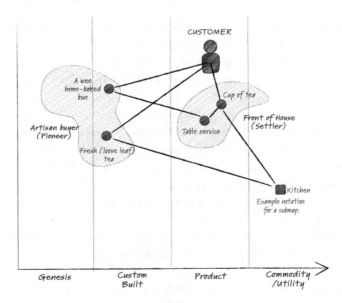

Figure 3.7: Example of a Submap

Usually, this is illustrated on the main map by a square or simply via an annotation. You would then create the submap on a separate board or paper. Make sure to keep it close to your master map.

The Wardley Mapping Grid

Understanding Wardley Mapping is one thing. Having the courage to bring it into the company is another. Some have tried to bring it into leadership teams, which is very effective if you don't get thrown out. The "map your stack" technique (discussed later in this chapter and again in Chapter 15) is effective when mapping with engineers and will likely require a few architects, lead engineers, or tech leads to fully roll it out.

The Wardley Mapping Grid technique helps make the map more accessible and simplifies the conversation (see Figure 3.8). Break the mapping plane into a grid and give it a simple reference:

1. **Visible:** Nearest to the user; component is visible to user.
2. **Aware:** The user *may* be aware of this component.
3. **Unaware:** The user is likely unaware of the component.
4. **Invisible:** the user has no visibility, nor knowledge, of the component.

Next, mark Genesis as A, Custom Built as B, Product/Rental as C, and Commodity/Utility as D. The intent of this simple system is a little like playing Battleship. When discussing a tech stack (for example), the mappers can quickly get a mental model of systems and start from a common understanding. For example:

- The new machine-learning component is currently in A2: The user is aware of it and it's in Genesis. Good, we need to get better at this.
- The Java system written by contractors six years ago is in B3: The user is unaware and it's Custom Built. We need to move this. The time it takes to maintain it is blocking other things.
- The cool UI is in C1: The user can see it and we are very good at it. This is the sweet spot of a UI.
- The logging system is in D4: The user neither sees it nor cares about it, and it's totally a commodity. Please tell me we didn't build this ourselves.

This simple system can be used with teams, and it's easy to describe potential moves: "We need to refactor those rules, which will move the component from B3 to

C3; then we can upgrade it, which will be cheaper to run." After using this grid a few times, engineers may start to draw four-by-four grids on the board and draw in the stack during regular discussions. It's used to debate what to refactor and chart a path through a modernization journey.

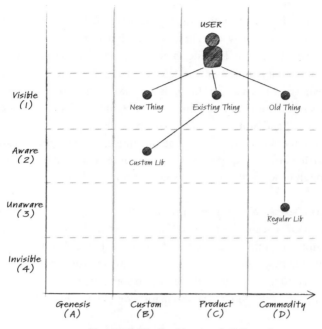

Figure 3.8: Wardley Mapping Grid Example

We created this technique and used it for many years to "meet the teams where they are" and help them decide what they need to do next. It works best when it's not too formal, drawn roughly on a board with sticky notes as the components, and it gets the team involved. Like event storming, this strategy gets people involved and interacting quickly.

Tips to Get Started

The best way to start mapping is to go to a board or grab a pencil and paper and just try it. There are some fantastic tools available for virtual mapping, but it's important to keep early sessions simple.

When mapping, think about these three phrases:

Harvest other ideas: Don't copy a map. Use another map or document to understand your organization's dependencies. For example, a mobile app may have some key dependencies. In time, the mapping community will share these common patterns to accelerate first-time mappers.

Collaborate on the map: Designing a practical collaboration session is essential. There are a few key areas to consider. First, ensure all participants are willing to try the session. Provide some simple preparation work or contextual materials that people can read ahead of time. Allocate enough time to create the map; don't rush. Set the right tone: everyone is participating in the map—it's not a presentation. Finally, facilitate fairly—let people speak, make their point, and add to the map. Welcome all suggestions and don't dismiss ideas out of hand. Just like a good meeting, a good mapping session relies on participants being prepared to contribute. The facilitator should allocate enough time so everyone can share without rushing the work.

Present it as a story: Weeks or months after the fact, you may well come back to the map to see if the story still makes sense. If the map instantly builds the story in your head, then that's a good sign. If it takes time to understand your map, then you might need to revisit the map or make a new one. A second test is to present the map to someone who was not at the initial meeting and ask them to tell the map's story. Did they get it?

Applying the Value Flywheel Effect to Wardley Mapping

Often, the story of how a company came to be is told as a straightforward series of events with a specific starting point. There are many smaller, interconnected, or diffuse events that impact other events. These are often overlooked when companies tell their "transformation story." The Value Flywheel Effect is one of those events. It exists outside of the company strategy and often acts as the engine that drives transformation and success. To get your flywheel started, it's important that the organization has a strong value chain, a desire to execute, and the will to continue the journey. A simple Wardley Map can get us started.

First, we must start by identifying your value chain (see Figure 3.9). The value chain is quite simple. For the stakeholder of your company, there must be a clear business goal, a plan. For this plan to execute correctly, the plan will need some effective people or teams of people. Those teams will need technology to help them, and the technology will need to work effectively (i.e., not keep falling over).

STAKEHOLDER

Needs

BUSINESS GOAL

Needs

STRONG
TEAMS

Needs

APPROPRIATE
TECHNOLOGY

Needs

RELIABLE
SYSTEMS

Figure 3.9: Simple Stakeholder
Value Chain

If we take the value chain from Figure 3.9 and turn it into a Wardley Map (Figure 3.10), we can assess what we need to focus on as well as the potential inertia points. We'll map our value chain on the map with the stakeholder at the top. Positioning the elements left to right (or along the *x*-axis) depends on how well developed that element is.

Let's work through our approach. First, your organization needs to have a clear business goal and single-threaded leadership committed to delivering (the first phase of the Value Flywheel). In Figure 3.10, this is shown as a pipeline. The business goal is represented as a cascading value, with the most ambitious (difficult) goal to the far left (in Genesis) and the tamer achievable goal to the far right (Commodity).

Teams need to be crystal clear on their goal. The North Star Framework can help (see Chapter 5). It should be possible to link the lagging output metrics in the high-level vision to smaller leading input metrics that the teams can track and improve. In saying that, all metrics must be observable—presented in real-time and in dashboards. A transparent system of telemetry across the entire system will keep everyone focused on the goal at hand. If business results are not presented in real-time or if they need to be generated manually, you are not a data-driven company. Remember, all software in the cloud has fine-grained audit trails; you just need to tap into them.

The more the goal or north star of the organization moves to the left on the map (toward Genesis), the more unique that goal is on the market (and potentially more valuable). But, if the components below the goal are also situated too far to the left (i.e., if the elements needed to achieve the goal are still too expensive, require too much toil, etc.), then the business goal may seem too far-fetched—it will not get the support required.

The best outcome for this map is the business goal to the left and everything else to the right. This would represent a goal that is unique on the market and potentially highly valuable (in Genesis on the map) but can be easily supported through the consumption of products and commodities (i.e., nothing must be custom built to support the business goal).

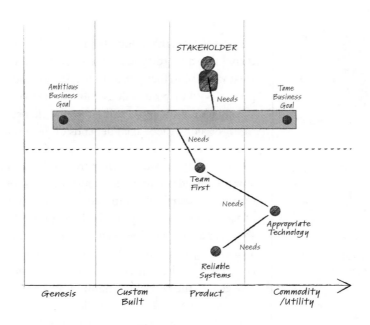

Figure 3.10: Simple Stakeholder Wardley Map

Let's take a moment to look at that in another way. Why did it take Tesla to change the electric vehicle market? Many tried before and failed. When Tesla was founded in 2003, the idea (business goal) was to produce electric vehicles that were better, quicker, and more fun. In 2003, this idea was firmly in Genesis. Tesla also recognized that three underlying components would need to evolve to deliver on their idea: the battery, the car software, and the motor. Tesla was designed to spend the early years of its existence moving these underlying components to the right, so it could pull the electric car into Product (through Genesis and Custom Built).

Once we have established clarity of purpose, we need to think about our people (phase two of the Value Flywheel: Challenge and Landscape). A team-first focus encourages strong units of delivery, as has been observed repeatedly in numerous organizations. But diverse and cross-functional teams can only be effective if they are supported—if an environment of psychological safety is created. These two elements (creating a team-first, psychologically safe environment) create the necessary environment to confront the business challenge.

Next, these teams must work in a low-friction environment, somewhere that they can experiment and do their jobs efficiently, without lots of unnecessary overhead and hand-offs. (Hint: one way to achieve low friction is for other teams, enablement teams, to help them with their work—good old continuous improvement.)

With a team-first environment, great things can happen, but we must also ensure that the technology strategy deployed will move the team forward, not impede their progress (phase three of the Value Flywheel: Next Best Action). The level of engineering in the team must be held to a high standard—not just technology from yesteryear shifted onto a different platform. A serverless-first approach helps here.

Now that you've thought about your people and the technology they'll use, it's time to think about how to address risk. When building complex cloud systems, for example, risk must be mitigated quickly. The landscape is always changing, so it's essential to constantly assess and get ahead of risk—security risk, business risk, maintenance risk, and compliance risk. Reduced risk leads to sustained long-term value (phase four of the Value Flywheel: Long-Term Value).

Next on the list of map components is your platform. This system must be maintainable and sustainable. What happens if your customer base triples in size quickly—Can everything scale? There is no point in having a great software system if the manual onboarding process prevents customers from using it. Your platform needs to be to the right on your map as much as possible—well known, well understood, and well practiced. If it's new and novel (on the left of your map), there will be mistakes (or system failures).

Three Styles of Maps

Throughout this book, we will use three different "styles" of maps to illustrate concepts and improve our situational awareness during the different phases of the Value Flywheel: mapping the stack, mapping the organization, and mapping the market. The three styles employ varying levels of detail.

Mapping the Stack

The lowest level of detail is *mapping the stack*. This map has quite a narrow scope and is relatively well defined. "Mapping the stack" typically happens within a software team. It's a way to look at the software stack and predict movement and inertia as software evolves. After all, software systems are never static and require constant maintenance.

Example
A bank has an aging system and needs to update its digital channels. The original site is part of the core system and hasn't been updated in over ten years. The engineers say it's too complex; in fact, it's so complex that it'll take five years to rewrite. The business owner is beyond frustrated and pays a lot of money to run the system every day; she reads customer feedback about poor experiences and reports of failures. The only option is to bring in an army of consultants. We now have a five-year

plan and a beautiful PowerPoint presentation championing the move, but we are still unsure how to start (and we also have a hefty bill from the consultants).

A second approach would be to take the technical leads and map out the stack. Starting from the customer (user), draw out the value chain of UX from the front end to the different API calls to the underlying, downstream systems. This will show us two things: (1) how well the system is broken up, and (2) if the responsibilities are split nicely between teams.

A typical pattern here is the "big ball of mud"—everything depends on everything else, and everyone is doing everything. This may sound like a great definition of "fungibility," but fungibility only works when everything is a commodity; it's a disaster when there are complicated or complex systems.

Once the value chain is mapped out and we identify the components and how evolved they are, we can add inertia points. A common inertia point is a system constraint: "We can't replace X because it depends on Y." Often, replacing a system will involve breaking dependencies—then it's easy to replace components.

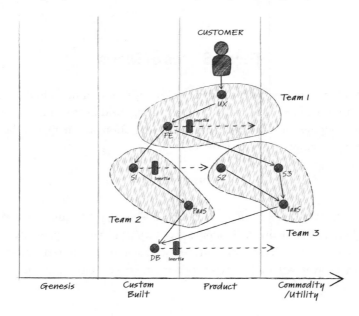

Figure 3.11: Mapping the Stack Example

Most importantly, at this point, we now have a room full of technical leads who have a picture (like Figure 3.11) in front of them that answers these questions:

- What are the key components of the tech stack?
- Are the teams correctly aligned?

- Which components are differentiators to our business? (A cool logging framework might keep developers happy, but your CFO won't notice.)
- What do we need to move to evolve the architecture?
- What are the inertia points?*

Actions

Moving a system forward is like maintaining and upgrading an old house while you're still living in it. You're aware of many things that need to be fixed: some are significant (turning your attic into a livable loft) and some are small (removing a small tree from the garden). Some jobs are urgent (replacing a leaking shower) and some are not (repainting a window frame). Performing a proper inventory and understanding that when you fix the shower, you should also replace the taps in the sink, is important. Painting the window frame may expose rot, which is a much bigger job. Mapping out the areas that require work and deciding how important they are and how to chunk up the work is the key to making progress.

With the stack mapped out, the technical leads now have a list of key observations and needs, and they can tackle them in an order that makes sense. Each of these observations has a ton of technical details that also need to be worked through, but the map will offer insights that will be new to the technical leads.

Mapping the Organization

The next level is *mapping the organization*. It's a good idea to do this step after you've mapped the stack, as the teams may not have the structure or correct capabilities to perform the work required. But you can also map how teams will organize around a product or event. This map will shed light on how the organization is structured and who can do what. Most importantly, it starts to address the question: "Are we working on the right thing?"

Example

A project's technical leads have just reached a major milestone, and the cloud-native system they created is performing way beyond initial expectations. During the change, they decided to run a few internal tech conference events to help staff understand the new tech and get comfortable with the paradigm shift. Everyone loved the internal events. A day to hear from your peers, lots of snacks, and a party at the end—best event ever! Now there's an opportunity to organize an external technical conference. A very different proposition. "Can we just use the same playbook?" one

---

* Learn more about the answers to the questions on page 186. And read a real life scenario in the Liberty Mutual case study in Chapter 16.

of the organizers asks. It might be tempting to do so, but an external conference has different needs than an internal one. A wise head, at this point, will suggest mapping out what needs to happen. Let's map the capabilities we need.

Starting with the customer need, the first questions are about the content: Will this event be attractive? Is it worth a day off work and the cost of the ticket? This is a deal-breaker. Next, are the speakers going to be any good? Next, how do we market to the attendees—no point in having a great event if no one knows about it! Will the venue be good enough? How can a customer buy a ticket? Will there be food? Is there any swag? What about public liability insurance? What about a code of conduct? And what about a map of the venue? So many questions that didn't apply when everyone worked at the same company.

You can see how it might be useful to map how your people will be organized around this specific event. When mapping how people are organized, it's possible just to map for a specific project or work area. In our example, we start with the conference attendee and map out their needs. Some needs are immediate (quality of the content) and some are buried (food quality). You must also factor in your budget.

Now you can draw several value chains, and some areas can be shown as sliding scales (pipelines). We can mark things that are critical to the event's success that only the organizers can do, as well as other items that can be off loaded (e.g., you don't want a bunch of software architects making lunch). This map will help manage the conference and ensure there's clear responsibility for different areas.

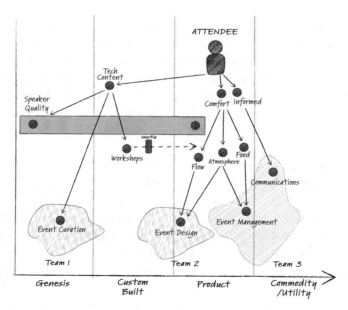

Figure 3.12: Mapping the Organization for an Event

At this point, after your map looks like Figure 3.12, you can make some key observations:

- The curation of the event is a key indicator of success.
- Tech leads will not be able to manage the event by themselves.
- There is a sliding scale for speaker quality; you must decide which topics to include and who to invite.
- The teams outlined should be formed, and the event will execute with these assumptions.

Actions

The example we gave above might be a simplistic story, but teams and capabilities are difficult to illustrate at the best of times. The map gives a clear picture of the customer's needs, along with how evolved they are. Of course, all these needs are critically important—with no communication, there is no event. What is important here is the capability. Is it worth training a software architect in marketing, communications, and PR, or is it more efficient to hire an expert? The software architect is a subject matter expert in the topic of the event, not the organization of events.

The map clearly shows the capabilities required to run an event, so a sensible team will focus the technical experts on the content and potentially hire other jobs from an events company or similar. An essential addition here from the "mapping the stack" example is the continuous scale—this mustn't be a definitive attribute; it's part of a scale, and a decision is required on what to aim for.

Mapping the Market

The highest level of mapping is *mapping the market*. This is very complex, as it covers a vast scope. One of the key challenges with mapping is knowing what not to map. It's very easy to "boil the ocean" with maps—that's partly why the first question asks us to focus on the customer or user, not the company.

Example

The digitization of everything has been a constant topic of conversation for decades. The news around technical advancement is constant. Many personal banks have discussed closing branches for many years—it's often reported as a failure for customers. The gradual shift to digital channels has been imminent but just waiting on a significant forcing function. When the global COVID-19 pandemic forced all branches to close for months, the digital systems of many banks were tested.

The pattern of walking into a branch and queuing has been around for many years. We often have complex actions to carry out and require the advice of a teller.

Everyone knows there are things the teller can do that you can't do on the website. At the same time, it's only a matter of time before you can do everything on the website, and the face-to-face experience evolves into something else.

The customer need for banking is primarily personal finance management: Help me manage my money and financial affairs. Don't talk to me about bank products and services; just help me with my savings, salary, spending, and long-term purchases (like a house). If a customer-centric view is taken, then it's easy to map these needs. These needs then depend on other components, and most can be performed online. There are some enabling dependencies—security, user experience, and responsiveness.

But what about disruptions? Could there be challenges from other banks, startups, or even big tech companies? Are there points of inertia that will prevent progress? What are they, and should we wait until they are resolved—or do we preempt them and gain a first-mover advantage? What are the weak signals that we should look out for? We don't want to be surprised. Will AI completely revolutionize personal banking? If so, in what way? What is even possible? What kind of AI—voice, computer image, machine learning, or even robotics? Could it even be as simple as an existing channel (like voice) appearing on a new device (like a television)? It's a minefield of decisions and developments—certainly not something that a two-by-two SWOT analysis will solve. "Our strength is technology, so we'll be okay." No.

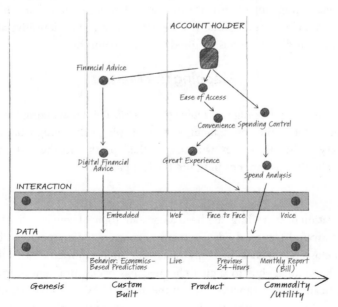

Figure 3.13: Mapping the Market Example

Actions

The pipelines illustrated in Figure 3.13 show how two key components will evolve. The *interaction* will evolve with the *user experience* market. We are moving from traditional interactions to those embedded in other places. So how will that affect digital banking? For *data*, we are evolving from monthly to real-time. What can we do with that?

Showing a pipeline can often give us a way to predict how a capability will evolve by taking examples from other industries. We can see from social media how interaction is evolving and how that same evolution affects our industry. We can ask ourselves questions like, "What happens when banking is embedded in a watch? What about identity, security, and user experience? What else can we do? Payments, approvals, notifications?" A pipeline provides the constraint for ideation.

Takeaways

This has been a dense section, so thank you for sticking with it! We've described the basics of Wardley Mapping and tried to make it real with some examples. We also explored how you can apply the Value Flywheel Effect to Wardley Mapping, and the three types of maps we'll be using throughout the book to help us gain situational awareness.

But, as we said in the last chapter, often the mapping session itself is more valuable than the map created at the end. So, in the next chapter, we've created a fictional mapping session to not only help you with how to map but also to show you the larger value that can be gained by mapping with your team.

CHAPTER 4
EXAMPLE MAPPING SESSION

As we stated already, the conversation that takes place during the mapping session is often more important than the final artifact. With that in mind, let's look at an example mapping session before moving on to the four phases of the Value Flywheel Effect.

In this scenario, the lead engineer, Laura, and one of the cloud engineers, Clive, (of a normal company, not a tech company) have been asked to "be more innovative." They know that doing a quick AI prototype will make the question go away for six months, but they want to change things properly.

They also know that if they drive transformation in the engineering department, it will be better for everyone. They want to map out the landscape from the business owner's perspective. They know that once they get started, the language will become very technical, so creating a map will help align them on the high-level moves and messaging they need.

User Need

Laura: Our user should be the CIO. They'll care most about cloud transformation and benefits.

Clive: No, I think it needs to be the head of the business. They care about cost and speed, which is what the cloud can give.

Laura: Okay, I can work with that. Which do you think is more advanced—speed or time to value?

Clive: Cost for sure. We could still increase our speed.

Laura: I agree. Okay, let's put cost slightly to the right on our map.

Clive: Yeah, good start.

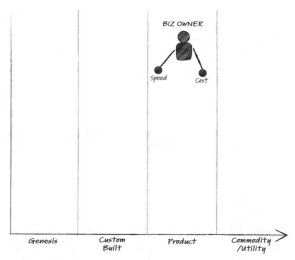

Figure 4.1: Example Story Map: User Need

Dependencies

Clive: Cost needs to choose the right type of technology. It's not only build cost; it's also run cost.

Laura: Yes, we should separate those.

Clive: Run cost is lower when it's pay per use. Some self-run services are more expensive to run as there is a team involved.

Laura: And for speed, you need the organization to be well-coordinated and orchestrated in the work. A real agile system.

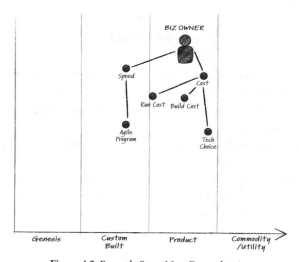

Figure 4.2: Example Story Map: Dependencies

Further Dependencies

Clive: For some of those tech choices to work well, you need strong engineering practice.

Laura: Yes, it feels like some of these needs eventually merge. And you also need decent cloud infrastructure. But that's a lot of work, so it will suck up time from everything else if it's not in place.

Clive: And what about business alignment?

Laura: Maybe we reflect it as leadership? It spans technology and business. It's also a rabbit hole we don't want to go down!

Clive: Yes, but we should separate it from architectural leadership, as that affects all of these.

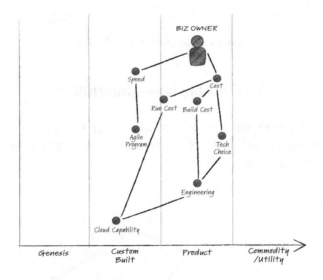

Figure 4.3: Example Story Map: Further Dependencies

The Pipeline...

Laura: For movement, I think that cloud needs to move over to Commodity quickly. I'm going to include a pipeline running along the x-axis to represent that. This movement is going to include things like networking, security, guardrails, operations. . . . Adding "Capability" to the name makes it a higher level component, so we remember there are a number of dependencies required to move Cloud Capability along the pipeline. What do you think of that solution?

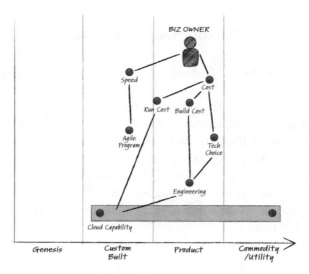

Figure 4.4: Example Story Map: Pipeline

. . . Enables New Capability

Clive: Exactly, which then acts as an enabler for a new capability (serverless) that comes in from Genesis. It's Custom Built at the start but will still help speed (and cost, I suppose).

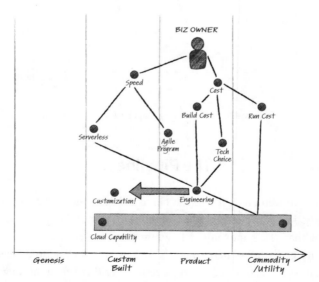

Figure 4.5: Story Map: New Capability

Inertia

Laura: But there is an inertia point we missed. If the org isn't willing to commoditize its cloud offering, it could be blocked.

Clive: What do you mean, not willing to commoditize? Do you mean to refuse to get adequately trained?

Laura: Maybe, but I was thinking more about "treating the cloud as a datacenter." Trying to repeat on-prem patterns, lots of IaaS and manual processes, not embracing cloud-native principles. That could drag engineering back over into Custom Built—which would act as an anchor on the other higher-order needs, like speed and cost.

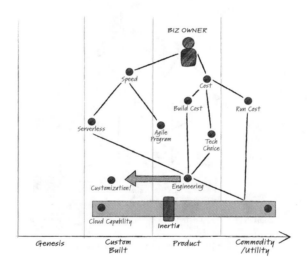

Figure 4.6: Example Story Map: Inertia Points

Clive: Very good. And it's unlikely they would be spotted in the organization. The impacts wouldn't be felt until it was too late, and the root cause may never be fully understood.

Laura: There's another inertia point around the Agile program. For many companies, it's not trivial to get Agile working right at a team level. Getting it working at a program level is way more complicated. I think very few companies have Agile working well at the program level. And this can slow things down far more than any tech. This is the "bad big Agile" inertia— basically, companies treating big Agile like a waterfall program but with no documents.

Clive: So, a combination of poor engineering and bad Agile will impact speed. Which severely affects the ability of the business to get new products and features to market.

Laura: Okay, so we have Agile and engineering as key enablers, which we can explore separately. We also have cloud capability, which seems like a vast area—there's a much bigger submap in that.

Clive: Yes, but we're saying that if engineering and cloud capability are correct, they enable serverless, which starts a Value Flywheel Effect, with speed and cost being massive benefits. There are others, but let's stay focused on the business need.

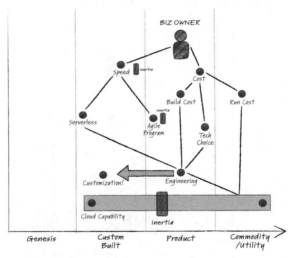

Figure 4.7: Example Story Map: More Inertia Points

Movement

Laura: Did we miss anything? Feels like cost should be moving.

Clive: Yes, I still don't like the way engineering is sitting. Let's clean up the movement.

Laura: Let's highlight the relationship to serverless as well. If engineering is in Custom Built, then it's possible to enable serverless, but very difficult. Maybe we should annotate that.

Clive: Yes, that's starting to look better. With the movement and inertia added, it almost looks like how things are now. Let's draw what we want to get to.

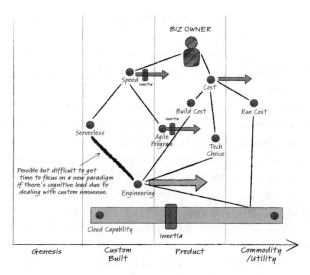

Figure 4.8: Example Story Map: Movement

Laura: That's a very different picture now. You can now declare and gather momentum around a serverless-first strategy.

Clive: Yes, as opposed to just experimenting with serverless.

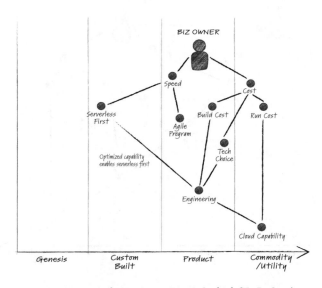

Figure 4.9: Example Story Map: Future Outlook (To-Be State)

Gameplay

Laura: So, what next? Our business owner is fast and cheap—time to go home?

Clive: Haha! Absolutely not. Let's think about what emerging capability they can build next.

Laura: It depends on the business domain, but there are always ideas for innovative business capability. If the core is running well, there's time to experiment—especially if it's fast and cheap.

Clive: The best way to experiment is to bring in innovative tech, such as applied AI, and test out a few use cases.

Laura: So, because there's a serverless-first strategy already in place, it's easy to integrate AI, ML, quantum, analytics, you name it. All the big cloud providers have a host of emerging tech services, and it's a "safe to fail" environment.

Clive: It certainly is. Remember the good old days when it took six months to get your hands on a new piece of tech? Now you can stand up a POT (proof of technology) in minutes.

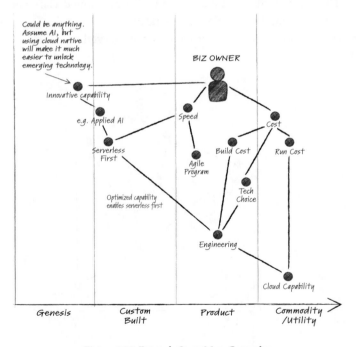

Figure 4.10: Example Story Map: Gameplay

Takeaways

In this chapter, we provided a short example of a mapping session to help illustrate the type of conversations that happen (and that are so beneficial) during mapping. The conversation is informal, respectful, and probing. The mappers explore something and then return to the original question. The map anchors them to the problem at hand, allowing them to peek into the rabbit holes without getting lost.

Mapping sessions are never perfect; they are exploratory. A map will always be produced, and it is always insightful. Never beat yourself up because the map is poor or it's not pretty. Wardley Mapping is simply there to give you a frame for exploration. No matter what you discover, it's always a discovery that will help you make a better decision.

Next, we'll begin to explore the Value Flywheel Effect in more detail, starting with Phase 1: Clarity of Purpose.

II

PHASE 1
Clarity of Purpose

PERSONA: CEO

KEY TENETS

Clarity of purpose: A data-informed north star.

Obsess over your time to value: Innovation is a lagging metric.

Map the market: Can you differentiate in the market?

CHAPTER 5
FINDING YOUR NORTH STAR

There is nothing more important than purpose and vision. A team must have clarity of purpose. If not, stop everything. I was once in a situation where the team had no idea why they were doing the tasks they were doing. This didn't sit well with me. I was a senior engineer, not a team leader, but I could foresee problems. Without clarity of purpose, the team would not be able to fill in the gaps between requirements.

I ran a short exercise with the team around "start with why." We looked at the why, the how, and the what, just to connect the dots. To my surprise, the manager pulled me aside afterward and said, "That's not your job. Stop it."

Of course, I didn't. The team needed the context to complete their tasks. Engineers are problem-solvers first; solution creation comes second. Good leadership provides clarity of purpose. You cannot tell smart people what to do without the "why."

Often a company will have a north star metric that is compelling but hard to directly link to software. For example, Spotify has "time spent listening," Airbnb has "number of nights booked," and I'm sure fast-food companies have "burgers eaten." The metric is very effective for people working on the content (music, rooms, or burgers), but could be disconnected for software engineers.

Software departments will often create their own north star. Spotify might work on uptime (which helps listening time) and Airbnb might work on UX (which helps bookings). During a cloud transformation, many companies will use a % of workloads in the public cloud as a metric.

Liberty Mutual tracked this number, and moving a workload from on-prem to cloud was always a celebration. A simple north star metric of "% in the cloud" was easy to remember and measure. It also enabled many other business metrics (cost, innovation, speed, availability), but that came later.

The Value Flywheel Starts with Clarity of Purpose

One of the hardest things to grasp about technology is the lack of definite answers. The worst response to any technology question is, "It depends. . . ." "What computer should I buy?" is a particular chestnut that can go many ways and, in most cases, will leave the enquirer more confused.

Of course, this isn't because it's a tricky question, but because this seemingly simple question leads to exponentially more questions, like a four-year-old in an endless loop of asking why. The thirty-nine questions that follow the first will likely be around "What do you intend to do?" and "How much money would you like to spend?"

Many conversations and strategic planning sessions should focus on the people, not the technology. The technology is definitive and straightforward; people tend to be continuous and complex, especially as the number of people on a team increases.

By the time a strategy is presented to a wider audience, it is often simplified greatly. Much of the nuance is removed to aid the presenter. Sometimes the original depth is lost as the simplified picture becomes "the strategy." A big part of the strategy is the narrative, which is repeated in town hall meetings many times. The detailed strategy then becomes just another picture on a slide. But it's rarely that simple. A strategic plan is a stream of activity and interactions that can change course at any point in time.

Setting this clear *purpose* is logically the first phase of the Value Flywheel Effect. If you don't have a singular, clear purpose—a guiding light, a north star—the rest is just chaos.

North Star Framework

The North Star Framework is a model for managing products by first identifying a single, crucial metric (a north star). The framework is a collaborative effort by Amplitude and led by product evangelist John Cutler. It helps organizations become more product-led and to optimize their structure and processes with a product focus. The North Star Framework also helps teams prioritize, communicate, and focus on impact.[1]

The framework starts by visualizing your product's north star metric. This metric should be a leading indicator of long-term (sustainable) business value. It should directly address a customer problem that your product seeks to solve.

Next, three to five input metrics should be included. These are influential, complementary factors that directly affect the north star metric. These inputs are typically just as important as the north star metric itself, as they directly affect your product.

For example, in 2015 when I was at Liberty Mutual, James McGlennon, the company's chief information officer, pushed for the organization to become more agile and customer-centric in the cloud. That goal, that north star (% of workloads in the cloud), is what pushed our team to discover the serverless-first approach that brought us so much success.

What's important here is that we were given a purpose, a why. Not a how. We were not told to go serverless; we were told to become more agile and customer-centric in the cloud. Through our own research and experiments, we discovered that serverless was our next best action to achieve this north star.

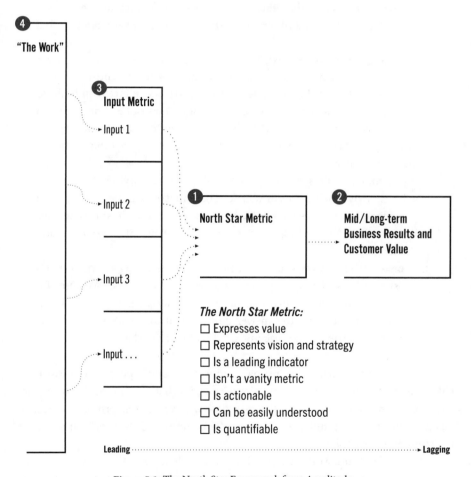

Figure 5.1: The North Star Framework from Amplitude
Source: North Star Framework by Amplitude, https://amplitude.com/north-star /about-the-north-star-framework.

The North Star Framework is best used in a workshop and works with experienced product people as well as people who are new to product (but know their company). Figure 5.1 shows the sequence.

1. **North star metric:** First, we ask a simple question: "What is our north star metric?" There's some advice on the template to help us: The north star metric is neither a leading nor a lagging metric, it's in the middle. It should be an actionable metric that is important to the business. Hopefully, we can answer this question quickly. When a business doesn't know its north star metric, then there is work to do. Often teams can be misaligned, each chasing a different north star metric, but we can talk that out.
2. **Mid/long-term value:** Next, we extend the scope to stretch the north star metric and consider how pursuing it might affect the business. This is a great test, as it should show how the north star metric can build to realize more value for the business. We sometimes put a time frame on this—three to five years—just to encourage a little creative thinking. It's okay for this to be a little fuzzy. It's only a test to verify that the north star metric is strategic.
3. **Input metrics:** This is the fun step. We start identifying metrics that will help drive the north star metric. These metrics can be derived from the customer, our internal teams, our partners, our leadership—anyone. We're looking for leading metrics, so expect plenty of suggestions and challenge.
4. **"The work":** Not always necessary but always interesting as a final step is to list "the work." It's not important that we do this step last. We know for certain the current initiatives and work underway; what we don't know (but we can often find the answer quickly) is if this work will drive the north star metric. Ideally, each phase directly drives the next.

It goes without saying that teams (engineers, product people, and executives alike) often struggle to define these simple metrics that run the business. A north star workshop can help you find the executive who values self-promotion over the business, but tread carefully, as exposure often comes with fireworks and outright rejection of the workshop.

Amplitude's framework also provides an excellent checklist for deciding your organization's north star, if you happen to find yourself lucky enough to be in on one of these meetings:[2]

1. It expresses **value**. We can see why it matters to customers.
2. It represents **vision and strategy**. Our company's product and business strategy are reflected in it.
3. It's an **indicator** of success. It predicts future results, rather than reflecting past results.
4. It's **actionable**. We can take action to influence it.
5. It's **understandable**. It's framed in plain language that non-technical partners can understand.
6. It's **measurable**. We can instrument our products to track it.
7. It's **not a vanity metric**. When it changes, we can be confident that the change is meaningful and valuable, rather than something that won't predict long-term success—even if it makes the team feel good about itself.

The workshop described in Amplitude's *Product Analytics Playbook* allows the product team to explore and discuss different facets of the purpose. It's also a way to make the north star metric real. For example, it might show the engineering team that the features they build in the platform will decrease transaction times, which increases the north star metric.

Many teams don't understand the purpose or north star of an organization or even their own team. Some companies have lost sight or disagree with their purpose for various reasons: poor communication, a clash of egos, executive takeovers, challenging markets—the list is endless. As a result, many teams don't understand why they build what they build. The North Star Framework is a great place to start the conversation. Remember, if you start a mapping session and no one can agree on the purpose, then the only objective of the session is to illustrate the misalignment.

Leading and Lagging Metrics

One of the main problems with setting goals and communicating mission and vision is metrics—specifically, the difference between leading and lagging metrics. We discuss, share, and celebrate achievements via lagging metrics (e.g., the sprinter won a gold medal at the Olympics; it's her third gold medal). What's often not as obvious, especially to those outside a tiny inner circle, are the leading metrics that made that achievement happen. In the case of the sprinter, what's the secret that led to her success? Was it training a particular muscle or area? Was it a type of equipment? Was it a mental technique or even an amount of funding for training? Or maybe it was all of those.

The North Star Framework is one of many approaches that attempt to teach us how to think differently, training us to push against a human attribute: focusing on the effect, not the cause. Most people will celebrate and discuss lagging metrics but do not discuss leading metrics with the wider team. Leading metrics aren't as exciting or might be a "best-kept secret."

Impact Mapping is one way to help focus metrics on leading indicators instead of lagging indicators. The creator of Impact Mapping, Gojko Adzic, describes the technique as a "lightweight, collaborative planning technique for teams that want to make a big impact with software products."[3] Software teams often struggle to tie the work they do (the deliverable) to the goal they want to achieve. The goal is usually achieved via a key user or actor, so the framework lets the team draw a tree out from the goal through the actor, the impact, and the deliverables (illustrated in Figure 5.2).

Teams usually do the exercise with stickies or on a dry-erase board, and it's quite informal. The very act of a team visualizing their goal, how it can be impacted via the actor, and what software deliverable will drive it rewards the team and provides insight into their actions. It's a session of ideation ("What if we did this?"), a session of focus ("Let's focus on this actor."), and a session of feedback ("I don't think that has an impact."). Teams can reach a level of clarity and alignment much quicker than by simply writing documents and code. Remember, software teams have a habit of going deep and can also sometimes lose stakeholders. Impact mapping lifts heads and discusses ideas with stakeholders; the time is not wasted.

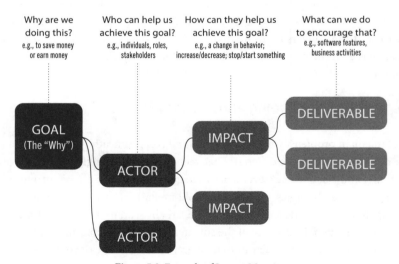

Figure 5.2: Example of Impact Mapping

Source: Impact Mapping: Making a Big Impact with Software Products and Projects *by Gojko Adzic.*

Impact Mapping is like Opportunity Solution Trees from Teresa Torres, author of *Continuous Discovery Habits: Discover Products that Create Customer Value and Business Value*. Both frameworks facilitate critical thinking and help identify leading metrics. An Opportunity Solution Tree as "a visual aid that helps enable the product discovery process through the non-linear organization of ideation flows, experimentation, and identification of gaps. Simply put, an opportunity solution tree is a visual plan for how you will then reach a clear desired outcome."[4]

Torres frames the Opportunity Solution Tree technique as part of "continuous discovery," which is a key activity of the product team. The language is also different in the sense that it talks about opportunities and experiments. By opening the idea of an "experiment," we are accepting that nothing is certain, and we can think of ideas to find value. The technique is like Impact Mapping but focuses on discovery instead of delivery. (An example is provided in Figure 5.3.)

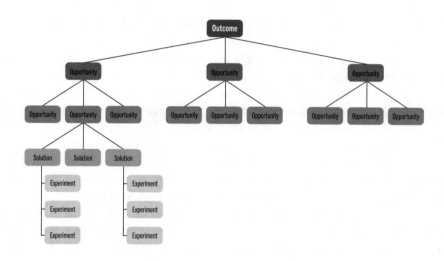

Figure 5.3: Example Opportunity Solution Tree
Source: https://www.productplan.com/glossary/opportunity-solution-tree/.

According to Torres, there are the four steps to creating an Opportunity Solution Tree:[5]

- **Step 1:** Identify the desired outcome: Narrow your goal to a single metric you want to improve (e.g., revenue, customer satisfaction, retention, etc.).

- **Step 2:** Recognize opportunities that emerge from generative research: Dig in deep to understand the needs and pain points of your customers. Keep in mind that pain points are opportunities!
- **Step 3:** Be open to solutions from everywhere: The caveat, however, is that a potential solution must directly link to an opportunity—otherwise, it's just a distraction from the primary goal of your opportunity solution tree.
- **Step 4:** Experiment to evaluate and evolve your solutions: Now, it's time to test a single solution with sets of experiments.

Before tools like Impact Mapping and Opportunity Solution Trees, product management and business analysis focused on this simple message: when communicating a mission or a task, focus on the problem and clarify the metrics that the solution will influence. The team needs space to explore the problem and solve it in the best possible way. Or, as Simon Sinek says, the team must start with why.

Balance is critical when exploring a problem and creating the solution to it. People tend to be obsessed with solutions, not necessarily the *path* to the solution. We don't want the solution to be complicated. In other words, we love the idea of the silver bullet, the magic key, $a + b = c$.

As part of the clarity of purpose discussion, we have looked at three techniques: the North Star Framework, Impact Mapping, and Opportunity Solution Trees. All have one thing in common: they attempt to slow down the desire to build something quickly. We should always pause, ensure we have identified leading and lagging metrics, and allow some ideation in both the discovery and delivery phases. Even if we have completed all our homework, these techniques offer a great chance to communicate with the team and key stakeholders to ensure everyone is informed.

Like most ideas, none of this is new. The British Design Council, established after the Second World War to support economic recovery, published its design methodology in 2004: the Double Diamond (see Figure 5.4). The Double Diamond is probably the cleanest representation of a complete innovation or design thinking approach. The Double Diamond creates space first to explore and understand the problem (discover and define) and then experiment with solutions (develop and deliver). Both diamonds contain phases to diverge (think deeply) and converge (act).

Although it seems to be changing now, it feels like the business was always associated with a culture of "go-getting" and "making things happen." These phrases indicate, again, a focus on lagging metrics. Hopefully, this is behind us, but maybe the product and design disciplines are still not as mature or prevalent in business as they should be. Product and Design departments tend to spend more time thinking about the problem (discovery) as opposed to Sales, Engineering, and Management, who are often focused on the solution (delivery). Focusing metrics on product and design can help keep teams and the organization focused on their north star and their leading metrics.

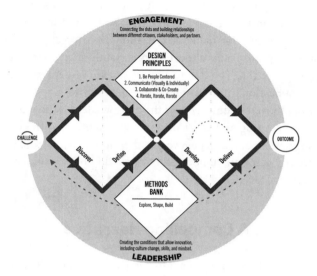

Figure 5.4: The Double Diamond
Source: https://www.designcouncil.org.uk/news-opinion/what-framework-innovation-design-councils-evolved-double-diamond.

There are many techniques for framing work in a manner that empowers teams—from the popular Objectives and Key Results system to the four disciplines of execution from Sean Covey.[6] Regardless of the technique used, it's critical to align around lagging metrics and act on the leading metrics. Often, poor organizational structure can be attributed to a poor understanding of leading metrics.

Alignment and Structure

An interesting test for any team is a conversation about their purpose, how they think about their purpose, and what metrics they use to track how they are achieving their purpose.

How well a software team comprehends business metrics is especially revealing. Someone might be able to repeat what the CEO said at the last town hall, but this is only a sign of effective communication. The next observation point is how they relate that message to their team and the work they do. Many will say, "What the

CEO said sounds great, but then we have to go back to our desks and work on stuff that's not related to it." It's doubtful that the team's work isn't related to the CEO's message, but if the team can't make the connection, then the team and the message are misaligned.

The ultimate test is around metrics. A disciplined team should track specific leading metrics that influence the lagging metrics. But too few teams possess this mindset. A common trap for many organizations is to organize around workflow and not around purpose. Teams and workers certainly share capabilities, so organization design is not trivial. The trap to avoid is a team or department performing a task with zero connection to a meaningful business metric.

Software has moved so quickly over the past two decades that teams often optimize for the wrong thing and don't pay enough attention to the customer or the company. Some developer teams believe that their top metric should make their jobs easier. Productivity gains are important, but they do not outrank customer experience or company success.

A Compelling Narrative

Great leaders can craft a story and tie it to company outcomes. The best leaders can tell and sell that story—and make it work. Another class of leaders is great at selling the story but doesn't do much else. Unfortunately, these leaders are more successful than you would imagine, but that's another story.

Successful companies have figured out their "why" and have scaled around it. Famous examples are Apple, Disney, Nike, and Amazon. These organizations are often driven by a founder who maintains and evolves that original narrative for many years. Absolute clarity on that narrative and the why is often the guiding light (or north star) through more challenging times. It provides the organization its clarity of purpose.

The truly great companies will hold on to that clarity of purpose, create a core value offering around it, and then invest in future value as they either move with the market or create new markets. Sometimes referred to as the "innovate, leverage, commoditize" cycle, investing in this future value is critical to prevent an organization from falling into the one-hit-wonder trap. Remember, our goal is to create sustainable, long-term value for the organization. As Simon Wardley describes it:

> The model is simple: what you do is you provide a commodity service; you enable everybody else to innovate on top of it. They are your research and development group. You do not bother to do it yourself; you get everybody

else to build on your services. Anything which is successful and starts to spread in your ecosystem, you can identify through consumption information, so you can leverage the ecosystem to spot successful development and then you commoditize these new components.[7]

There are several models (coincidentally, most have three phases) that describe the creation of future value (the practice of evolving a product, ideally with the market as it becomes more popular):

- Innovate, leverage, commoditize
- Pioneer, settler, town planner
- Explore, expand, extract
- Desirability, feasibility, viability
- Horizons 1, 2, 3

Regardless of the model, the principle of leading and lagging metrics is critical to quantifying your north star, as is the importance of creating a narrative around it and evolving it.

We are moving away from the command-and-control manner of working, but it's a profound shift. We must overcome decades of waiting to be told what to do. Too often, we have relied on a talented leader to help us work autonomously. How do we enable teams everywhere to own a part of their story, understand the difference they are making, and make it happen? Crafting a compelling narrative is one clear way to bring your teams along for the ride through invitation instead of coercion.

In the book *Extreme Ownership: How U.S. Navy SEALs Lead and Win* by Jocko Willink and Leif Babin, one of the core principles called out is decentralized command.

Junior leaders must be empowered to make decisions on key tasks necessary to accomplish the mission in the most effective and efficient manner possible. Every tactical team leader must understand not just what to do, but why they are doing it. [Junior leaders] must have implicit trust that their senior leaders will back their decisions. Without this trust, junior leaders cannot confidently execute.[8]

An organization that has clarity of purpose on its mission, but more importantly knows how to measure success against that clarity of purpose, can begin to leverage these models and empower its teams and leaders to make decisions on the ground that will drive success for the company. It will be the leaders of these companies that can produce the most compelling narratives.

Working Backwards

One example of this technique (crafting a compelling narrative and investing in future value) comes from Amazon, which only recently started publicly sharing its "working backwards" technique. Amazon codified the method internally as the organization grew (circa 2000–2010). Some early clues toward the approach started to leak in various blogs in the mid-2010s. Amazon started to document and share the process in the later 2010s. The best description of the entire technique is in *Working Backwards* by ex-Amazon executives Colin Bryar and Bill Carr.[9]

The technique captures a customer's need, explores that need in detail from every angle (empathy, market size, competition, growth), creates team alignment and a common understanding around the need, and then solves the problem. It sounds straightforward, but two essential functions make it work.

The Amazon Press Release

The Amazon Press Release (or the PRFAQ: Press Release and Frequently Asked Questions document) is a powerful concept and is detailed in *Working Backwards*. But let us summarize.

Amazon has been customer-obsessed from day one and always starts with the customer's need. Instead of proposing a new product by a slide deck or a pitch, Amazon writes the press release for the new product first, including precise details like the release date, accurate stats, and any FAQs. The fake press release (like real ones) has a specific template and is quite restricted with words—no filler words (Amazon uses the term weasel words) allowed.

After a team writes the press release, another group reviews it in a meeting. Everyone reads the press release in silence. Note: the press release is not presented. The written word should be able to communicate everything that is required. A successful press release is followed up by a six-pager, which fleshes the concept out further.

The press release written at the project inception is usually the press release used for the actual press release. In fact, the press release for the first Amazon Kindle in 2007 used this process.[10] The goal is that very little is changed in the press release through product development. Quotes from customers will be added to the final version, but otherwise, there should be few changes unless the project pivots. It's the ultimate customer-centric technique: start with the end user in mind and work backwards.

Single-Threaded Leadership

A second technique from Amazon and detailed in *Working Backwards* is "single-threaded leadership." In this technique, a single leader is responsible for a product. This is quite an ideal concept, but it also helps understand why Amazon uses the "two-pizza team" model (the idea that a team should never grow so big that it can't order two [American] pizzas for lunch). It is also good practice to give a team a single goal or a single product to work on. The two-pizza team model is a great concept, as there is lots of research on the ideal team size (around four to seven people), but many companies struggle to hire engineers and don't have the luxury or scale for that flexibility—many teams are overloaded with too much responsibility.

This sounds like fun, but both single-threaded leadership and two-pizza teams are real lessons in accountability and responsibility—create an environment of focus and clear priorities. It's all very well having a north star, but if your leader has three different priorities or products, you have an immediate problem.

Takeaways

Many in business will talk about a north star, but few will have the discipline and rigor to lay it out and describe it in detail and with metrics. It requires considerable courage, as starting with a north star makes it pretty apparent when things don't go well. Mistakes can't be covered up with executive trickery.

Many of the frameworks and techniques touched on in this chapter are very well understood in the product and design disciplines, but not so much in traditional management. The CEO may have a compelling narrative, but will they start at the end and work backwards? Will they lay out the vision in metrics and track it in a radically transparent manner?

The Value Flywheel Effect starts with this clarity of purpose. If we don't have that, it's hard for teams to make progress. There is no shortage of good practice to help with clarity of purpose, but do you have the leadership to see it through?

Hand in hand with clarity of purpose is an obsession with time to value. Having a great purpose but taking a decade to achieve it won't do any organization any good. Let's explore how time to value is essential in this initial phase of the Value Flywheel Effect.

CHAPTER 6
OBSESS OVER TIME TO VALUE

A major part of clarity of purpose is value. We start spinning our flywheel by talking about purpose, but what we really mean is delivering value. Unfortunately, value is one of the most overused words in business. The concept of shortening time to market is not new, but we assume that the value of our product has already been identified before we hit the market. With modern cloud systems, it's tempting to get to market very quickly and skip discovery. But the delivery of a feature does not necessarily mean that we have discovered its value.

In this chapter, we'll explore the need for velocity in business, not just in delivery but in discovery and delivery combined—and repeated. Time to value is the key measure of success here. After all, clarity of purpose implies that we have identified the value proposition, that we can recognize it and can rally around it.

The Problem with Innovation

Every CEO wants innovation. Every employee wants innovation. It's one of the catch-all concepts that's hard to argue against. As a concept, innovation has captured the imagination of every industry, and it is no coincidence that its ubiquity rose alongside the digital revolution. We have access to capabilities now that our predecessors could only dream of.

But what does innovation promise an organization? Value.

Due to the hype around the value of innovation, the excitement in the boardroom, and the size of "digital transformation" budgets, there has been a rise in "innovation theater." Many older companies are creating "labs," which are primarily a marketing ploy to hire a few smart people, give them a great office, and use them as a source for exciting news stories. Sadly, such efforts rarely make a positive impact on the company's revenue and usually make the people working on the core products furious and disgruntled. "Why are *they* sitting in a fancy office, getting paid loads, and playing with robots while we work the weekends and debug fifteen-year-old code?"

The disruptive function of these innovation labs certainly has a place in an organization, but it must be effective. And to be effective, it must be tied to the organization's clarity of purpose. It must be driving real value.

Agile transformation offices can sometimes fall into the same trap of obsessing over "progress" without truly changing how people get things done or what they work on. Talk of sticky notes, patterns, and product is always compelling, but once the transformation starts, the clock is ticking to show real value.

Accelerate by Dr. Nicole Forsgren, Jez Humble, and Gene Kim is a seminal book about building and scaling high-performing technology organizations. Two fundamental ideas must be the bedrock of any innovative behavior within an organization. First, technology is not a cost center; it's a value-creation function. Second, the age of questioning "Should we go fast or go safe?" has been answered. A digital environment set up correctly enables teams to work with speed *and* safety.

So how do we innovate? To cut a long story short, become fast, become safe, and you'll find the value. Amazon isn't an innovation company; it's a high-performing technology organization that repeatedly finds innovative value.

Rate of Turn

As a leader looking to affect change within an organization, a useful concept or metric is to try and ascertain the organization's rate of turn. Rate of turn measures the time it takes to decide on a change before making that change within the organization. This metric represents the organization's ability to deliver value quickly.

You can measure rate of turn in two ways:

1. **The time it takes to enact a change from the top down:** Organizational leadership has spoken in support of a change or evolution. How long does it take to carry out that change within the organization?
2. **The time it takes to enact a change from the bottom up:** An individual or group on the ground floor has suggested a change. How long does it take for that change to be enacted within the organization?

Why is rate of turn an important metric for a leader to surface? On the *Titanic* (as depicted in the 1997 film), the barrel man sat in the crow's nest and was responsible for identifying obstacles that posed a threat to the safe passage of the ship (like icebergs). Upon spotting an obstacle (in this case the fateful iceberg), the barrel man sounded the bell to alert the bridge. Thirty seconds to one minute later, with the ship still sailing toward the iceberg, the barrel man made a phone call to the bridge to make sure they had heard the bell. At the same time, the *Titanic* began to turn to the left, but their fate was sealed. Their ship's rate of turn was too slow to avoid the iceberg once it had come into view. This is a dramatic and likely incorrect version of events, but it demonstrates how important it is to know about your organization's rate of turn.

Knowing the ship's rate of turn, could the crew have put better operating procedures in place to ensure the ship's safety? In other words, could the crew have established a better, safer doctrine? For example, given the visibility of the crow's nest in various weather conditions, could they have applied a safe sailing speed at which the ship could avoid any identified threats? Alternatively, if the captain wanted to maintain the pace of the ship to the destination and take the ship's slow rate of turn into account, could they have empowered the barrel man with authority to order a change, allowing the ship to react earlier to avoid hazardous obstacles such as icebergs or other vessels?

Rate of turn is the same even in the digital age. Organizations can become locked in process and bureaucracy, hindering their ability to react to hazardous situations or change course to take advantage of new opportunities. In other words, their rate of turn is slow.

As a leader in an organization with a slow rate of turn, you may be frustrated with your organization's lack of ability to carry out what you feel are straightforward instructions. You might find yourself saying, "It shouldn't be this problematic. Why can't we take this direction?" Similarly, as an employee, you may experience frustrations when your ideas don't impact the organization, or the impact takes too much time and toil to enact and isn't worth the effort.

Ideally, leadership within an organization should have a good idea of the organization's rate of turn and should always endeavor to improve their rate of turn. Digital organizations are currently all the rage. They're all about being able to adapt to market conditions, customer demands, and changes in technology and industry. But how does a leader identify the things affecting their organization's rate of turn?

Increasing the Rate of Turn for Your Organization

Most people who find themselves in a leadership position will have a subliminal understanding of their organization's rate of turn; however, it can be helpful to try and identify actual physical measures that make it visible. A practical method to identify issues or opportunities within an organization is Wardley Mapping. Mapping can be a powerful technique for visualizing the organizational landscape through introspection of the value chains. Studying these value chains can in many cases highlight areas of inertia, duplication, or opportunity that may be ripe for some strategic gameplay. These observations are points of action that can help improve or deal with your organization's rate-of-turn metric.

To make this a bit more real, let's look at an example. The CTO of an organization might become frustrated when it takes eighteen months to roll out a countrywide addition to their main product (rate of turn = 18 months). Why does it take so long?

The CTO could bring in a few critical subject matter experts and create a Wardley Map of their product tech stack. Looking at the core components on their value chain, they see they have a duplication problem. The changes they are rolling out must be replicated in several parts of the system. This is their main point of inertia.

To correct this issue, the subject matter experts decide to create a central product engine that all teams within the organization will use. It requires some investment, but the organization will get their product release rate of turn down from eighteen months to three months. They'll also benefit from freeing up more engineering talent to invest in more future value through development efforts.

This is an example of a Wardley Map applied to a scenario of slow rate of turn in a technical value chain. But mapping can be used across nearly every dimension to help leaders make decisions and improve their organizations.

To solve points of inertia or to take advantage of opportunities identified in slow rate-of-turn scenarios, an organization can use other techniques to facilitate Agile-like experimentation, like the North Star Framework or Impact Mapping. It's not simply good enough to spot the problems; you must create solutions to these problems.

The most effective leaders will not simply throw money at a problem or trust an external consultancy or entity to tell them why they have a slow rate of turn. They will act and decide from a position of complete situational awareness. They will zero in on areas that need addressing. As captains of their ship, they will adopt doctrines to look after a vessel with a slow rate of turn while applying strategies and decisions that chart a path to success for the future.

Time to Value

The concept of time to market has been very well covered, but in a world of continuous delivery, there may be more to it. There is lots of material around cycle time and lead time, but these important measures can often be lost in the complexities of how we measure, especially if we're working in a very bureaucratic Agile process (yes, "bureaucratic Agile process" is a strange term, but lots of Agile is far from responsive or agile, but that's a different book).

As companies embrace the modern cloud, the term "time to value" is gaining traction. There is a rising call to deconstruct the silos and focus on value for our customer. Instead of asking if teams are doing their share, the organizations should ask if the company achieved the desired outcome.

The modern cloud enables organizations to offload tech and infrastructure work to the cloud provider, meaning the organization has more time to focus on the quality of their product, functional and nonfunctional. The modern environments also allow the organization to ship several times a day. We can sense and respond at a pace that was unheard of several years ago. The challenge for companies now is not delivery; it's value realization. Startups are very good at this. Well, if they aren't, then they don't last very long.

If we state the value of a product or feature up front, right at the inception, then we should be able to measure how long it took us to create the intended value. When Amazon writes that first press release, they put a date on it: the date of the publication of both the real press release and the product. Usually, a product will be in the hands of customers when that date arrives. Value has started and the flywheel is turning.

Time to value is not completing the epic or delivering to a test team. It is not how quickly an idea flows from the executive to the engineering team or from the engineering team to production. It's end to end. Time to value is a powerful test of organizational effectiveness. Weeks or months are good, years are not.

There is no reason that a CEO cannot measure time to value. In its most basic format, time to value is how long it took to see customer feedback from the day the CEO first heard this idea. For some CEOs, this will be years. Time to value is the measure that we can use to judge the efficiency of our company's Value Flywheel. We can track the movement through the phases and observe slowdown or deviation.

Takeaways

In this chapter, we explored innovation and the need for it. We hope the complete obsession with innovation will have gone out of fashion by the time you read this, but we doubt it. Demanding innovation may be the sign of a good executive, but achieving innovation by capitalizing on the Value Flywheel Effect is the sign of a great executive.

You can measure how well you've innovated with your rate of turn. Every ship (sea and air) has a rate of turn: how quickly can that ship turn to avoid an oncoming obstacle. Your company has a similar measure that you should be aware of. It's not an exact science, but it can be helpful. Simply having the ability to see that measure will enable you to improve it.

You should also recognize time to value as a critical metric in your organization. This is something you can and should measure, but remember to establish what you mean by *value* up front.

Next, let's look at an example Wardley Map that can help us gain situational awareness in the first phase of the Value Flywheel.

CHAPTER 7
MAP THE MARKET COMPETITION

In the first phase of the Value Flywheel Effect, we'll use a map to flesh out our clarity of purpose. Often a map of the competitive market will help identify gaps in the market that your business could choose to address. It's important in this stage to think about what your differentiators are and if you understand what customer needs you're solving.

Sense Making the Competition

One of the phrases experienced mappers often use to describe what mapping accomplishes is "sense making." The very nature of technology means that someone who is trained in computer science is often sitting with peers in very specific domains, like pharma, finance, entertainment, marketing, or telecom. The people building the system that will make or break your company are not experts in the domain. Sure, they understand it, but it's unlikely they have the same depth of expertise as others.

A Wardley Map can help make sense of a complex or emerging area of your market. It can help provide words and concepts to things that have not been created yet. The map can separate the wood from the trees. The map can then highlight gaps in the market, or areas that can help build clarity of purpose, the first phase of the Value Flywheel Effect.

We often default to the thing we know. Mapping is no different. A bunch of engineers will end up mapping how they deploy code or evolve the system. They may need coaching to come back to the business problem or customer need they are looking to solve. It's important to use the techniques we describe in this chapter early, so everyone can agree on the opportunity: the problem we need to solve, not the things that we think we need to build. We are, in effect, making our north star real by mapping the space around us in the market and delineating the problems we won't pursue.

The Value Flywheel Effects starts with clarity of purpose. Map the problem space and discuss how you'll move in that market. This conversation might take several hours but will potentially save you millions by anchoring the team on the appropriate user need and not building the wrong thing.

Start with the Customer Need

Starting with customer needs is usually not how engineers think about many things. We often approach things from the "builder" persona, from the inside out. "We will create this service by doing X, Y, and Z. We assume customers will use it in this manner." If the team includes a designer, then the chance of success is much higher—designers excel at focusing on the customer need. One excellent example of this is the jobs-to-be-done framework.

Jobs-to-be-done (JTBD) is a framework to define, categorize, capture, and organize customer needs. It was created by Clayton Christensen, author of *The Innovator's Dilemma*. To put it simply, this concept is a light-bulb moment. People are either aware of this approach or not. If not, learning about it is often mind blowing.

The impactful question in the JTBD Framework is: What is the customer need when someone goes into a hardware store to buy a quarter-inch drill? The answer is not a quarter-inch drill bit. What the customer needs is a quarter-inch hole. See, light-bulb moment.

This example likely originates from the 1940s or 1950s sales industry, but it's attributed to Harvard Business School marketing professor Theodore Levitt.[1] It has been the mantra for sales and marketing people for almost a century, but in many cases, software people are still making the mental transition from builder to user.

With the Jobs-to-be-Done Framework, a developer looks at the functional elements of the task and the social and emotional elements. The theory is that customers don't buy products; they rent products for a specific job. If we can understand that job, it'll be easier to meet the underlying customer need.

One of the best examples of the JTBD Framework, is Christensen's "The Milkshake Dilemma," which he explains in a brief YouTube video.[2] The project was for a fast-food restaurant, and a milkshake was created for breakfast. In short, commuters with a long drive wanted something that would fill them up for the day, entertain them during the drive, and be easy to "use" while sitting in traffic. The whole story is worth a listen and shows the importance of creating empathy with the customer, spending time working out what is needed, and starting from their point of view.

Many books are written on JTBD, but the same basic principle applies to mapping. Every map and value chain starts with the customer need.

Identify the Value Chain

Each customer need will have activities or capabilities needed to enable it. A milkshake needs ice cream, other ingredients, a cup, a straw, and a blender. A website needs a designer, a server, and a developer. Each of these represents a value chain.

Value chains do not have to be precise; we suggest keeping the total number of components in the value chain between three and six. Some maps have over ten, but they start getting hard to read. For example, don't start breaking a computer down (e.g., screen, keyboard, disk, CPU) when that detail isn't required. It's better to simplify and aggregate it all as "computer."

Let's use our electric vehicle value chain as an example. We have four essential user needs, which we've drawn out in Figure 7.1:

- comfortable car
- electric powered
- smart technology
- low running costs

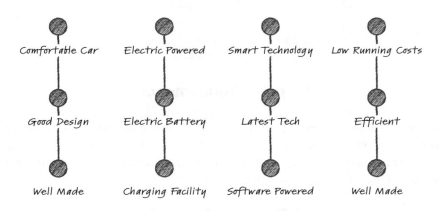

Figure 7.1: Electric Vehicle User Needs Value Chains

Once we have the value chain, we can drop it into a map (see Figure 7.2) and identify each component's phase in the evolutionary axis (*x*-axis). As before, this is always a challenging exercise, so go easy on yourself and guess. It's easy to come back and change them. No map is correct, but they are all useful. Maps are constantly evolving, so you will find that a single map will have many versions. The picture is not important. It's the insights and observations that should be captured. These insights and observations will create alignment.

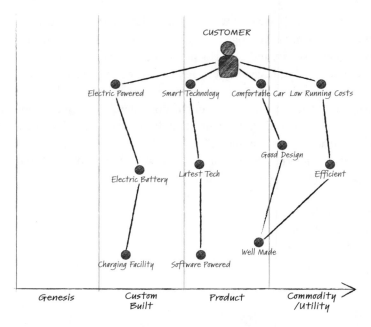

Figure 7.2: Electric Vehicle Value Chain Mapped
(One possible variation)

Mapping Your Impact

Once you've drawn a map, the fun starts. You and your compatriots should debate the placement of components, challenge what has been included or excluded, and have sidebar conversations. As an organization, step back and start looking at the market and the impact the company can have.

Introduce Movement

The customer's needs may evolve, depending on the maturity of the market and any number of climatic patterns or an event outside your control that forces a component to move to a new category. What *will* evolve are the underlying capabilities. One of the most significant forcing factors will be advancing technology. We can now rent for a few dollars what were new and novel capabilities ten years ago.

Climatic patterns will constantly come up through the exercise: "What about the change in the stock market?" "What about Amazon?" "What about 5G?" "What about the IPO?" It's best to capture these in a bulleted list beside the map. For example, 5G could be the driving force that starts moving a broadband component into Commodity or makes video calls a commodity. It's a climatic pattern because you can't control it (even though you might wish you could).

During this exercise, you might be tempted to debate how fast a component will move to a new category. Don't be tempted to try and predict when something will move. The fact that it will move eventually is enough to drive the "what if" discussion, and that's the real goal.

We can often capture inertia at this point. Inertia is usually represented as a vertical black line or box that stops the movement of a point on the map. The inertia point for Charging Facility is the cost of building new infrastructure, which will slow evolution. (See "Charging Facility" in Figure 7.3).

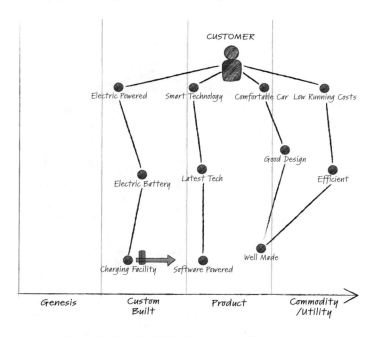

Figure 7.3: Electric Vehicle Value Chain with Inertia Point

For another example, 5G may have the ability to make video calls a commodity, but perhaps 70% of your customers are in rural areas that won't get 5G for another few years. That's an inertia point. Inertia points either stop or slow movement, and it's important to know what they are ahead of time. Sometimes the mapping discussion surfaces an inertia point, and someone in the room knows how to overcome that. Also note that when something moves to Commodity, it can enable a new component in the Genesis space.

Capture Observations

The end of the mapping session is both the most satisfying and the most important. Before the session ends, analyze the shape of the map and capture your team's key observations in a list. Take a step back and see what else you can see. Observations are best annotated with a number and written off to the side.

Look for patterns on the map. Are there any groupings of components? Does your product fit in a particular area? It might be helpful to think in terms of pioneers, settlers, and town planners. We discussed in Chapter 3 how teams can be classified into these three groups. But you can also classify components and products as pioneers, settlers, and town planners as in Figure 7.4.

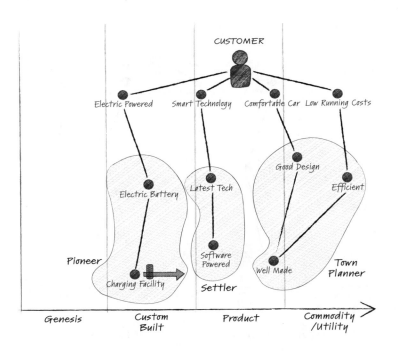

Figure 7.4: Electric Vehicle Finished Map

Pioneers build new things. They find value quickly and fail fast. Products in this space are not made with quality in mind; they are built to test the market. What components on the map are pioneering?

Settlers take successful components from pioneers and refine them for the customers. They productize things. This reduces the cost, improves quality, and improves customer satisfaction. What components on the map are settlers?

Finally, **town planners** bake quality into products. They harden, optimize, and up the quantity; in other words, they scale the product. Town planners know the demand is there, drastically reducing the unit price. What components on the map are town planners?

All three groups are essential and equally important, but they behave differently. There are fundamental questions: Is your new product being built by town planners? Are your pioneers trying to scale something? If these three groups exist, it should be clear how they pass off to each other, moving from left to right.

Takeaways

In this chapter, you learned some new techniques that will help launch your team in the right direction and start your Value Flywheel turning. When a big effort starts, we build excitement and want to jump into the plan right away. Be sure to take some time to talk through the problem space with the team to ensure they all understand their purpose in the same way. It's important to map the market before you start, as it will frame what you're doing and what you don't intend to do. It should be a relatively quick exercise (resist the temptation to dive into too much detail) and will raise lots of good questions. What are the product's inertia points? How do we start planning for this product and how quickly can we/should we make an impact? This exercise will lead nicely into the second phase of the Value Flywheel (Landscape and Challenge) as we start to wonder, "Do I have what I need to achieve this?"

CHAPTER 8
CASE STUDY—A CLOUD GURU

Our first study is an excellent illustration of the first phase of the Value Flywheel Effect: Clarity of Purpose. A Cloud Guru was formed in 2015 from an idea, a clear north star purpose that drove everything the company did. By 2021, it sold for almost $2 billion. Simon Wardley famously said in 2018 that people will go nuts "when a two-person company that produces a single function that everyone uses gets acquired for $1 billion. It's only a matter of years."[1]

Yes, Simon's prediction came to life just three years later, and A Cloud Guru was that company. They epitomized the Value Flywheel Effect, including using a serverless technical strategy, but—most importantly—they had an absolute laser focus on their clarity of purpose.

In this case study, the founders of A Cloud Guru generously sat down with us to tell us the story of how clarity of purpose shot them on a one-way trip to success.

The public cloud has been available for companies to take advantage of for years. But one of the largest roadblocks to cloud adoption has been a lack of qualified staff. You can't move to the cloud if no one on your staff knows how to do it. And, as we've mentioned in the earlier chapters and will dive into more in later chapters, using the cloud effectively requires more than just lifting and shifting your database from on-premise to the cloud.

This cloud skills gap has been an urgent concern for years. But finding the time and effective materials to quickly educate a workforce on new, burgeoning technology is an obstacle in and of itself. The founders of the online education platform A Cloud Guru decided to do something about it.

In 2015, frustrated with the dull and expensive cloud training options available at the time, brothers Ryan and Sam Kroonenburg launched a business to quite simply "teach people about cloud." The initial idea was to build a business around an AWS certification course. A Cloud Guru grew into an online education platform for anyone who wanted to learn Amazon Web Services, Microsoft Azure, Google Cloud Platform, and other cloud-related technologies.

The core features of the platform include:

- on-demand video courses
- practice exams and quizzes
- a real-time discussion forum
- dashboards and reporting
- user profiles and gamification
- educational features like learning paths
- interactive sandbox environments for students to test their skills

The way the business grew was quite specific and represented a change in how modern companies buy services. The technology platform that A Cloud Guru was built upon (serverless) allowed the business to scale quickly as demand grew while still maintaining a lean workforce. In 2019, they had ninety employees, and by 2020 they had four hundred (after the acquisition of Linux Academy). With just four hundred employees, their content figures were quite impressive (these numbers are as of 2020):

- 2.2M+ learners
- 4,000+ businesses
- 100+ certifications
- 250+ courses
- 1,500+ hands-on labs
- 450+ quizzes and exams

How were they able to build so much with so few employees? Importantly, A Cloud Guru chose its engineering strategy with an obvious goal in mind. A goal that was directly linked to the singular customer need A Cloud Guru was looking to address, their north star: teach people about cloud.

How did this happen? Let's explore some of the backstory.

Content and Vision

The vision and value proposition for A Cloud Guru is straightforward and plastered all over their website: *To enable anyone, anywhere to become a cloud guru and achieve a brighter future.*

There are three critical properties in the vision (their north star) that we will examine in this case study.

1. **Enable:** There is an enablement mindset here that puts the customer, the student, first. The solution must make it easy for the student to learn.
2. **Anyone:** The platform must be accessible. It shouldn't be behind large corporate agreements or only cater to students—the content must be consumable.
3. **Anywhere:** By using the cloud as a technology enabler, a global delivery mechanism becomes possible. The cloud is a global platform with global interest.

Pretty much every engineer on the planet wants to be "a cloud guru." Engineers are busy people and finding the time to take four or five days to attend a class is a considerable investment of time, money, and mental acuity. Instead, A Cloud Guru offered a service that could allow you to dip into great content as much or as little as you wanted when you wanted and where you wanted, a service that worked on a laptop, tablet, or mobile device—online or offline.

Founder Ryan Kroonenberg had already experimented with creating AWS courses on Udemy, an online learning and teaching site, so he knew there was a demand for this content. He also knew he needed to strip the content to its bare bones and focus on the experts who create and deliver that content.

But cloud technology was changing quickly. Almost every week, either a price, feature, or option would change for cloud services. To keep their educational content fresh, up to date, and good, A Cloud Guru would need to be able to update its platform often and quickly while still maintaining quality and reliability.

And it was essential that the system made it easy for the content creators who would be the ones adding and updating that content.

Technology and Scaling for the Enterprise

The founders of A Cloud Guru knew that the courses worked—as Ryan had provided Udemy content in the past. But now, they needed a platform that would help them achieve the core values set up in their vision. So, co-founder (and later CEO of A Cloud Guru) Sam Kroonenberg famously decided to take four weeks to build a platform—in the cloud, of course—that would meet their needs, focused on the value of enabling anyone, anywhere to learn. (There is a great talk from Serverless-Conf where Sam describes this journey in detail.[2]) Invention is born of necessity.

Sam frequently says that "there was no serverless epiphany." There was no idea to build a "serverless company." The idea was to build a company that enables anyone, anywhere to learn about the cloud. That vision (necessity) dictated the invention (a serverless learning platform). The truth is that serverless was the only approach that could achieve the values they set for themselves in their original vision. Using technology services such as Lambda, Auth0, Firebase, and Stripe, a single developer (Sam) was able to build a fully featured, video-based training platform that was secure enough to collect user payment credentials. A system that, for very low cost, had excellent performance, resilience, and operational qualities—as they are guaranteed by cloud service providers. A remarkable feat that shows the true power of the cloud.

Once the team had the platform working, they started to market the product to developers. Peter Sbarski, VP of Education and Research at A Cloud Guru, tells a story about the end of 2016, as they began to ramp up the marketing.

> We decided to use Black Friday as a way to attract more customers. We put our AWS certification course on sale; I think it was 90% reduced. The plan worked, and we had an unprecedented number of sales. Our traffic grew many times more than we expected. The only problem was, the entire company was attending the AWS technology conference, re:Invent. We sat during some of the talks, watching the traffic rise and the platform scaled beautifully—no issues. That evening we all sat around, with nothing to do— both shocked and satisfied that the platform scaled with the customers, and we didn't need a fire drill.[3]

The serverless platform was a game changer. The team didn't need to worry about system capacity. Any big sales or holiday promotions didn't cause any extra pressure. To quote Drew Firment, Senior Vice President of A Cloud Guru, "A Cloud Guru had a zero-dollar cloud compute bill for the first 300,000 customers."[4] Compare that to the cost of legacy cloud compute costs or even on-prem compute costs—traditional bills may have run into millions, sometimes before any revenue had been received. Serverless effectively bootstrapped the business: the team didn't need to worry about huge IT bills, which meant they could run lean and avoid spending other people's money. This created absolute focus so the team could capture intent and act on their clarity of purpose.

The real benefit to serverless was not cost, it was the capacity to keep their focus on other work—to stay focused on their clarity of purpose. Every hour saved on operations or dollar saved on compute was put into new features or new content to address the customer need instead of wasted on just keeping the lights on.

By 2019, the developer market had grown significantly for A Cloud Guru. The next stage was "A Cloud Guru for Business," which targeted the business and enterprise market as opposed to individual engineers. Again, the performance, operations, cost, and security standards would also need to meet enterprises' stringent demands, and cloud providers offer best-in-class service-level agreements on these points. Again, going serverless meant the team could focus on navigating the various procurement processes for large companies and building relationships during the sales process. An efficient onboarding process often makes or breaks an enterprise sale.

Mapping the Market

As a side note, the A Cloud Guru co-founders created a conference, ServerlessConf, in 2017. This conference became a great way to engage in the community and get feedback on the emerging area of serverless architecture. In 2017, Simon Wardley was invited to speak at one of the conferences, and in a back room, he "mapped the market" with the founders of A Cloud Guru.

Mapping the market is an essential exercise when developing an organization's clarity of purpose or north star (the first phase of the Value Flywheel). A map of the competitive market helps identify gaps that your business can try and fill. It can also help answer the questions: What are your differentiators? Do you understand what customer needs you are solving? Etc.

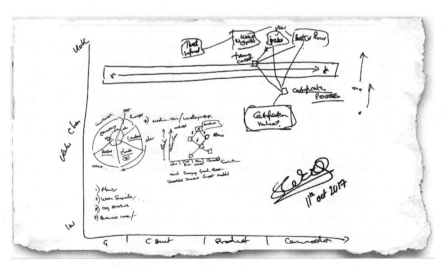

Figure 8.1: Simon Wardley's Map the Market for A Cloud Guru
Source: Used with Permission of Simon Wardley.

Paraphrasing the map shown in Figure 8.1 (this is a copy of the actual map, and it is quite hard to read), you can spend all your time building a neat architecture or you can build content. If your customer is a person who needs to become a cloud guru, which is more important to them? Architecture or content?? Focusing on the customer need first, the team doubled down on content. An engineer who is nervous about being left behind because they don't know AWS doesn't really care what database the course is stored on; they just need to get their cloud certification!

Marketing to Developers

Software and software services have gone through a dramatic evolution as they have moved to cloud-based and pay-per-use models. Previously, when the platforms for such services were created on-premises, costs to run and operate them were high. Thus, the software service was incentivized to sell large, bulk purchases to support their operating costs. The sales team would lead the process and sell directly to the CIO in a big, upfront purchase.

Later as software services moved into the cloud and costs were a bit lower, the sales process was led by marketing, as software now became a smaller recurring annual purchase. But it was still a reasonably senior sale, typically requiring purchase by an executive.

A Cloud Guru knew that the end users, the developers, could drive sales if the product was good and if it was easy and cost-effective enough for them to purchase on their own (either from their own money or if the purchase was small enough to fit onto their usual expense accounts). In fact, A Cloud Guru had this customer need clearly stated in their vision when they said they wanted to enable *anyone* anywhere to learn, not enable anyone whose boss has decided to purchase this software to learn. *Anyone.* A product-led process would give developers access to the platform first and then A Cloud Guru could grow into selling to full organizations.

Again, serverless was the answer to the customer need. Its pricing model supported this strategy, as operating costs for the software would only increase as customers increased, allowing A Cloud Guru to sell individual subscriptions in a way that was cost-effective for the company.

As part of this vision to sell directly to developers, A Cloud Guru had a significant presence at many cloud conferences and even organized their own series of events: ServerlessConf, the original serverless event. They also encouraged their trainers, like co-founder Ryan Kroonenberg, to present at the expo stand wearing the same A Cloud Guru T-shirt he wears in the training videos. This resulted in many selfies shared around social media of developers with "the cloud guru guy."

With a clever sales strategy (involving flash sales and quick and easy digital purchases), developers didn't have to wait for their training department or executives to "procure" A Cloud Guru services; they just bought their own license on their phone while sitting at home or in a conference audience. The value proposition of "becoming a cloud guru" was so attractive for many developers that they would just grab it and self-study when they saw an A Cloud Guru course on a flash sale for $10.

The map in Figure 8.2, which Drew Firment, SVP Cloud Transformation at A Cloud Guru, presented in Map Camp London in 2018, clearly shows that the IT systems (front end and back end) are on the bottom right of the map: they have been commoditized. In other words, the platform itself is something that A Cloud Guru can consume as easily and simply as electricity or telecom services. The platform functions (serving the users), however, are custom built to support features, partners, and channels: they drive the unique value the business offers to customers. And it all has been mapped and built to fulfill upon a singular clear purpose: *To enable anyone, anywhere to become a cloud guru and achieve a brighter future.*

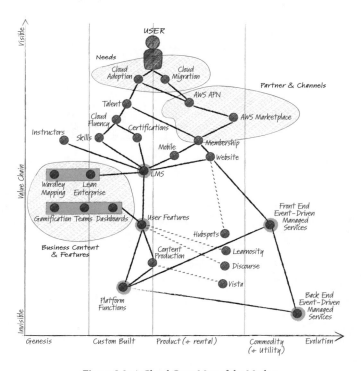

Figure 8.2: A Cloud Guru Map of the Market
Source: Used with permission from a talk that Drew Firment
gave in Map Camp in London in 2018.

Takeaways

Serverless enabled A Cloud Guru to fulfill on its vision and to do it fast. One person in four weeks was able to build the low-cost, high-performing, resilient platform that powered A Cloud Guru's success. The serverless platform was a game changer. Even on Black Friday, the A Cloud Guru team didn't need to worry about system capacity or scale! Serverless also freed up capacity to do other, more critical and impactful work, such as new features and content to address customer needs, procurement, sales, relationship building, etc. With their serverless approach, A Cloud Guru could easily meet the most stringent enterprise demands around security, performance, reliability, cost, and operational excellence.

But none of this would have been possible without first identifying and focusing on a singular clear purpose. By focusing on meeting their customer needs and adopting a serverless-first approach, A Cloud Guru has become a multibillion-dollar company, recently acquired by Pluralsight.

III

PHASE 2
Challenge and Landscape

PERSONA: ENGINEERS

KEY TENETS

Psychological safety: Team-first environments always win.
The system is the asset: A sociotechnical systems view.
Map the org for enablement: Enable empowered engineers.

CHAPTER 9
ENVIRONMENT FOR SUCCESS

Challenge and landscape are so important. We rarely have all the capabilities that we need. The concepts of challenging an idea and building situational awareness are vital. I was once told that "challenge" did not mean what I thought it meant. That some people found it offensive. Then I was told that collaboration is a dirty word—it's almost like people are sneaking around. Creating an environment for success means people will bring themselves to the work. Let's hope that person is keen to work in a team, as opposed to disrupting it.

In the first phase of the Value Flywheel Effect, we focused on finding and clearly communicating purpose—finding your team's or organization's north star. In other words, identify what you value as an organization. But purpose alone isn't enough.

In the second phase of the Value Flywheel Effect, we must turn our attention to the importance of *challenge* and *landscape*. To achieve an organization's stated purpose, we must lay the groundwork for success. After all, if the road to value is riddled with potholes and obstacles, it doesn't matter that you have a north star. You'll never reach that goal. Or you'll only reach it after a long, arduous journey, and by then someone else may have beat you to the goal.

Creating an environment for success is like paving the road and sweeping away obstacles. The scene must be set for people to be their best, to challenge one another responsibly, to work with psychological safety, and to have the technological tools necessary to complete their jobs easily and efficiently. After all, there's no point in knowing what the right thing to do is if you're afraid to say it or if you don't have the tools to build it. In a truly supportive environment, everyone can build and react to these feedback loops. Only by building a holistic sociotechnical (people and technology) view of the system can you get your flywheel turning.

So how do we pave the road? What does an environment for success look like? Well, it should come as no surprise that adopting a team-first approach is the best path forward.

The Team

The concept and construct of a team are so fundamental in business (and life) that we don't need to cover them here. But why do so many companies get it wrong? We all have many stories about the superstar team with huge salaries who didn't win anything. And there's the team of so-called nobodies, no superstars, who do well. Teamwork makes the dream work. We teach it to kids. So, does it even have a place in a book like this? Unfortunately, yes—"unfortunately" because it should be a solved problem.

The team must be a first-class citizen in the company. You need other constructs too, but teams are non-negotiable. Human beings work well as a group when they feel like they belong in that group and when they can bring their best versions of themselves into that group. With that said, what are the team antipatterns that we often see?

The rock star: This is a case of an individual who is bigger than the team. Team success is largely because of this person. This also extends to the team dynamic. Strong teams are diverse and inclusive; weak teams are closed and exclusive.

Tiny team: In general, a team should be at least three or four people. A collection of pairs is just that; it's not a collection of teams. Capacity will suffer if teams are too small.

Huge team: Once a team grows to over ten people, it's two or three sub-teams. See Amazon's two-pizza teams, not three- or four-pizza teams.

Bob's team: This is the idea that all the people who report to Bob are a team—all six of them. This isn't necessarily true (or a good idea). We can have six individuals sitting together, working on similar things, and all are reporting to Bob. But that doesn't make them a team. A team needs to have team working agreements, interactions, discussions, debates, a common purpose, and togetherness. The fact that Bob approves their leave doesn't make them a team. This fallacy can often be found among executive teams (who often go to considerable lengths to outmaneuver their "teammates").

My work: Work should be assigned to the team, and it should be worked on as a team. If the team has a common goal, it will work together. If a team has a bunch of tasks that individuals own, there will be no shared sense of achievement.

Johnny's bonus: Teams should get rewarded for performance. Individual awards do have a place for exceptional achievement, but the team should have a team incentive for performance.

The magic manager: In this antipattern, every successful delivery is due to the skill of the manager. This is especially destructive in traditional companies. When a manager does nothing, the team must "manage up" and perform well against all odds. The manager thinks they're a great servant leader by making the tea and listening to the team. The team is perplexed why this highly paid individual is making them tea yet doesn't understand what they are doing. In this scenario, the team is flying blind as the manager is not really helping them, so they need to babysit the manager, self-manage, and go directly to stakeholders. It's twice the work and adds considerable risk to the project. This antipattern is more common in technology than you might think. It is often paired with headship, posterior protection, and an inability to make a decision.

Team Topologies by Matthew Skelton and Manuel Pais does a terrific job of describing how to create a great environment for teams to flourish.[1] There are many other excellent references about building teams, but the bottom line is this: leadership must recognize that the team is the unit of delivery, not the individual. It really is that simple. It's a team-first approach. Focus on building teams, give them a good environment and a purpose, and enable them to get the work done.

Accepting Challenge

Giving a person feedback is often difficult, even during a one-on-one session. When someone shares an idea that they've invested time in, it's often tricky to respectfully point out an alternative approach to that idea, even more so when the idea is presented in a highly polished presentation, and more so again when it's presented to a room full of people. It's hard to try to phrase your feedback, ensuring that you fully understand the idea, and attempt to think through an alternative suggestion, all while trying to respect the fact that only five minutes have been allowed for questions.

Most people attending these presentations simply don't attempt to ask a question or challenge the presenter's opinions. It takes great courage to raise an alternative point of view, especially when a leader is sharing an idea. Truthfully, many presenters love to hear a polite challenge when presenting, but the format of the meeting makes discussion difficult.

Let's also look at politics. We must acknowledge that it exists. Some people will fault the presenter and ask an awkward question just to "score a point" in front of the boss. Yes, this is old-fashioned, but it happens. If a leader has expertise in the presented topic, however, it's straightforward to address these "questions" and move on.

We work in complex environments with experts in the domain and technology, so we need feedback on ideas. We need an environment where everyone invites challenge and everyone feels comfortable challenging others' ideas, as often the most junior person (i.e., the person closest to the work) is the expert. Without a safe environment in which people can speak up, we miss out on valuable feedback. It is often as hard to criticize an idea presented to three people as when the idea is presented to one hundred people. Anything other than a reinforcing comment is often seen as an attack, as are alternative ideas. How many times has an engineer listened to an idea that they were pretty sure wouldn't work, no one offered an alternative idea, and money was wasted in executing the flawed idea?

In many cultures, just the word "challenge" has a negative connotation, as in "me challenging you." This is political point-scoring; it's not healthy. The environment for success should support a healthy challenge, where a person can challenge an idea with an alternative view without offending the presenter. The alternative idea may be rejected for good reason, but sharing that thought process will increase everyone's confidence in the proposed idea.

It turns out that maps provide an ideal mechanism for challenge (as we'll explore throughout this book and as we pointed out in Chapter 2). We cocreate them; we admit they are wrong, and we evolve them rapidly. They are not linear, so they facilitate exploring different avenues. As effective as slides are for presenting an idea to an audience, they fail as a tool to promote thinking because they lack context, promote spin, and evade challenge. Jeff Bezos famously banned PowerPoint presentations in favor of the written word. If you present an idea, write it down so there is little margin for error.

Work Level Mismatches

Another hindrance to accepting challenge into a team is the fear of bad optics. How many of us want to "look bad" at work? Probably none of us. But we are also encouraged to fail fast. It takes quite a progressive environment to be able to fail fast without the fear of looking bad or losing your position. To achieve this progressive environment where people can experiment and fail fast without fear of optics, there must first be clarity of purpose in the team and organization (phase one of our Value Flywheel), but the environment (the culture) must also be supportive and provide psychological safety (phase two of our Value Flywheel).

What happens when a team's or organization's purpose is unclear? Shreyas Doshi, a product leader who is well worth a follow on Twitter (@shreyas), has a wonderful model around the three levels of product work: execution, impact, and optics.[2] As he explains, when an individual or team becomes fixated on a different level of work (i.e., execution, impact, or optics), there will likely be conflict, as priorities and actions may work against each other. Imagine trying to rebuild an entire website to improve customer experience, and one of the front-end engineers spent all their time fixing bugs on the old site? The short-term gain (fixing bugs) may be very execution-oriented, but the long-term gain of rebuilding the website will likely deliver a much bigger impact.

Let's expand on these levels slightly to consider who is the primary consumer of the work:

- **Execution level:** We execute to keep the manager happy. *Not a flawed approach, but a little outdated and traditional.*
- **Impact level:** We create impact for the customer. *A very product-centric approach.*
- **Optics level:** Regardless of what happens, we don't look bad. *This is self-serving. Unfortunately, it works but doesn't move the company forward.*

So, what does this look like in action? Doshi has a great example he shared via Twitter,[2] which we'll rephrase here. Imagine a product manager is fixated on the execution level of work. She focuses on making compromises. This is justified because execution is hard. Since she was able to execute against the odds, she's proud of the upcoming launch. The VP/CEO reviews it but fixates on the impact level of the work. He tells the product manager that her work isn't good enough. The launch is a no-go, and everyone is frustrated.

According to Doshi, the main problem here isn't paying attention to multiple levels of work. After all, any healthy team must balance its attention across all three levels. The problem is twofold. (1) When an individual or team becomes *fixated* on a particular level—that is, when someone has an obsession or bias toward one level of work—imbalance is inevitable. (2) The fixation on a single level of work is not stated outright. If we don't clearly express our bias, there will be conflict and we will challenge the minutia. What the team needs instead is to be explicit about the real issue at hand: a levels mismatch.

A team-first approach can help, as the team must have a shared understanding of their goals. If the correct constructs are there (see *Team Topologies*), then the team is clear on the purpose for their existence. The team can achieve further alignment via the North Star Framework we looked at in Chapter 5 during the first phase of the

Value Flywheel. Everyone should be able to honestly say, for example, "As a team, we are focused on this value chain, and that's the metric we'll pursue over the next six months." This simple statement will help bring the team together.

Leaders must make the critical decision of what kind of environment they want to create for their teams. Discussing organizational culture can be difficult and emotionally charged, but everyone comes out of that discussion better for it. Leaders at all levels should clearly communicate what they prioritize and tolerate as a leadership team to create a supportive environment that paves a path to success.

Culture Shift

Dr. Mik Kersten has been credited with shepherding the "project to product movement"; in fact, he wrote the book on it.[3] Shifting from a project model to a product model is critical for engineering and IT, because it helps to define the flow of value in your company and optimize for it. Again, we organize around value (the value the end product will bring the customer), not function (completing one teams' portion of the product, like screwing in a screw).

The first step in creating an environment for success is to ensure the team and the whole organization has absolute clarity and alignment on the value proposition—clarity of purpose. FYI: the value is not completing the project (I checked off my box, so I did my job).

But this paradigm shift is not straightforward. We have one-hundred-year-old *product* companies (successfully focused on delivering value) and five-year-old *project* companies (teams and individuals are focused on completing their tasks as opposed to having a holistic view and stake in the whole product).

When we organize around a product, anyone in the organization should be able to challenge the thinking and the value proposition. The whole team/organization discusses better ways to achieve the outcome, is involved in innovating, and is empowered to challenge assumptions. When a team or organization is structured around a project instead of a product, they may be able to challenge an estimate, but expect a healthy argument with the project manager (unless you are reducing it). They are never allowed to challenge the plan itself.

Behaviors Supporting Challenge

To create an environment of success, we also need to establish basic behaviors in the company that are rarely discussed outside a small leadership group. Simon Wardley compiled a list of supportive behaviors team members will perform when they feel psychologically safe (see Table 9.1). The behaviors are split into categories of communication, development, operation, learning, leading, and structure.

Table 9.1: Wardley's Doctrine

Reprinted with permission, Simon Wardley and Chris Daniel, Doctrine.WardleyMaps.com/.

Wardley's Doctrine (universally useful patterns that a user can apply regardless of context)

CATEGORY	COMMUNICATION	DEVELOPMENT	OPERATION	LEARNING	LEADING	STRUCTURE
PHASE I	Use a common language (necessary for collaboration); Challenge assumptions (speak up and question); Focus on high situational awareness (understand what is being considered)	Know your users (e.g. customers, shareholders, regulars, staff); Focus on user needs; Use appropriate methods (e.g. agile vs. lean vs. six sigma)	Think small (as in know the details)	Use a systematic mechanism of learning (a bias towards data)		
PHASE II	Be transparent (a bias towards open)	Focus on the outcome not a contract (e.g. worth based development); Think fast, inexpensive, restrained and elegant, (FIRE, formerly FIST); Use appropriate tools (e.g. mapping, financial models); Be pragmatic (it doesn't matter if the cat is black or white as long as it catches mice); Use standards where appropriate	Manage inertia (e.g. existing practice, political capital, previous investment); Managing failure; Effectiveness over efficiency	A bias towards action (learn by playing the game)	Move fast (an imperfect plan executed today is better than a perfect plan executed tomorrow); Strategy is iterative not linear (fast reactive cycles)	Think small (as in teams); Distribute power and decision making; Think aptitude and attitude
PHASE III			Optimize flow (remove bottlenecks); Do better with less (continual improvement); Set exceptional standards (great is just not good enough)	A bias towards the new (be curious, take appropriate risks)	Commit to the direction, be adaptive along the path (crossing the river by feeling the stones); Be the owner (take responsibility); Think big (inspire others, provide direction); Strategy is complex (embrace uncertainty); Be humble (listen, be selfless, have fortitude)	Provide purpose, mastery, and autonomy; Seek the best
PHASE IV				Listen to your ecosystem (acts a future sensing engine	Exploit the landscape; There is no core (everything is transient)	There is no one culture (e.g. pioneers, settlers, and town planners); Design for constant evolution

Behaviors are also organized by phase: a team that's just starting to develop a supportive culture will use behaviors from phase I, while a team that's an old hat at psychological safety will use all the behaviors through phase V. The doctrine is interesting as it describes the environment for success in an organization. The behaviors may not be present in your company.

Wardley's Doctrine summarizes behaviors that help establish a culture in which challenge is welcomed. Look at each entry and ask yourself, "Does my organization/team do this?" This is also a good group exercise. Ask the team to identify all the patterns that the organization practices.

Often, an organization's executive team will have many tasks that they can do and many ways to improve the working environment. As we already discussed, their most important job is to create clarity of purpose. This second stage of the Value Flywheel Effect will seriously test that understanding. Has the purpose been clearly communicated throughout the organization? Does everyone know how their work helps achieve that purpose? If executives don't clearly define the company's purpose and communicate it well in the first phase, your flywheel will come to a screeching halt here. Go back to phase one and refocus on your clarity of purpose.

Psychological Safety

Psychological safety is an essential part of a team-first approach and is critical to creating an environment for success. This is a very complex topic, and there are many great books and blogs written covering many aspects of psychological safety. But at its core, psychological safety is the feeling that you won't be punished or ostracized for being yourself and sharing your opinions. In a psychologically safe environment, a person feels comfortable taking risks, experimenting, and questioning others. They know their teammates will treat failure as learning and not judge.

According to Greek mythology, Narcissus was so obsessed with his beauty and reflection that he spent his entire life looking at himself. He was so consumed with his appearance that he eventually withered away and died, and a flower appeared. This story represents emotional immaturity.

In my experience, many developers will put their desire to work on technology X before the need of the customer or the company. (vanity) We often call it "résumé-driven development." A developer wants to use technology X because it's cool. Part of the job of a technical lead is to spot this and stop it. When the CTO is practicing résumé-driven development, it's a massive problem and can put a company out of business.

In the business world, we have talked a lot about emotional intelligence. Maybe more so in technology, where we create unique business environments—software-driven ecosystems, if you will. The customer is king in software more so than in many other industries. Why do we spend so much time encouraging tech teams to think about the customer? Why is it so revolutionary to "think outside-in"? Do we have a failure in leadership that we continually think about optics and execution before the customer?

If we have a safe environment to work in, we should feel confident to focus on the customer and not worry about friendly fire from our own team. Do we obsess about ourselves because we lack the emotional maturity in work to put the customer first? Or do we worry as we believe our peers (and some leaders) lack that emotional maturity? Regardless, creating psychological safety at work is required to start building empathy for others. Building empathy and starting to mature as an industry, we can also begin to treat diversity, equity, and inclusion as primary considerations in how we behave at work.

The concept of psychological safety is starting to become valued in the C-suite, thanks to the fantastic work of people like Dr. Amy Edmondson. We are finally beginning to recognize that diversity is more than a tagline.

In software, the team's importance cannot be understated. Teams create software, and the balance of the team is critical. How many managers and leaders prioritize team effectiveness over the plan? A genuinely high-performing organization is diverse. The mix of different views, backgrounds, cultures, skills, and experiences help inform, challenge, and shape good decision-making, ensuring that the best outcomes are achieved.

Amy Edmondson talks about failure at work, the dangerous silence, and the importance of candor in her excellent book *The Fearless Organization: Creating Psychological Safety in the Workplace for Learning, Innovation, and Growth.*[4] There's no point in having a diverse team if half the people are afraid to speak up. Both leaders and team members must create transparency in the workplace—radical transparency.

It's a topic that is well worth further study and cannot be adequately covered in a page, but the traditional model where no one tells the boss bad news is fundamentally broken. Every business has problems that need to be discussed and understood from different perspectives. We need to think ahead and surface challenges as we find them.

Safe to Experiment

"Fail fast" is a wonderful idea and phrase, but (as with many wonderful phrases) the business media has completely killed it. This is not the fault of the business media; it's the inertia of traditional leadership. When a new term pops up, every executive wants to use it first and claim that they "brought it to the table." "Fail fast," or experimentation, requires a significant foundation to implement correctly—it can't just be rolled out at an all-hands meeting.

Experimentation is linked to performance appraisal. The best way to assess the "fail fast" environment is to examine the incentive system at an organization. Yearly reviews with targets and performance-related pay can make it very difficult to experiment unless considerable expertise and effort are made to planning. If an individual is incentivized to experiment, then they likely have a very clear business objective.

The Objectives and Key Results (OKRs) framework has become popular, but it too can be abused. The objective must be an outcome: What do we need to achieve? The key results will indicate how we will achieve it (in detail). If a team has an objective and a good environment within which to move quickly, they can start thinking in bets. If we try this, what outcome do we observe? Good, let's add to that. If a team is locked into a plan, then if the objective is not met, it's because the plan was flawed!

Ethics

Ethics is moving away from checkbox compliance. The idea that, as an employee, you can watch a video once a year and you are compliant is a bit ridiculous when you think about it. This is a relatively lazy sheep-dipping of "ethics and compliance," but some large companies rely on this method because the alternative is expensive and time-consuming—it's easier to just mandate that every employee watches that one-hour video. To truly consider ethics when creating software requires a deep understanding of ethics as well as how your people, technology, business domain, and customers interact. The pressure builds considerably when dealing with large amounts of data or AI/machine learning systems.

Unfortunately, there is no easy fix or cool technique for ethics. It's hard and requires focus, expertise, and investment. Don't just append "do no evil" to your list of forty-three company principles—it's not going to work! You must spend time considering your customers, the common good, and your staff. What issues did you uncover? How can you ensure your teams work with integrity and respect their customers? In short, ethics requires deep thought about the systems you are building and how they affect users.

Diversity

Diversity has always been an important and valuable quality in teams. There are countless examples where a diverse team has produced better results than a homogeneous team. Diversity is a very complex term as it has many meanings. Diversity means different—whatever that may be. It could be a team that contains people with differences spanning gender, ethnicity, sexuality, functionality (i.e., by role), background (i.e., education and upbringing)—even physical and neurological differences.

Let's focus on neurodiversity for a second, or the idea that all human brains are different and have different strengths. Some excel in social interaction, some excel in conceptual work, and others excel in deep analytical work—the combinations of these strengths and other diverse attributes make for a solid team.

Diversity is an attribute to be celebrated, not a weakness to be avoided. Sometimes a team's makeup may not be suited to the task at hand (think back to the pioneer/settler/town planner lens). Take appropriate care that teams gel and focus on the right type of work.

Learning or Generative Organizations

Dr. Ron Westrum created a very insightful model commonly referred to as Westrum Organizational Culture (see Table 9.2).[5] It focuses on how information flows through the company but acts as a great indicator of culture. It has been heavily used in the DevOps community, specifically in the DORA (DevOps Research and Assessment) State of DevOps research program.

For a business to break into new ground, it must be able to try things, make mistakes, and learn from them. Dr. Westrum describes this as a generative organization, which is the ability to produce or create something. The table below describes other characteristics of a generative culture and highlights two other culture types—pathological and bureaucratic.

Table 9.2: Westrum Organizational Culture

Pathological (power-oriented)	Bureaucratic (rule-oriented)	Generative (performance-oriented)
Low cooperation	Modest cooperation	High cooperation
Messengers shot	Messengers neglected	Messengers trained
Responsibilities shirked	Narrow responsibilities	Risks are shared
Bridging discouraged	Bridging tolerated	Bridging encouraged
Failure leads to scapegoating	Failure leads to justice	Failure leads to inquiry
Novelty crushed	Novelty leads to problems	Novelty implemented

Mapping Psychological Safety

Let's work on a quick map that shows how we might cultivate a culture of psychological safety. With Wardley Mapping, you can take a quality like psychological safety and map out what the dependencies are and how mature they are in your organization. We refer to this as "mapping a capability." It's a great way to take a theory read from a book and quickly assess how close you are to accomplishing that theory. So, what would it look like if we mapped for psychological safety?

We'll use the characters we met back in Chapter 4, Laura and Clive. They want to explore how far their organization has come and where they still need to work to better create a psychologically safe environment.

User Need

Laura: We need a good anchor. The team member is ultimately the primary beneficiary of psychological safety. What do you think?

Clive: I suppose it must be the "general" team member. Then we can talk about general leadership requirements without getting into the myriad of roles—project manager, scrum master, product manager, tech lead, top banana.

Laura: Yeah, so what does the team member need? I'd say trust is first. That and clarity of purpose. Do I know what I'm supposed to be doing? And do I feel my manager trusts me to accomplish it? I'd place clarity of purpose in Product on the *x*-axis, since it's something we get from leadership.

Clive: I agree. But trust must come from the inside out, right? Teams must build trust themselves. You can't buy it off the shelf. Should we put it in Custom Built?

Laura: There is also the work environment. You want to "be able" to do your job—without lots of stuff in the way. That would include having the tools you need as well as the time you need.

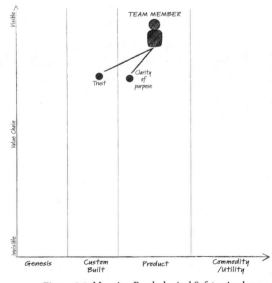

Figure 9.1: Mapping Psychological Safety: Anchor

Clive: Yes, and you want the ability to speak your mind. Pretty much nothing should be left unsaid. That doesn't mean you always get your way, but you shouldn't be afraid to speak up.

Laura: Absolutely! And feedback must be given in a kind, respectful way. How would you stack those four from most common to least common?*

Clive: Hmm, almost like a hierarchy of needs? I'd say being heard is the most common. It should be placed furthest to the right, followed by the environment, then trust, and then clarity of purpose to the left.

Laura: I agree on the first two, but I think trust isn't as common as you think. I'd flip the last two. And let's just line them up. I think they're all equally visible to the team member. How's that?

Clive: Yes, that's a start.

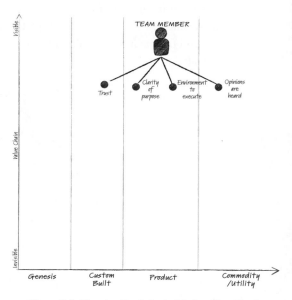

Figure 9.2: Mapping Psychological Safety: User Needs

Dependencies

Laura: Okay, next we need to list the dependencies required for the team member to receive each of these needs.

Clive: I think "trust" requires leadership, and that requires a "safe to fail" environment.

Laura: And a "safe to fail" environment requires a space to learn.

Clive: I think those two always need to go hand in hand. You can't fail safely if you're not given the time afterward to investigate what happened and why.

Laura: Yes, and leadership is in control of providing that environment. Not just in the team but also with stakeholders outside the team. I've experienced environments that suffered from a relatively toxic blame culture with

---

* Remember: this is sometimes an easy way to start a map—least common to the left (still being discovered or created) and most common to the right (as ubiquitous as water and electricity).

failure. That always brought work to a screeching halt. The inertia blocks all the benefits you get from a safe-to-fail/learning environment.

Clive: Yeah, and we should define "failure" here. Failure could simply mean missing a sprint deadline or a low-risk experiment—not putting the organization out of business. Sometimes I think failure sounds too big. You can have small failures too.

Laura: Absolutely. And I think each of those dependencies you mentioned would all fall in Custom Built on the *x*-axis. You can't buy them; they must be created.

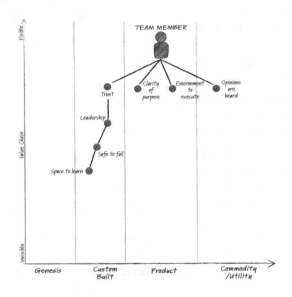

Figure 9.3: Mapping Psychological Safety: Dependencies

Further Dependencies

Laura: I think we should bring in the idea of being "team first" here.

Clive: Yes. I know it's different if you're working on your own, but we need to write software as part of a team. I think that's an essential part of the puzzle. And if that's the case, then a good team should also embrace diversity. Great teams always bring a diverse set of voices to the product.

Laura: And diverse in every way. It's nearly impossible to say what the right mix is as it depends on the problem, but what I think you're saying here is we need to avoid groupthink or "more of the same."

Clive: Yes! And you also must have decent team norms or standards.

Laura: The old "working agreement." These work best if the standard is measured and tracked. I've experienced many working agreements that are just stuck on the wall and then forgotten.

Clive: Yeah, you must measure and celebrate progress on the team. It's the heartbeat that keeps everything moving. Not silly manual tasks or mountains of red tape. What we need is a decent delivery pipeline with good tools and processes tuned to the work. It always irritates me when a flawed process slows me down. I don't mind governance, but a lousy process grates on me.

Laura: Agreed. An excellent partner to that is sharing. We need a collaborative environment where people can jump in and pair if anyone has trouble.

Clive: Yes. And I think all those dependencies should be placed in Product on the *x*-axis, since you get them from the team itself. But diversity is different. You can't just buy diversity; it needs to be created by the team. I'd place it in Custom Built.

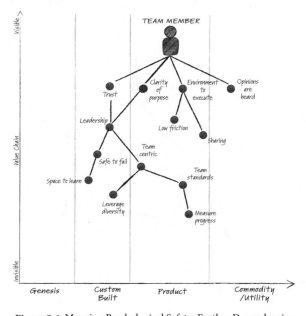

Figure 9.4: Mapping Psychological Safety: Further Dependencies

Laura: Great—this is shaping up nicely. Now, looking at our user need of being heard, I think feedback must be a big part of that. But I think we also need to be careful with that phrase.

Clive: Why is that?

Laura: Sometimes we can use feedback almost like a power play. "I HAVE FEEDBACK FOR YOU." I think what is needed is for people to feel they can speak to each other directly and politely and not be afraid of honest communication. I guess you want team members to appreciate, coach, and evaluate ideas as they come up—not afterward in a one-on-one meeting or over coffee. Give feedback in the moment, in the team environment, so everyone will also learn from it.

Clive: Yes, I know what you mean. We need a very short feedback cycle, so we aren't "waiting for a good opportunity." I think sensitive feedback is different, but you must start with the simple stuff.

Laura: And do you think feedback cycles also link back into being team centric?

Clive: Certainly. Well, everything links to everything—but let's not get carried away.

Laura: Definitely not. Okay, so feedback would need to be freely given and easy, so I'd place it in Commodity. Everything else feels like a product, with feedback cycles linking with team centricity.

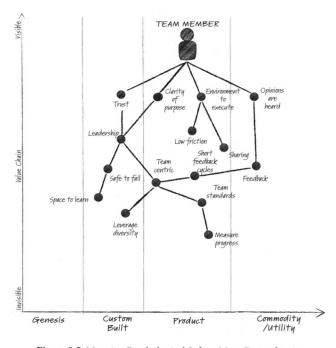

Figure 9.5: Mapping Psychological Safety: More Dependencies

Laura: That has a nice shape to it. What do you think of the placement from left to right—the evolution?

Clive: Hmm. Maybe a few tweaks. Let's bring some of the measuring and sharing left a little. They aren't super common, unfortunately.

Laura: Anything else to add?

Clive: I wonder if there is something under space to learn. I always think a good team has the confidence to slow down when they need to. It's quite rare, in my experience, but it can be powerful.

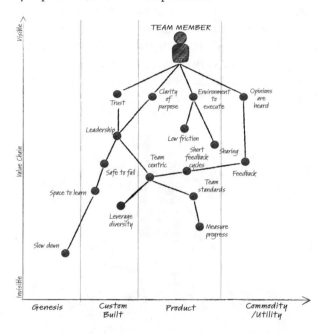

Figure 9.6: Mapping Psychological Safety: Dependencies Complete

Adding a Pioneer/Settler/Town Planner Overlay

Laura: So, the three needs that are deep down, out of immediate sight of the team member, are: (1) the ability to slow down when the team needs to, (2) leveraging diversity in the team, and (3) measuring progress. And number three is obviously in a fair and transparent way, not a sneaky way.

Clive: Very interesting. Now that you say it, those three points are very insightful and not immediately obvious. Slowing down to speed up is so important, but I've never thought of doing it in this environment. We need to celebrate that our team is so diverse and that we have open and honest discussions, which can look like arguments, but we all respect each other. And the last one is interesting. Story points are not progress. So, what is? I wonder if we could put a pioneer/settler/town planner lens on this map.

Laura: Draw a few boxes? Yes, it might be interesting. So, pioneering needs are advanced and rare. Settler needs are common but need work to refine them. Town planners should be part of every team but may need a little localization?

Clive: Yes, exactly. Let's just lay them on the map in equal rectangles vertically and see if we agree with which dependencies fall into pioneer/settler/or town planner. This is an interesting trick as we can see if there's a hidden grouping. We may need to tweak the rectangles, but labeling needs as Pioneer, Settler, or Town Planner tells us how we can treat them.

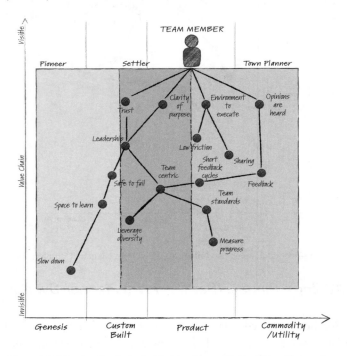

Figure 9.7: Mapping Psychological Safety: Pioneer/Settler/Town Planner Lens

Tweaking the Map

Laura: I think this makes sense, but it probably needs a few tweaks.

Clive: Let's bring the trust and diversity dependencies into pioneering. I still think they are not as common as they should be.

Laura: Okay, and I don't think low friction is in the right place. I feel like it should be more to the left, as it's still not as common as it should be. And let's throw some labels on these boxes. I always forget which is which.

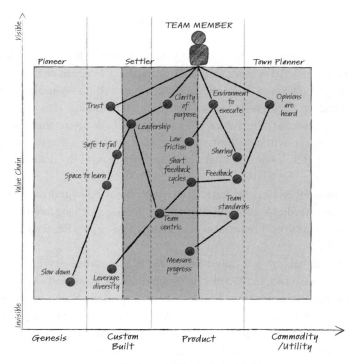

Figure 9.8: Mapping Psychological Safety: Tweaking the Dependencies with the PST Lens

Clive: Looks good. The question is—would this map be accurate for every team?

Laura: Not a chance! But I think it's general enough that it could give people a place to start. I think working out the initial shape of the map is often the most challenging part.

Clive: In summary, the dependencies in the box on the right (the team planner box) should be in place for every team to create psychological safety. The stuff in the middle box (settler) might be present, and the things on the left (pioneering) are likely not present but are worth aiming for.

Laura: Yes! And the needs at the very bottom of the map can help a team work their way up—they're the basic building blocks, if you will. Start slowing down to create the space to learn, for example.

Clive: Brilliant! I think we've got it.

Takeaways

The first tenet of the second phase of the Value Flywheel Effect is creating an environment for success. To achieve this, it's important to establish that the team is a first-class citizen, always. A team-first approach is critical in technology—building in the open and on a team will always win over the solo build.

It's also important to introduce the concept of challenge in this stage. Part of inviting challenge in will help shift your organization from a *project* mindset to a *product* mindset. This organizational structure must be right to create that environment for success.

When assessing your organization's progress toward a supportive culture, you can use Simon Wardley's doctrine of patterns. It's a quick list, intended to drive conversation about your organization's strengths and gaps. (Remember, it's not a maturity model!)

Challenge is healthy, but only when there is appropriate psychological safety present. Team members must feel comfortable taking risks and being their full selves. When everyone on a team feels heard and respected by their peers, the group can be more experimental and innovative. And that risk-taking attitude sets up the team (and eventually, the whole organization) to quickly adapt when the market calls for it, priming developers to proactively address needs and seek continuous improvement.

CHAPTER 10
A SOCIOTECHNICAL SYSTEM FOR CHANGE

An oft-repeated pattern in companies today is disconnection. A key responsibility for leadership is to ensure that the organization runs effectively. But it can be hard to both run your organization effectively and keep everyone aligned with so many departments focused on different responsibilities—Talent, Finance, Operations, Sales, Marketing, Technology, and others.

Often, the revenue stream (what the company does to make money) and the supporting technology platform (the tech the company uses to enable this revenue stream) are woefully disconnected. They are seen as separate entities. Often the technology is seen as something more akin to overhead, like the building that houses a restaurant. The building is seen as little more than a necessary cost of doing business. Necessary but not part of the value the business is delivering. The value is the food (revenue stream). Today, most companies use technology to *support* their revenue stream. They hire experts to create, customize, and run the tech. But technology should be a key component in the business's success, not an overhead.

Let's look at our restaurant example again. A restaurant that views and treats the building it's located in, the servers and chefs who make and serve the food, and even the technology that is used to process payments as equally important is set up for long-term success. In this restaurant, the environment is as much a part of the value the customer is consuming as the food. And it is this collective value that brings the customer back again and again. This takes the restaurant from a short-term gain (customer comes in for one meal service) to a long-term, sustainable success (a dedicated customer base that returns frequently).

To achieve the long-term value promised by the Value Flywheel Effect, organizations must bring all the various departments (people, the socio) together to provide a connected view of the technology and business at its core: a sociotechnical system.

Sociotechnical System

The system within a company (the way that organization conducts its work) should create cohesion between the people and the technology, hence the advent of the term sociotechnical system. This cohesion is essential for creating a team-first culture and creating an environment for success. The effectiveness (or lack thereof) of this system can make or break the company.

Here are some guiding principles of a resilient sociotechnical system for change. After all, any organization can have people and technology. But how these two are brought together is what truly makes a sociotechnical system built to withstand and embrace change.

1. **Socio:** The people in the system must have a specific mindset that contributes, collaborates, and enables. This is the starting point, and it is critical.
2. **Technical:** The technology approach fits the purpose (north star metric) and enables the company to move quickly.
3. **Problem prevention:** Team members anticipate problems in the system's architecture and eradicate them proactively.
4. **Time to value:** When the previous principles are in place, the Value Flywheel Effect will take hold and feedback cycles will become shorter, leading to true agility and a low time to value. This allows proactive behavior, quick pivots, the ability to fail fast, effective scaling, and all the other good stuff. Better time to value will differentiate next-generation companies from their traditional rivals.

The order of these guiding principles is essential to ensure sustainable growth that all team members are responsible for (rather than one person being the sole change agent). There is also an orchestration to the change that is important to embed and get right. Change must start with people (socio), be supported by the right technology (technical), and have the right problem-prevention environment in place. Then time to value will shorten, and you'll be in place to face any change coming your way. (See Figure 10.1)

While it may be well and good to hear and understand these principles of a sociotechnical system for change, the question remains: How do you get there? How can you build a sociotechnical system for change in your organization? As with most things, it starts with your people. Let's dive in in more detail.

Socio

It seems unnecessary and trite to state that companies must be people-centric, but even today many systems are not. The difference between having people "in the system" versus having people "evolving the system" is enormous. Most organizations will say they have a people focus, but it's often hard to separate employees from contributors. *Employees* work for the company and are obliged to "follow" the direction of leadership. *Contributors* are given an order to achieve something. The employee's goal can simply be "to get paid," so maybe they need some more direction. It really depends on the role and expectation.

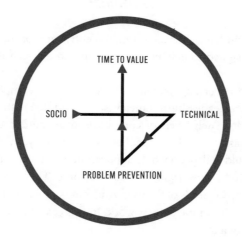

Figure 10.1: Guiding Principles of a Sociotechnical System for Change

From a socio perspective, it's simple—any software system must have significant customer input and critical user personas. It's not acceptable to build software in isolation. We need to know what the customer need is and know that what we're building is going to solve that need. Despite this, it's not uncommon for software to be treated as a "closed box." The user or the developer feels like they can't change the technology to better meet user needs because it's too slow, too expensive, or not a priority.

This is not acceptable.

The industry has also designed frameworks (e.g., Scrum, Kanban, SAFe) to try and "shield the team from interruptions" so they can focus on delivering user needs. But if the team is too busy with low-level software details to talk to their people (stakeholders, peers, customers), then the architecture is wrong and the whole system collapses.

As we have discussed previously, clarity of purpose (see Chapter 5) and an environment for success achieved through psychological safety (see Chapter 9) will help align a team on a purpose and allow them the space to experiment and meet challenges. This is successful *socio* in a sociotechnical system for change. A human-centric approach aligns people on a purpose and creates an environment in which they feel happy and safe. Only when this is present can we move on to supportive technology.

Technical

Once an organization has achieved a human-centric approach, the tech stack and process must be designed to help empower people to deliver value faster, not slow things down.

Too often, teams over-engineer and create accidental complexity (this is also a sign of poor technical leadership).* Enterprises are riddled with Custom Built software that has reached such levels of complexity over the decades that they more closely resemble massive bowls of spaghetti or knots of yarn. If you pull on one thread here, you could collapse a whole application over there. Therefore, enterprise IT is often known to be slow, rigid, and cumbersome. This is often why enterprise software fails to meet the needs of the user. And, often, much of this software hinders a team's ability to easily complete their work. In this case, the technical has become an obstacle instead of a tool.

Reducing this complexity is essential to creating a successful sociotechnical system for change. If the tech isn't so complex and hard to change, then the technology could more easily change to meet user needs and become a tool instead of a burden. Public cloud vendors today can look after an awful lot of the operational concerns of a software team.† Giving up some control to cloud vendors can serve your business and your customers. It often feels easier to build rather than use, but it's the maintenance that will get you. When you use a service from the cloud, you aren't saving in build costs; you're saving in operations costs—one less thing to worry about, which frees time to focus on delivering value (your north star) for your users.

In support of this, engineers and product people must be joined at the hip—this is an example of an excellent sociotechnical system. Technology does not lead; it is

---

* Remember, just because you can, doesn't mean you should. Always invest in technical leadership: it should be clear to stakeholders why things are happening. If a technical lead makes you feel stupid or can't explain something in a simple manner, then they need training. Pat Kua has more great material on building technical leaders at PatKua.com.
† Only a tiny percentage of companies need to perform infrastructure engineering at a higher level than the public cloud vendors can provide; you are likely not in that small group.

not the driving factor. Appropriate technology choices combined with a high-quality working environment will maximize return with a well-defined business goal.

Technology does not exist in a vacuum. Look at the successful tech companies: Apple, Tesla, Amazon, Google, Netflix, the list is endless. The technical solution is so well suited to the product vision that the company name replaces the capability. We watch Netflix over watching internet-streamed HD video. We drive a Tesla over driving a software-powered electric car. We Google things instead of looking them up on a pulsating brain that indexes the entire internet. The point is, do not let the tech team run wild; technology is the business.

Wardley Mapping is among the best tools available to help leaders make these types of effective technology decisions. Chapter 11 will help walk you through this type of map.

Problem Prevention

When socio and technical combine, it creates an environment for success—it is a builders' paradise. But every builder requires constraints and standards for risk mitigation. This is especially true if you're looking to build a sociotechnical system for *change*. After all, we need to be able to meet the needs of tomorrow head-on, not stagnate in the needs of today.

With the advent of the full-stack engineer, the role of the architect is often poorly understood. If an engineer can do everything, then (some may assume) complicated architecture isn't needed. But even if you have no architects, there is still architecture. The problem is you can't see it. Maybe architects have never been understood, but they are needed now more than ever to ensure the third guiding principle of a sociotechnical system for change: a problem prevention culture.

Architects have a very busy job, which includes writing code. But their primary responsibility is to reduce risk by communicating. Their ability to do this requires extensive system building, designing, and hard work—often decades' worth. The architect team will usually have the only sociotechnical map of the entire company, but this team is rarely leveraged properly.

Historically, a software architect oversaw making high-level design choices and enforcing technical standards like software coding standards, tools, and platforms. But as Gregory Hohpe points out in *The Software Architect Elevator: Redefining the Architect's Role in the Digital Enterprise*, which describes how we use architects in modern companies, this role is evolving.

As the digital economy changes the rules of the game for traditional enterprises, the role of architects also fundamentally changes. Rather than focus on technical implementations alone, they must connect the organization's penthouse, where the business strategy is set, with the technical engine room, where the enabling technologies are implemented. Only if both parts are connected can IT change its role from a cost center to a competitive digital advantage.[1]

Unfortunately, many still think either architects are unnecessary because we don't need diagrams anymore, or that they should join the team as engineers. Regardless of who fills the architecture function, someone needs to prevent bad things from happening.

There are many risks when building software—security, poor performance, outages, erratic behavior, and high run costs. But many companies incentivize *solving* problems over problem *prevention* (what's known as the problem-prevention paradox); thus, they are incentivizing the *creation* of the problem in the first place. We are all familiar with the superstar who saved the day, the hero who landed the plane or brought the system back up. But why don't we give equal merit to the steady heads who check and triple check limits? Those who audit and test the system? The engineers who prevent problems from happening?

There is a growing culture of postmortems and premortems in software, which seek to understand how we can prevent problems from happening and recognize great systems appropriately. This is where atomic behaviors like well-architected systems come into play—continuous resilience should be front of mind. It's not glamorous, but it's the bedrock of great systems. Some companies will spend years trying to decide what good architecture is (and to be fair, it's not a perfect link to building architects, but it's the term that we have). Using an industry-defined standard for good architecture (like AWS's Well-Architected Framework, explained in more detail in Chapter 17) removes a huge amount of argument and wheel-spinning.

Time to Value

As we saw in Chapter 6, great companies act on leading metrics; they are proactive. They don't wait until the quarterly results come in before they decide what they're going to do next to continue delivering value to their customers. They are aware, they anticipate, and they preempt customer needs.

A critical component of this is the feedback loop, or as Jeff Gothelf puts it "Ship -> Sense -> Respond" (and then repeat indefinitely).[2] In other words, ship value to your customer, sense what value they need next, then respond by building the next feature or value to meet customer needs. This feedback loop gives your business goal every chance to succeed no matter what change is on the horizon.

But too many companies don't behave this way or don't have the sociotechnical capability in place to behave this way. Many are more focused on reacting to results, on waiting for the customer to tell them a need instead of anticipating it. Thus, they are slow to market with the answer. Others are hindered by their overly complex technology stack to ship quality value sooner, safer, and happier (as Jon Smart might say).[3]

Ask yourself this question. You have an idea for a product or feature. How long does it take to ship and then to see some feedback? Is it hours, days, weeks, months, or years? It depends on your business domain, of course, but for many companies, the answer is more like months or years. However, when you have the first three guiding principles of a sociotechnical system for change in place, you can shorten your time value and stay competitive in the market.

The Intersection of People and Technology

Often organizations make the mistake of starting with the tech and don't focus on people, problem prevention, or time to value. Many of the organizations that are obsessed with the latest tech will lose sight of the other areas. Below are some strategies for helping your organization keep the socio in sociotechnical system of change:

1. Taking an outside-in approach will ensure that user need is driving the work. An inclusive nature to socio factors will help.
2. The correct technology choices will prevent your teams from being laid down with legacy decisions and enable rapid movement.
3. Good technical leadership will apply standards and good practice to prevent bad things from happening.
4. A drive for improved time to value will keep everything connected to business outcomes. This connects back to user need.
5. The lack of legacy tech means more time to focus.
6. Lightweight governance and standards mean expertise is valued over red tape. This creates an effective time-to-value flywheel.

The Value Flywheel Effect will ultimately help organizations maintain a balance and focus on creating a true sociotechnical system.

The first two phases of the Value Flywheel Effect—clarity of purpose and challenge and landscape—focus on a human-centric business strategy and how a healthy environment can help a business get the most out of that strategy. This is the socio strategy focused on user need (clarity of purpose) and providing teams with the environment the need to succeed (challenge and landscape).

The second two phases of the Value Flywheel Effect, which are the focus of the next two parts of this book, focus on the *technical* strategy and creating a healthy environment for *technology teams* to execute in. Let's imagine what that might look like.

The technical teams have a modern cloud platform with an exceptional developer experience. The engineers can work at a high level of abstraction when building software (you don't need to type every line of code or worry about maintenance). Instead of writing oceans of code, they reuse components and libraries to do the same job. They move fast and things just work. It's the epitome of work smarter, not harder.

Combine abstraction with a serverless-first strategy, and technical teams are using all the latest and greatest products from the public cloud provider. When a disruptive product is released, they're using it effectively to build value for their business the next day. With a lack of operational overhead and low-level work, the team is free to think about the bigger system, ensure it is well architected, and deliver for their business partners ahead of time.

When a team has absolute clarity of purpose regarding the business problem and they are experts on market-leading technology, they can make a huge impact. They can deliver value quicker than anyone else.

It's not a pipe dream to think of your organization as a sociotechnical system. In fact, the only question is, why aren't you doing this? Technical debt? No, that's not a good enough excuse. Creating a sociotechnical system for change will work equally as well on an older system as with any digital native.

Purpose vs. Function (DP1 and DP2)

In the early 1960s, there was a breakthrough in organizational development by Australian psychologist Fred Emery. He identified three organization types (design principle 1, design principle 2, and laissez-faire)[4] that still ring true today and provide another lens for viewing the connection between people and technology:

> **Design principle 1 (DP1)** is named "redundancy of parts." In this type of organization, there are more people (referred to as parts) than are necessary to complete the work. As people are classified by "function," there is coordination and control required to "do the work," e.g., a manager is required to ensure the designer and the developer work together. This results in fragmented work, unclear purpose, and a hierarchical, controlling environment.

Design principle 2 (DP2) is named "redundancy of functions." Quite simply, we train people with the skills required, and they self-manage to complete a goal. Organized into groups of people (teams), there is negotiation, responsibility, and a sense of purpose.

The third type is named **laissez-faire**, which is the "no design principle." In short, an absence of one of the design principles results in a lack of structure, with people working independently. This might seem desirable but often leads to confusion.

With a purposeful organization (DP2), there is cooperation, collaboration, achievement, and a sense of pride. There is ownership of the problem, empowerment, and the motivation to meet the goal.

With many traditional organizations (DP1), there is a gradual deskilling of staff, demotivation, and little understanding of motivation (apart from salary). Applying a DP1 system to the creation of software is wholly disastrous. It didn't work decades ago, which is one of the reasons the Agile Manifesto came about.

Many organizations become laissez-faire about their structure, not by design but usually due to the executives having a lack of technical expertise and inadvertently letting the structure break down. Daniel Pink covers a very simple model in *Drive: The Surprising Truth about What Motivates Us.* According to Pink, people are motivated by autonomy, mastery, and sense of purpose (intrinsic motives), not by "fear of punishment or the promise of a reward" (extrinsic motivation).[5]

For a very simple example of the importance of purpose, look at many of the roles that have deep-rooted meaning, like firefighters. Many roles that can be classed as a vocation or have deep meaning will look to the functions as a way of meeting the goal of saving a life.

We are not defined by the functions we perform in our work. As we look to the future of work, a sense of belonging, ownership, and purpose will be more important than learning skills. We could argue that this has already happened. Maybe in patches, but certainly not across all industries in all global locations.

Your Organization Is a System

We often think of software as a system and the people in the organization as a hierarchy. We believe that the people can be controlled and the software has a life of its own. It's the opposite, and this is important to understand as we strive to create sociotechnical systems for change. There are two interesting models that explain this: the Cynefin framework and complex adaptive systems (CAS).

The Cynefin framework is a decision-making model created by Dave Snowden.[6] It's often referred to as a sensemaking device. In short, there are five different domains, or contexts, that a component can be in:

1. **Clear:** We understand what is happening and can apply best practice.
2. **Complicated:** Governance and analysis are required.
3. **Complex:** Hard to predict; we need to probe and respond.
4. **Chaotic:** Lack of control; there are no effective constraints.
5. **Confused:** A state of not knowing where one is; not good.

In organizations, people are usually in the Complex domain and the software is only in the Complicated domain, not the other way around.

But every organization is a complex adaptive system (CAS). Any illusion of control is exactly that, an illusion. Some of the clearest examples of a CAS are a flock of starlings or a school of fish: hundreds of independent agents moving as one.

The Human Systems Dynamics (HSD) Institute is worth quoting on this topic, and their site contains many excellent tools.

> As early as 1997, Kevin Dooley, defined Complex Adaptive System (CAS) as a group of semi-autonomous agents who interact in interdependent ways to produce system-wide patterns, such that those patterns then influence behavior of the agents. In human systems at all scales, you see patterns that emerge from the interactions of agents in that system. Thoughts, experiences, perceptions interact to create patterns of thought. Shared attitudes toward diet, exercise, and physical awareness interact to shape patterns of health in team or community. In an organization or business, individuals play out their roles, relationships, and expectations to generate patterns of competition or innovation. In organizations and communities, history, traditions, and expectations all influence behavior to shape dominant patterns we see as the culture of that group.[7]

How many CEOs think of their companies as a collection of patterns performed by independent agents? Well, maybe a lot do, but this should dictate how leadership leads—creating similar patterns of thought is more important than control, or purpose over function.

What Are Feedback Loops?

Returning to the Cynefin framework, Snowden provides very clear guidance on how one interacts in this domain: probe, sense, and respond.[8] Said another way, observe, gather evidence and hypotheses, and then act. The "probe, sense, and respond" directive is a feedback loop of sorts. Feedback loops are what allow an organization to pivot and respond to change effectively instead of being blindsided. It's important for an organization to think about what feedback loops are currently in effect, how fast they are, and who is aware of them.

Once we start thinking in feedback loops within an organization, we can look out for weak signals that supply early warnings. We can think ahead of the response to an action. We can consider adaptation within the company—responding to change in a positive or negative manner. We can create *leading* metrics that we believe will influence *lagging* metrics. We can shorten our time to value, the fourth principle of creating a sociotechnical system for change.

Takeaways

The concept of sociotechnical design has been around for a long time, but we have always found it useful in technical groups. Specifically, as it makes us think of the social side. In this chapter, we dissected the term down into a simple diagram that walks through the guiding principles to create a sociotechnical system for change: socio (people), technical (the system), problem prevention (the culture), and time to value (the flow). This simple mechanism is intended to quickly check the environment and hopefully flag any challenges.

This chapter has condensed around three PhDs, so has been purposely a quick skim. There is a wealth of information out there on the concept of sociotechnical systems. This chapter barely scratches the surface. I highly encourage any readers who find it interesting to dive into the research.

That said, it's clear that viewing our organizations as more than socio and technical but a combined and aligned sociotechnical system will help organizations prepare for and meet the demands of tomorrow and is essential in facing the second phase of the Value Flywheel.

CHAPTER 11
MAP YOUR ORG CAPABILITY

The ability to map the capability of your organization is crucial in the second phase of the Value Flywheel Effect. Ask yourself the following questions: Do you have the people or capability to do what you need to do to meet your north star? How can you grow the skills of your people to meet your needs?

An organization is more than a group of people working together. And it's more than the products it churns out. Think about the companies that people admire or the brands you love best. Most people don't have a deep understanding of how that company is organized or what its strategy is. It's the organization's capabilities that lead to success. According to an article from *Harvard Business Review*:

> If you ask them which companies they admire, people quickly point to organizations like General Electric, Starbucks, Nordstrom, or Microsoft. Ask how many layers of management these companies have, though, or how they set strategy, and you'll discover that few know or care. What people respect about the companies is not how they are structured or their specific approaches to management, but their capabilities—an ability to innovate, for example, or to respond to changing customer needs. Such *organizational capabilities*, as we call them, are key intangible assets. You can't see or touch them, yet they can make all the difference in the world when it comes to market value.[1]

An organization's capabilities are made up of its unique combination of people, skills, technologies, processes, and shared mindsets. These intangible assets, and their unique combination in an individual organization, are true differentiators of success or failure in the market.

In the second phase of the Value Flywheel Effect, as we look at Challenge and Landscape, mapping your organization's capabilities is a way to find the strengths and weaknesses present in your environment. It's a way of getting an unbiased snapshot of your organization's culture. With it, you can start to plot a path forward to success.

Mapping a Capability

Let's take two relatively robust areas and map them out for a company either embarking on these as a new venture or assessing their own adoption path. The method shown here is important to learn, as it can quickly make sense of a brand-new area for both an individual and for a team building a shared understanding.

There is a simple pattern here for mapping a capability:

1. Use a different evolutionary axis (*x*-axis) for the map: Concept, Hypothesis, Theory, Accepted instead of the traditional (Genesis, Custom Built, Product, Commodity.
2. It may be easier to take a description of the capability from a trusted third party—either a vendor or a standards body.
3. Map the components out with respect to how much work is needed to introduce them and change them. Some components can be used off the shelf (like a checklist) others will need to be changed for your context (like an architecture blueprint).
4. Finally, add in supporting components.

Secure Development

The first example takes a company introducing security into the software development life cycle. For this example, we have taken the excellent Microsoft Security Development Lifecycle (SDL)[2] practices as a starting point.

Here are the twelve practices in full:

- **Practice #1**: Provide Training
- **Practice #2**: Define Security Requirements
- **Practice #3**: Define Metrics and Compliance Reporting
- **Practice #4**: Perform Threat Modeling
- **Practice #5**: Establish Design Requirements
- **Practice #6**: Define and Use Cryptography Standards
- **Practice #7**: Manage the Security Risk of Using Third-Party Components
- **Practice #8**: Use Approved Tools
- **Practice #9**: Perform Static Analysis Security Testing (SAST)

- **Practice #10:** Perform Dynamic Analysis Security Testing (DAST)
- **Practice #11:** Perform Penetration Testing
- **Practice #12:** Establish a Standard Incident Response Process

For the map (Figure 11.1), we have simplified the components and added an anchor (a senior leader) to determine which practices are more visible. We also ordered them along the evolutionary axis. Penetration testing can be rented from a vendor with little effort while threat modeling requires training, effort, and experimentation. The components marked in gray instead of blue are enabling components—they help realize the others.

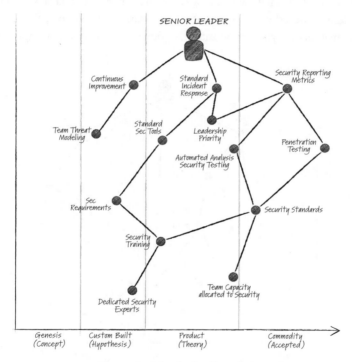

Figure 11.1: Map the Org Example 1

Cloud-Native Development

For the second example, we can look at a company moving toward a fully cloud-native development environment. There are many opinions and ways to do this. This example shows a Microsoft Azure definition of cloud native from the .NET documentation.[3]

The description starts with six areas that feature in this description:

- cloud infrastructure
- modern design
- microservices
- containers
- backing services
- automation

Each of these areas has one or two dependencies, as outlined in the documentation. At this stage (especially with a new capability), it's best to take a relatively simple and well-defined description to start the conversation. Remember, this is a new or emerging capability for your organization, so don't over complicate things at the start.

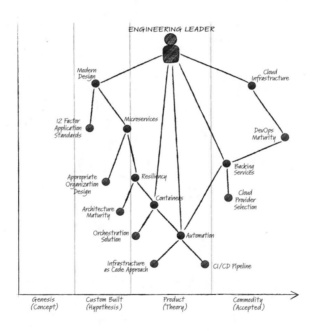

Figure 11.2: Mapping the Org Example 2

The anchor in this map (Figure 11.2) is an engineering leader and the six areas are directly linked to that role. They have been ordered along the evolutionary axis based on how much work is needed to "change the hearts and minds" of the engineers. Cloud infrastructure will be bought, but modern design will need to be created specifically for the company. In this map, there are also dependencies.

The six areas mapped out in this manner clearly show the dependencies and there are enabling components marked in gray. This example is more fluid than the Secure Development example (Figure 11.1), as there are many, many decision points.

Takeaways

Things move fast in the cloud. We often need to dip into new areas and do it quickly—security being the prime example. Learning a brand new technology space is also very daunting. Mapping your capability is a straightforward yet powerful technique to objectively look at an industry definition (like a framework or a standard) and map how the different elements of components exist in your company.

A helpful addition is using a slightly different labeling system on the evolutionary axis: Concept, Hypothesis, Theory, and Accepted. I have observed experienced developers treat well-established secure coding practices as Concept purely because they didn't have any secure development experience. Of course, with some training, these elements can quickly move to Accepted.

Mapping your capability is also an excellent way to take an industry-standard framework or even a book and break the composite parts into a map. We then link them together in a rough value chain (it can be approximate) and position them from the left to the right along the evolutionary axis. Try it with a framework you are familiar with now, just with pen and paper. I bet it will result in an insight you have not considered.

CHAPTER 12
CASE STUDY—WORKGRID

O ur second case study is from the enterprise software startup Workgrid Software, which aims to simplify the digital workplace, unify and deliver important information seamlessly, reduce digital friction, and meet employees where they are. Founded in 2017 with a very small number of people, the company had ambitious plans but faced a challenging landscape.

The Workgrid story illustrates the importance of successfully navigating the second phase of the Value Flywheel Effect: Challenge and Landscape. If Workgrid hadn't created an environment for success on day one, they certainly would have failed. In this case study, we'll examine how Workgrid's technical leaders created an environment that valued high standards, created space to respectfully challenge each other's thinking, and made technology work for them instead of against them.

Workgrid Software spun out of an innovation project at Liberty Mutual. They sought to solve the complexity of the enterprise ecosystem.

At Liberty Mutual, for example, there are many applications that employees are expected to use. Each of these applications provides key functions for the digitization of the organization's processes and procurement. Together, these best-of-breed systems for HR, the help desk, procurement, finance, collaboration, and communication add complexity to the overall workplace and increase the cognitive burden of even the simplest tasks. It's hard needing to switch between six or more different systems every day in the course of your normal work. And this complexity inherently creates waste, including:

- missed communications in emails
- delayed approvals
- too many screens and too many steps to navigate

- time wasted switching between systems
- hidden, difficult-to-find, siloed information
- navigating different vendors' requirements, passwords, etc.

Workgrid believed that the workplace was moving into a new era. But each era doesn't replace or erase the previous era; it builds upon and evolves it. The early internet was the foundation for the more complex digital landscape we have today.

The modern workplace digitized the organization's processes and tools. But Workgrid wanted to take it a step farther and create an intelligent workplace that would make sense of, streamline, and connect current and future technologies in a way that simplified employees' lives and provided a more seamless and enjoyable experience.

What Workgrid created was a single pane of glass—one piece of software, one console—that simplified the workday. The experience layer that Workgrid provides unifies digital information and reduces friction for employees. Workgrid's robust software can also meet employees wherever they are with multiple different channels.

The Backstory

The founding Workgrid team consisted of seven people from within Liberty Mutual, including the CTO, Gillian McCann. They had their clarity of purpose: to create one piece of software, one console, that simplifies the workday. Now they needed to face the second phase of the Value Flywheel: Challenge and Landscape.

The engineering team at Workgrid consisted of just four people. These engineers each had many years of experience across a multitude of enterprise applications—they knew how to build complex, large-scale systems with quality and security baked in. However, McCann was the only one with in-depth knowledge of AWS, and they knew that to achieve their goal they would need to leverage the cloud.

In that first week, the four engineers discussed what needed to be the key drivers in making initial architecture choices.

- **Speed:** The team wanted to get the product into the marketplace fast to get feedback, traction, and—ultimately—customer buy-in.
- **Low cost:** The initial funding the team received needed to stretch as far as possible, so they couldn't afford to spend time or money on anything that wouldn't set their product ahead of the competition.
- **Autonomy:** Dependencies needed to be kept to a minimum so the team could move as fast as possible and make decisions quickly. As much as possible, the core team had to have end-to-end ownership of decisions,

and they wanted to limit the need for procurement of external products or lengthy contract negotiations. Again, speed was key.

- **Scalability:** The team prioritized more flexibility and quicker time to release, all at a reduced cost.

The Compute Experiment

Based on their architecture decision to focus on speed, low cost, autonomy, and scalability, the team knew they would build a SaaS (software as a service) in AWS, and they would leverage as much out-of-the-box functionality as possible, but some discussion was needed on exactly *what* that was. McCann was very much in the serverless camp, but she didn't have complete team buy-in. With the intention of enablement and empowerment, she knew it was better to bring the team on the journey instead of forcing them down the road, as it would be a long road. So, the team did what McCann refers to now as the *compute experiment*.

The team played around with using AWS products, such as EC2, AMIs, load balancers, and autoscaling policies, but they also thought about Lambda as the compute layer. Remember, this was 2017, so Lambda and serverless architecture were very different from what they are today. After a day of deliberation, the consensus was to go serverless. The team had been given the environment of psychological safety necessary to experiment and then make the best decision to meet the user need.

Of course, viewing this decision through rose-tinted glasses, it appears like a success. But the engineers really made a leap of faith that day. It's possible they could have gone way down the serverless road and found out it was a huge mistake. The important thing to learn here is that they were given space to experiment without fear; thus, they were the best equipped to face challenges and make smart decisions. The team had started to establish psychological safety by making it okay to disagree, experiment, and learn.

Serverless is not just about the Lambda functions. Some choices need to be made across key components, such as data, logging, events, and deployments. It's more than the compute. And as most operational responsibilities stayed with AWS, the team could focus on the product.

Architecture Philosophy

Since 2017, Workgrid has matured their architectural philosophy from their original bullets. In other words, they faced challenges, pivoted where necessary, and grew to continuously meet the needs of their user. Their new architectural philosophy was as follows:

- **Serverless-first:** Leverage serverless tech as much as possible.
- **Managed services over managed infrastructure:** Build business features and add value rather than run infrastructure.
- **Pragmatic architecture:** Architect what is right for right now (also known as the *Frozen 2* evolutionary architecture strategy). This recognizes that sometimes the group will make choices that they know they'll need to change in the longer term. Sometimes the tactical solution is the best solution at that given time. The question always asked is, "Is this the simplest version of what can be built today?"
- **Evolving architecture:** Do the next right thing. The team is not afraid to throw code away. AWS releases new services and features constantly; assess these and remove code as necessary.
- **Modular/"Lego™" design:** Don't be afraid to remove pieces of architecture that are no longer fit for purpose.
- **Security and operations are everyone's job:** Workgrid engineers deploy their code and infrastructure.
- **Cost-aware:** Total cost of ownership is an architectural concern, and high expense is considered a defect.
- **Industry-aware:** Leverage common patterns and approaches shared by AWS practitioners.

Underscoring all of this is Workgrid's endeavor to remove as many Lambda instances as possible from their serverless architecture. Maybe architectures of the future can avoid servers, Lambda, and functions? Maybe they'll be able to bypass the compute layer completely?

It turned out that this transformation was easier said than done. Workgrid hasn't been without growing pains and challenges. Taking on the end-to-end ownership of building an external product and a company, exploring product-market fit, and building engineering teams is not without challenges. Workgrid challenged the enterprise's thinking of what was possible with serverless architecture. Then they showed that serverless can meet all the enterprise controls and compliance and security standards. And finally, the group had to work closely with Security and Legal and privacy teams in many enterprise companies, which included earning SOC2 compliance certification—something that full organizations struggle to accomplish, let alone a small team of individuals.

Serverless SaaS—Enabling a Global Company

A significant part of Workgrid's technology journey evolved around how to change an application that served a single customer—Liberty Mutual—to serving many customers across the world. The group needed to build a multitenant SaaS solution. They researched SaaS architectures and leveraged AWS resources, white papers, re:Invent talks, and the AWS SaaS Factory to understand what this meant.

The upsides of cost, fault tolerance, deployment agility, and managed scale made continuing to leverage serverless computing an attractive model.

- No need for tenant-specific provisioning of compute services.
- IAM (identity and access management) policies can control scoped access to AWS resources.
- Easier to experiment with different tenant isolation models.

In a SaaS model, there tends to be a higher reliance or need to focus on more operational aspects, and management and monitoring look different from traditional software applications.

As Workgrid grew, the group set up a small team of engineers to manage these SaaS operational aspects. As the team embraced the serverless SaaS concept, the engineers could focus only on business functionality—the challenge and creating an environment for success in the early days built a solid foundation for the future growth of the business. Succeeding at the second phase of the Value Flywheel Effect lay the groundwork for successful third phase, next-best action.

Scaling Serverless Teams—Our Learning Journey

In 2021, Workgrid now had twenty-five engineers spread across five teams. Their new challenge, (another iteration of Phase 2 of their Value Flywheel) was learning how to effectively spread serverless expertise and skills across five teams instead of one.

Realistically, you don't just hire twenty-five serverless cloud engineers. Building high-performing serverless-first teams is a journey. The mythical concept of a "full-stack engineer" is popular across businesses today, but adding serverless expertise to the stack made the myth a whole lot bigger and even more unrealistic! Instead of chasing twenty-five serverless unicorns, Workgrid provided training, support, and guidance in cloud and serverless technologies to their existing engineers, making sure they could all work with a serverless-first mindset and approach.

The teams were responsible for the entire end-to-end development life cycle, so the engineers needed to learn all the concerns around discovery and framing, coding, testing, performance, cloud security, scalability, cost optimization, infrastructure as code, CI/CD, AWS services and features, serverless architecture patterns, and more. It took a long time for everyone to develop these skills. But Workgrid's leadership helped lower the burden on the teams by creating the environment to meet these challenges (including time and space, giving the technology road map equal weight to the product road map in planning and budget, not being afraid to invest in help and training so skills are up to date, etc.).

Workgrid's aim is to create an environment where it is safe to learn fast, experiment with the latest services and features, rapidly prototype capabilities, and then rapidly get those prototypes into production with real users giving fast feedback. And as showcased earlier, leadership had set up the guardrails and a secure CI/CD pipeline to enable their teams to "go fast" with confidence.

Education is vital—but it's also important to leverage all the resources available to you. The Workgrid team learned to ask AWS first before building anything. The pace of change in the cloud is unbelievable, and AWS was much better poised than Workgrid's engineers to quickly provide new systems that responded to changes.* In the serverless and serviceful world, two weeks of research, learning, and experimentation is better than two months of coding.

Takeaways

Workgrid Software CTO Gillian McCann often compares serverless architecture to physical architecture: "I never once said it was easier . . . [but] I do think it is better."

By using serverless technology, Workgrid teams developed a complete end-to-end understanding of what it takes to deliver a product to production. Event-driven architecture always resulted in a complex distributed system, but the software tools to build event-driven systems are improving.

Workgrid came to learn that serverless teams are product teams. There is a high level of technical capability within each team, but also high velocity. Workgrid teams focus on the user need and don't get distracted with infrastructure tasks that can be offloaded to the cloud vendor. Recognizing that infrastructure could be offloaded on day one was a game changer for Workgrid Software.

But none of this learning and success would have been possible if Workgrid hadn't been set up to face the challenge and landscape in front of them. By successfully navigating the second phase of the Value Flywheel Effect, Workgrid built an environment for success based on psychological safety and stayed focused on crafting a sociotechnical system that could adapt and respond to change.

---

* It's important to reach out to developer advocates and account managers if you have questions, and to follow the AWS Heroes and Developer Advocates on Twitter and YouTube. Use sandbox and Dev environments that are safe for experimentation and learning. The Well-Architected Framework can help keep your teams aligned with architectural good practices. (More on this in Chapter 17.)

IV

PHASE 3
Next Best
Action

PERSONA: PRODUCT LEADERS

KEY TENETS

Code is a liability: A serverless-first mindset delivers value.

Frictionless developer experience: An easy path to production.

Map your solution: Align on how you will serve customers.

CHAPTER 13
THE SERVERLESS-FIRST EDGE

The next best action (the third phase of the Value Flywheel Effect) is about doing the simplest thing you can do *right now* to deliver value. Remove all the unnecessary baggage and just provide value. It's a shortcut around a lot of the waffly, strategic frameworks that we've seen in the past. The next best action really asks organizations to look at what they do now to create rapid impact. What's the most important, most impactful thing you as an individual, team, or organization can do to improve your organization's ability to deliver value?

Today, serverless-first is the perfect strategy to achieve this; it's a quiet revolution happening right in front of us.* A serverless-first mindset enables teams to focus on business outcomes and business impact, not keeping the lights on. It also has added benefits, including keeping your code low, your security high, and your cost liabilities under control. Serverless-first is a game changer that can allow organizations to move rapidly and sustainably. It also removes developer friction, as we'll discuss more in the next chapter.

As we mentioned earlier in the book, the last two phases of the Value Flywheel Effect focus on the technical strategy and creating a healthy environment for technology teams to execute in. So, you'll see these sections are more focused in that direction. But don't take it to mean that if you're not a technology leader, a CTO or CIO, you shouldn't read these chapters. As we settle into the Fourth Industrial Revolution, it has become clear than ever that every business is a technology business. And likely, every leader is or is becoming a technology leader. So, wherever you lie in the hierarchy, you should keep reading.

The goal in the third phase of the Value Flywheel Effect is to achieve fast flow efficiency, from idea to real user value and real impact for your business, using the next best action. Today that is serverless, but it won't always be. It's important to choose the right tool for the job. And in five or ten or twenty years, the next best

---

* I get equal praise and criticism for this opinion, but I don't mind. A lack of criticism is a dangerous place to be. I have seen countless serverless projects deliver way above and beyond. It's the future of software development, but serverless will continue to evolve.

action for any organization might be very different. The important thing is to keep your organization moving. Keep your flywheel spinning.

Next Best Action or Flimsy Trend

Software is eating the world (as has been famously said). A direct effect of that is that many companies have moved to the cloud. Hordes of organizations are migrating west like the gold rush of the twentieth century. The call was sent out: gold could be found in the beautiful wild mountains of "the cloud," and organizations clamored to seek their claim before investigating if it was the right move for them.

It's understandable. The technology landscape is so difficult to understand that very few have the perspective, visibility, and expertise to see what's happening. Hardly anyone truly understands new tech capabilities. In some ways, the HR industry is struggling to keep up. A new technology trend or even a conference talk can spawn a wave of new job titles. Is this a "new thing" or a "rebranded thing"? Is this the next best action our organization can take or is it an empty promise?

Technology experts don't do themselves any favors in this discussion. The vendors, the experts, and the IT department leaders love to confuse people with new terms, changing the meaning of things, and simply copying peers. IT vendors use "technology terminology marketing" to attack new ideas. Vendor A launches XYZ; Vendor B is also working on XYZ. Both products are slightly different. The vendors copy each other's work and try to use as many buzzwords as possible. Net result: no one knows what XYZ means, and the original product manager who had the groundbreaking idea has now left the tech industry to work on an organic farm—they've had enough!

When the migration is complete and all their applications are successfully in the cloud, what happens next? Do the organization's leaders understand the invisible force that now powers the company? Has the organization become over-reliant on the CTO? Is it even happy with its technology portfolio? Do the promises of lower time to value and total cost of ownership deliver or do technical, process, and business debts slow progress more than ever?

In successful organizations today, business and technical concerns combine to create great outcomes. From a leadership perspective, this sociotechnical system should be an asset (not a liability). The people, the tech they make, and the services that run it create value, not a cost to be squeezed. Likewise, the next best action should provide you with a robust technical strategy that helps lead to improved time to value. But many who have made the journey west and migrated to the cloud have yet to reap the benefits they were promised. Instead, they are left with questions:

- Why did we not speed up? *Answer: Product delivery still feels slow.*
- Why does the cost keep rising? *Answer: It didn't get any cheaper.*
- Why is it so much more complicated? *Answer: It was supposed to be easier.*
- If the tech is so great, why can't we hire people? *Answer: The salary asks are crazy.*
- Why is security and compliance so tricky? *Answer: It's never-ending.*
- And why do we keep rewriting everything? *Answer: Change is constant.*

Moving to the cloud is like getting on a rocket ship. It sounds like an exciting adventure, but guess what: once you commit, it's hard to get off—and it gets faster and faster. The fact is that simply moving to the cloud is not the next best action. Simply lifting and shifting your legacy applications to the cloud will not necessarily improve your time to value. The next best action is modernization, building applications with a serverless-first mindset to shift operational burdens to the vendors and free your developers to focus on delivering real value.

The Modern Cloud

Software and the cloud have a language problem. Both have been around for decades and are evolving rapidly. For software, it was mainly sensible to keep components similar, consistent, and close to each other. The introduction of the internet and the cloud started to drive the mass adoption of distributed systems instead.

When Sam Newman published *Building Microservices: Designing Fine-Grained Systems* in 2015, the concept took hold. Approaches before that, like component-based development and service-oriented architecture, had similar promises and paved the way for a microservice future. In other words, it's a little like the iPod. MP3 players and digital music advances happened for years, but Apple put the time and effort into putting the correct language, design, and innovation into the iPod. Marketing and product engineering are needed to change a market.

Many organizations are moving their legacy nondistributed systems to the cloud with cloud migration. These migrations look like cloud applications, but they're still built on legacy technology, causing the organization to lose out on the promised cost savings and increased delivery velocity.

The term *modern cloud* applies to applications and systems that embrace modern practices built for the cloud. Practices such as containers, managed services, event-driven programming, microservices, and serverless all fall under this umbrella. Of course, you can still drop a monolithic, legacy application into a container—but it's not modern until you break it up.

Modern cloud is hard to explain, but let's outline some characteristics. After all, understanding the details and benefits of the modern cloud are critical to the third phase of the Value Flywheel Effect if your organization is to avoid following trends and instead find your true next best action.

Here are some aspects of applications built in the modern cloud:

- **Microservices:** Break applications into components deployed separately containing the data they need and speak to other microservices via service calls.
- **Loosely coupled and scalable:** Ideally built on an event-driven architecture, but lack of a hard dependency means applications can scale as they need to (automated).
- **Cloud native:** Software is ephemeral, infrastructure as code, and resilient.
- **Abstracted:** Software is abstracted away from the OS via containers or serverless architecture.
- **Pay per use:** Only pay for what you need.
- **Low operational overhead:** Fully (or almost fully) automate operations. There's no longer a need to log into a computer and manually configure or install something.
- **Leverage the provider:** Use the services that the cloud provider offers to minimize overhead.

Modern Cloud Inertia Points

To keep our Value Flywheel turning, it's essential to acknowledge areas of possible inertia (blocks or bottlenecks). In the third phase, you'll encounter some specific obstacles that will slow your progress, like lack of skills, lack of capacity, security constraints, and under-investment in technical strategy.

Inertia points are different for every organization and can disrupt progress significantly. Mapping your organization will help you identify and discuss inertia points in the room ahead of time and work around them. We'll look at this mapping technique more in Chapter 15. But for now, let's work through a few common examples of inertia with technology in the cloud.

Legacy Cloud

If you've already completed a migration to serverless (the modern cloud), you are likely in a good place. Unfortunately, the cloud is evolving fast. A standard you put in place three years ago may now be outdated. "Legacy cloud technical debt" is very real.

Because you "migrated" your system to the cloud, you've benefited from some cost savings, but you must put in a significant amount of work to continuously move your system forward. Legacy cloud systems require constant modernization. Be wary of the sunk cost fallacy: you may have built something fantastic that worked a few years ago, but if it no longer makes sense, then let go of it and modernize; its purpose has been served. The process of ruthless simplification never ends.

The technology transformation process often *starts* with migration to the cloud, but migration is not the endpoint. It bears repeating. *Migration is not the endpoint.* Successful companies in the modern cloud begin with migration, then measure. Once everything is in the cloud, we can measure and observe the system's behaviors. Once we have telemetry, we can start transformation and modernization. Once modernization begins, it never ends, but the value unlocked through the effort should show a huge return on investment.

Lack of Business Alignment

You don't need to take your business partners through every low-level detail about your cloud offering, but they must be part of the cloud migration process. If your IT department has put a facade up in front of the business to obscure the specifics of their work, you'll need to deconstruct it. You must have a single-team mentality to get the most out of your modern cloud. When you have your principles in place, you must move your systems forward *with* your business partners, not *for* them.

But the pendulum can swing too far in either direction. Migrate with too little buy-in and you'll find it hard to explain the benefits. If you over-hype the migration and fail to release the promised benefits, you'll create pressure on your engineers. Instead, create a one-team mentality between the business and technology and keep a next-best-thing mindset to align your stakeholders.

Fear of Vendor Lock-In

Vendor lock-in is a genuine concern for many organizations today. Some industries have regulators that may require a plan to move your workload just in case you ever need to. This is sensible risk mitigation, but your time is better spent creating a system with clear boundaries and the ability to move, not creating a cloud-agnostic solution.

With other utilities (power, telephone, even banking), it took many decades to be able to provide a fast-switching mechanism. These companies needed to improve efficiencies and standardize or industrialize—only then could they build fast switching.

The cloud industry is still evolving, so it's premature to introduce extra complexity into your systems. It's easier to migrate a well-designed serverless system than a poorly designed traditional system. Use your capacity to strengthen API and service boundaries. Don't waste your time making everything agnostic. Ask any company that goes out of business with an agnostic cloud solution—was the extra spend worth it?

Serverless Is Not the Point!

It may seem like this chapter is being a tad overly prescriptive, but we don't intend for it to be. The last thing we are looking to do is *mandate* serverless. In fact, we don't care if your organization chooses to go serverless or not. What we want you to take away from this section is that in today's environment, the next best action for achieving faster value for your organization isn't necessarily to build everything yourself.

Do not underestimate the change of mindset required to truly embrace the modern cloud. Some engineers will have to give up some very familiar habits. (Maybe you can't test locally. No more manual configuration. No more blaming the Ops team!)

We've always believed that as software engineers our job is not to write code; our job is to help the business. Ben Kehoe, the lead researcher at iRobot, once said, "The point is not functions, managed services, operations, cost, code, or technology. The point is focus—that is the why of serverless."[1] Again, this bears repeating so let's break that down:

- Functions are not the point.
- Managed services are not the point.
- NoOps is not the point.
- Cost is not the point.
- Code is not the point.
- Technology is not the point.
- Events are not the point.
- Architecture is not the point.
- Mapping is not the point.
- Data is not the point.
- Innovation is not the point.
- Even sustainability is not the point!

Serverless is a consequence of focusing on business value and offloading everything else (infrastructure and operations, for example). Serverless-first should be a reminder to "not sweat the small stuff"—focus on your business and delivering value to your customer instead.

Serverless is a mindset. It's a realization that you will not rely on separate internal teams to run compute, database, or operations for you—the Dev team will handle it all. It's a realization that you have access to everything, and you will make sure that it all works for the business. It's also a realization that you are not going to be logging tickets and waiting for stuff. You will move quickly. You won't accept a three-day service-level agreement.

The power of the cloud is at your fingertips. You have the skills, and you have the business problem. Do not tolerate any slowdown. We've tried to describe this as a way for the enterprise to scale DevOps.

DevOps was a tremendous promise, but it relied on a significant specialty. We believe the perfect manifestation of DevOps is serverless. NoOps is a fallacy. You always need to run your systems, but utilizing the modern cloud will significantly reduce that burden. The serverless-first strategy says that any other implementation option is less optimal. If you need to fall back, you must have a good reason—and that's okay.

Serverless Myths

The term "serverless myths" could also be "modern cloud myths." The myths highlighted here also apply to a containerized, microservice, event-driven solution. The very nature of the cloud means it practically redefines itself every three to four years. The "old stuff" doesn't go away, but new things come along, and the problems of yesteryear are fixed behind the scenes.

The constantly evolving landscape makes it very hard to keep up with good practices, as the goalposts are constantly shifting. The myths presented here are either old issues that have since been addressed or were simply the result of a lack of knowledge by an engineer who has not kept up. Remember, two of the most challenging situations in software are a very experienced engineer with a legacy skill set and a very inexperienced engineer with a modern skill set. You need both the scars and the curious mind.

Engineering/Technical Myths

Myth: "Serverless has a cold-start problem. We can't afford slow performance in our system." —Engineer or architect

Context: When you own the server, it runs 24/7. When someone makes an API call, the code is ready to execute. But when you're using serverless technologies, the code is only primed once the API call is made. This causes a slight delay for the first call (known as a cold start). But once the "pump is primed," there's no delay for subsequent calls (warm start). Public cloud providers are constantly working to reduce the cold-start time. How you write and configure your code also has an impact.

Impact: Every technology has pros and cons. Cold starts are no longer a concern in the way they were in the early days of Lambda and function as a service. Cold starts are a solved problem, so this myth is incorrect. Serverless may not be the correct architectural choice, but not because of cold starts.

—

Myth: "Serverless is impossible to test, since you can't run it locally." —Engineer

Context: "It worked on my machine!" said every developer, always. Replicating a production environment on a local laptop has always been desirable. The developer can test the change and push it straight to production, right? Wrong. You cannot replicate "the cloud" on your laptop.

Impact: Software verification is complex and requires a different strategy than traditional unit testing. The system under test lives in the cloud and should be tested in the cloud; verification requires an alternate approach, designed by experts. "Running everything locally" is a lazy option and problematic. Efforts to run functions locally can help developers, but it's not the answer.

—

Myth: "You can't see what's happening with the modern cloud. You don't know what's running." —Engineer

Context: Many traditional monitoring approaches involved installing an agent or specific software in the application. This doesn't work for many modern cloud solutions, as you have no access to the underlying system. You must trust what's happening.

Impact: This inertia point happens when you fail to embrace the cloud as a platform. To use the cloud properly, you must also use an event-driven monitoring system, not an execution monitoring system. In many cases, the modern cloud platform has more data about the system available—it's just a matter of approaching observability differently.

—

Architectural Myths

Myth: "Serverless/Kubernetes is not the next big thing; it's technology X. I read a report that backs this up. Besides, our skill set is better matched to technology X." —Architect

Context: At a time of change, if your architect has not stayed relevant, then the architectural advice may be, "Let's not move to the new technology; we'll use the next version of our current technology." Consultants are also likely to give similar advice.

Impact: This is excellent advice for short-term goals, but it's more important to look at the long-term picture. It's worth mapping out the next five years of expected expenditures and deciding how much investment will go to training, development, operations, infrastructure, etc. Today, taking the hit on simplification and upskill may have a much better return on investment than business as usual.

—

Myth: "We don't want to be locked into X cloud provider. If we use their services, we can never change providers." —Everyone

Context: There are two essential terms to explore here—multicloud and cloud agnostic. Multicloud should be a typical strategy for a company. For example, many companies have office products running on Azure and workload running on AWS. This is multicloud. The cloud should be treated as a suite of services—from different vendors—and you use the best service you can. Cloud agnostic means you create a software component that can run on any cloud. Usually, this means building on an open-source platform, which the cloud provider supports. Of course, many of the cloud provider's features cannot be used. There is a widely held opinion that engineers should write code in a cloud-agnostic manner so that they can switch to Provider Y if Provider X hikes up their prices. It's a little like saying, "I won't drive a car because fuel prices might go up. I'll just walk everywhere." Sounds sensible, but it's entirely impractical.

Impact: First, the leading public cloud providers have a record of consistently lowering prices. Second, the goal of your software should be to solve important problems for your business. Let's take two scenarios:

Scenario A: To avoid being locked in, a company spends one million dollars extra. If something ever happens, they can change cloud providers. There's a very high chance that they will never change cloud providers.

Scenario B: The company uses the higher-order services in the cloud (including serverless). They ship six months ahead of Scenario A and save one million dollars. If something ever happens, they have a loosely coupled, well-designed system and can move quickly to adapt to new scenarios.

—

Myth: "We are different. We'll create custom standards to keep quality high." —Architect

Context: Some architecture teams believe that the problem they have has never been solved before. Usually, it has been solved—they just haven't researched appropriately.

Impact: Use industry standards. They are public, hardened, and understood by all. Custom standards need to be created and communicated; teams need to be trained and maintained. It's rarely worth the extra effort.

Engineering Management Myths

Myth: "Serverless/autoscaling is more expensive; there's no control over the costs." —Architect

Context: In this case, the architect has likely tried serverless previously or read about a project that generated a large cloud bill. Many cloud implementations, unfortunately, fall victim to poor cost optimization. To avoid this, you'll need to have the ability to predict traffic and cost. If there is an unexpected lift in traffic, this should mean more users—which is good.

Impact: Create a coherent cloud management strategy to ensure that your system can handle an increase in traffic and increase your costs at a proportional rate.

—

Myth: "The engineers won't do what I tell them to." —VP of Engineering

Context: The serverless paradigm demands teams that move fast. This VP has probably not worked in a technical environment before (unless they come from a big tech company). Making teams move in a pseudo-waterfall manner, with all their work planned out, will frustrate the developers. Give it whatever Agile buzzword works—SAFe, program increments, limit WIP, protect the team—but the impact is the same. We can micromanage the team and force them to make lousy technology choices, even in Agile. But we're hiring professional engineers; let them own their problem space.

Impact: If the engineers are skilled in serverless, give them a behavior or outcome to create—resist the temptation to specify every class or function. Great engineers need to be empowered. Don't slow them down.

—

Myth: "Our engineers are disconnected from the business." —VP of Engineering

Context: Engineers must deal with high cognitive load. The connection to the business offers the highest insight into what needs to be done next. If the engineers don't seem interested, it may be because it's hard for them to find out their next move. Do they have the metrics they need? Is there a clear purpose to their work? Are they included in the crucial discussions and decision-making? With some large-scale Agile frameworks, the teams are so busy with Agile ceremonies that they don't have the time to connect with the business.

Impact: If engineers don't have clarity of purpose, they will likely build the wrong thing.

—

Myth: "Technology X worked like a charm for me in my last role. Let's use that instead." —VP of Engineering

Context: Every project and problem should be assessed with context. Blindly using what worked before is not always a good strategy.

Impact: Architecture is about risk mitigation. Failing to modernize technology is a considerable risk. Support architecture to create and describe the technical strategy—including pros and cons.

—

Myth: "We only work on the cool stuff." —VP of Engineering

Context: A team has explored some new technology and doesn't want to go back to old technology. This opinion is often misinterpreted by engineering management. Good engineers should own the problem and use whatever technology makes sense.

Impact: The engineering management should not be dictating technology nor have the technology be dictated to them by engineers. Technical leadership needs to be involved, empowered, and driving the technology decisions.

—

Organizational Myths

Myth: "We are under capacity." —VP of Engineering

Context: Headcount allocations have been made, and they're not enough. The main topic of engineering management discussions is a lack of "resources" (an awful term for people)—a tell-tale sign of an insufficient focus on the work.

Impact: Building an empire does not drive business outcomes. If a team is given ownership of the problem and has an adequate number of people, they will find a solution. Good serverless teams should not need many people unless they are set up wrong.

—

Myth: "Security is blocking serverless." —Engineering

Context: There is a complex security monitoring system, and serverless is not supported. The engineers feel serverless is a good choice, but security will not approve the new technology.

Impact: The process implemented is blocking progress. Both engineering and security should revert to the control and reimplement the process with a serverless-friendly approach. Likely, the previous process is not cloud native.

—

Myth: "Our financial model does not support OpEx." —CFO

Context: The financial model was designed with CapEx, assets that depreciate over time. A variable bill every month makes the numbers look bad.

Impact: This is not a serverless problem; it's a blocker for cloud adoption. The focus needs to switch to the additional revenue that the cloud will generate.

—

Myth: "We spent two years building X. Was that a waste of money?" —Stakeholder

Context: When a decision is made to build something, what you learn during the build is often more important than the build itself. This is rarely acknowledged or understood. Technology must be viewed as a throwaway.

Impact: Holding on to previous investments with no additional value is a considerable expense.

—

Myth: "Consultancy X will engage for twelve weeks and set direction."
—Stakeholder.

Context: A consultancy house starts an open-ended project that could last for years with limited business outcomes. Often consultants are used to creating internal alignment, not advising on outcomes.

Impact: Own your technology and business strategy. It's essential to get an evaluation from external parties, but don't relinquish control.

Takeaways

Trying to define a cloud strategy for an organization is not easy. The ability to communicate that strategy in two words (serverless-first) is powerful, elegant, and memorable. Unfortunately, it may be too elegant and require some unpacking. Serverless-first is a strategy, mindset, and guiding principle. People need to be up to speed with what it means to be cloud native to understand serverless-first, engineers need to be sharp and well-rounded, and product teams need to trust that small teams can deliver tremendous value.

Serverless, or modern cloud, is not a trend; there is a set of revolutionary principles behind it, which we have explored in this chapter. Once these principles take hold and we forge a path forward, the most significant obstacle (as with any change) is the inherent inertia that exists in people. We often say that technology is simple and people are complex. In this chapter, we have laid out and dispelled many myths and arguments against modern cloud and serverless.

The simple truth is that technology evolves very quickly, and people rarely keep up to speed. Many will use myths in this chapter (and there will be new ones) to reason why it's not a good idea to change. But if you have a growth mindset, you can push through the fixed mindset and persevere. Leading change is hard: have strong opinions, hold them loosely, and expect to repeat arguments often!

CHAPTER 14
THE FRICTIONLESS DEV EXPERIENCE

One of the most effective paths to high performance is to consistently identify and remove impediments that stand in the way of your development teams delivering value. Any group involved in software creation, whether a team of four or an enterprise of several thousand, must have a collective agreement about software quality levels.

To ensure everyone moves at a sustainable pace, engineers must have harmony—in simple things like ways to format and document code, coding standards and testing standards, and even to architectural integrity. This is no different than Marketing adhering to brand standards or an editorial department choosing to abide by *Merriam-Webster Dictionary* instead of the *Oxford English Dictionary* or vice versa.

Creating software is a people-centric process. On top of that it requires the higher-order attribute of collaboration. Code at this level can't be written by just one developer. To pave the road ahead for groups to effectively deliver value, it's essential for an organization to define an engineering excellence mindset as an essential competency—including managers.

To enable the next best action, a key phase of the Value Flywheel Effect, it's critical that the developer experience is correct for your company's unique needs and culture. There are many ways to design a good developer experience, but the goal is to create an experience of *low friction*. Does it take developers a long time to do simple tasks? Are developers frustrated by any part of their workflow? Are there only certain people who can do certain things? Are there too many manual steps? If you answered yes to any of these, it's time to invest in improving your developer experience.

Engineering Excellence?

If we think of the creation of software as an organizational capability, then we can define it and celebrate it. Many companies do not have or need the capability of creating their own software. Many will decide to outsource it. Most will buy the finished product. But it's still an important area to understand.

Let's compare creating software to buying a car. When you buy a car, you need some knowledge and appreciation of what you want the car for and what attributes you need in the car. Levels of expertise range from a fully-fledged mechanic to a complete newbie. What is certain is that all levels will learn from this experience, because cars are complicated and are constantly changing.

Part of the experience of buying a car is the idea that you must maintain and look after it for years. Learning how that model works is part of the experience. Software is no different. A company cannot just purchase a year of software development and then forget about it. Once you buy software development or a car, you are committed to maintenance, learning, and general upkeep.

If you also have the *creation* of software as a capability, why not instill a sense of pride in your teams and set an expectation of—and enable them to deliver— excellent engineering? There are several key characteristics to consider when setting expectations of engineering excellence.

There is no finish line. Software creation is a never-ending journey of discovery and improvement. The trend is more important than the number. Marginal gains over a long period are an excellent and optimal result.

It's impossible to define. Once you take the time to describe precisely what engineering excellence is, then your definition will immediately become redundant due to a change in technology, people, or your system. A better way to manage engineering excellence is to think in goals or pillars—like the AWS Well-Architected Framework but at a more introductory level. For example, it's much better to set a goal or principle around security than to demand specific security measures.

Enable, not control. Finally, engineering excellence is a mechanism to help teams, not control them. There should be two levels of quality control. The first is within the team. This needs to be very well defined and specific. Driven by the technical lead, it very much depends on and can differ from team to team. The second is at a department or organizational level. This needs to be more of a probing conversation that highlights gaps or celebrates excellence for the team. When engineering excellence starts to feel like someone is marking your homework, then you have a problem.

The software industry is fickle. New techniques and frameworks will come and go. Some will be utterly revolutionary, and some will be terrible—no one can tell the difference in the early days, not even the experts. The best thing to do is create an environment that promotes learning and appreciation of what it takes to create great software. The fundamentals of creating good software have not changed over fifty years—just pick up a copy of Gerald Weinberg's *The Secrets of Consulting* from 1985. The fundamental principles he lays out will set your department up for success.

Celebrate Engineering Excellence

Engineers are not stupid. They'll know if you treat them like a cost and constantly try to box them in to save money, and there's a good chance they'll resent you for it. Engineers must be frugal, but frugality is hard to measure correctly. Sometimes $100 spent on a book can save your company $2 million. It's important to differentiate curiosity from idleness. Just like an organization must promote a culture of psychological safety, it is also important to celebrate the practices of excellent software engineer to help foster its adoption and encourage teams to continually seek out new practices of engineering excellence.

Clarifying Team First with Team Topologies

To elaborate on the team-first approach we covered in Chapter 9, we must now discuss a related concept outlined by Matthew Skelton and Manuel Pais in their book *Team Topologies: Organizing Business and Technology Teams for Fast Flow*, which describes an adaptive model for organizational design based on four fundamental team types and three team interaction patterns.

The four team types are:[1]

- **Stream-aligned team:** focused on a single flow of work from (usually) a segment of the business domain.
- **Enabling team:** helps a stream-aligned team overcome obstacles and shore up missing or lacking capabilities.
- **Complicated-subsystem team:** a team of specialists with significant mathematics/calculation/technical expertise.
- **Platform team:** a grouping of other team types that provide a compelling internal product to accelerate stream-aligned teams.

A team that executes well is usually quite clear on their main priority. It can be hard to tell if a team has a single objective, but the *Team Topologies* model can help you answer that question. Share the four team types with your team(s) and ask them to self-identify. Many teams will answer, "We are aligned to *this* value chain, but we're also helping other teams and we want to build a platform." The next piece of coaching is invaluable: *Do one thing and do it well.* Teams frequently overextend themselves, and engineering standards suffer as a result. Team-first means absolute clarity on the purpose of the team.

Motivation and Drive

As the software industry has grown, managers often struggle with how to keep their teams motivated. We can survey the team, but the answer that comes back is often, "Pay us more money and just leave us alone to write code." Companies that follow this advice end up paying huge sums of money for teams that build the wrong thing.

Daniel Pink's *Drive: The Surprising Truth about What Motivates Us* examines three elements of true motivation: autonomy, mastery, and purpose. Interestingly, *Drive* explains that once people are compensated fairly for their work, it is these other attributes that become their main motivators.[2] For software, autonomy is the freedom to build what is needed by the team, mastery is the support to develop their skills, and purpose is the compelling vision or reason *why* they build what they build.

Through the lens of engineering excellence, instead of arguing with individuals about pay raises, maybe there's a different approach? Talk to the team and ensure that they have the support to work autonomously. Learn what they need to do their job well—it might be time, or mentors, or resources, or something else. Discuss the vision and the purpose of their work. What is the customer impact? Who are we helping? Can we bring the engineers to meet the end users and build empathy for the people they're solving problems for?

DORA and the Four Key Metrics

Since the Agile Manifesto was drafted, the core measurement of "good" is working software—plain and simple. At any point in time, we should be able to use the software in a working environment. Once our software meets that baseline, we can start looking at the four key metrics from the DevOps Research and Assessment (DORA) group that are outlined in the book *Accelerate* by Dr. Nicole Forsgren, Jez Humble, and Gene Kim.[3]

Even though there are four metrics, we will split them into two categories. The first, throughput, is defined by deployment frequency and lead time. How often is new software delivered? Is it several times per hour/day/week/month/year? This is a straightforward question that has untold depth.

The second category is *stability*. You can't build software if your platform constantly breaks. Defined by change fail rate and mean time to resolution, stability will ensure that we have the correct quality processes in place.

It's not our place to mandate a practice, but it's essential to measure the outcome of your quality practices with stability. It is often thought that you can be either fast or safe. With software, it's a little different. You can move very quickly with safety. With continuous, minor corrections, you will stay on track and keep making progress, even if there are slight hiccups along the way.

Code Is a Liability

A key phrase when working in modern or serverless systems is "code is a liability." The statement itself is as deep as a well but is quite simple to explain. Suppose you're responsible for a business section, and you require a technical capability. You evaluate the market and decide that it can't be bought. You must hire some people to create it, to write the software. Software is not your expertise, so you naturally inquire what these people will do and produce. They are software developers or coders, so you assume that the code they write is valuable. You end up paying $1 million for this software, which is more than you initially budgeted for. You ask how much code was written, and the developers told you they wrote one million lines of code. This sounds reasonable. But a much better solution would have been ten thousand lines of code. Not unlike poetry, extraordinary code is elegant and precise.

We recommend keeping the following in mind when deciding the value of more lines of code:

- **Code is a liability:** every line of code that is written is an expense.
- **Engineers are paid well:** the time taken to write a line of code has a cost.
- **The code must be tested and documented:** this is an additional cost.
- **The code must be secured continuously:** code calls other code—there may be future vulnerabilities.
- **The code must be maintained:** libraries change and require updates; requirements change; more code requires more work to maintain.
- **There is an operational cost:** the code must be deployed, monitored, and updated, and the hosting needs to be paid for.

When you ask a software team to build something, they deliver a system, not lines of code. The asset is not the code; the asset is the system. The less code in the system, the less overhead you have bought. Some developers may brag about how much code they've written, but this isn't something to brag about. As Mark Twain said, "I didn't have time to write you a short letter, so I wrote you a long one."

Shared Outcomes and Recognition

Team success must align with organizational success. You don't want to create castaway teams that feel alienated. You might wonder whether you should organize your teams top-down or bottom-up—both are wrong. It's better to have decentralized, aligned goals, never us versus them. Avoid forming factions within the company. Sometimes a poor team creates profitable software; sometimes a great team creates software that loses money. Rewarding engineering efforts is different from rewarding business outcomes.

Sense Checking: The Miner's Canary

The technical leadership of the organization needs a way to check in with teams and the work they perform. Each team should have technical leadership, but the work must be cross-checked. This isn't just for software development. In the medical industry, for example, clinical peer review is welcomed. There are many ways of working this model, but the core principle of another medical professional reviewing your work is to ensure high performance and that safety remains.

Has this been lost as a practice in technology? Imagine if a mechanism were in place in which trusted professionals from the company but outside your department would review your work. The review would be transparent, constructive, and meaningful.

The exact implementation of this model will differ from team to team and much depends on personalities, maturity, the size of the company, culture, and the tools available. But the question is simple: What is the miner's canary for your engineering projects? What is the signal that first alerts leadership to a quality issue? Quality, in this sense, is very loosely defined. There are many ways that software can be poor. Often the team doesn't realize it, as they are too close to the problem and solution.

Method: How does "the organization" coach a team on their engineering quality? The direct leader of that team will be best positioned to do so, but they might be biased for or against a technique, product, or person. When a technology expert from a different area provides the team with feedback, it can help raise various issues and celebrate success with more impartiality. For this to work, you must start with an environment of psychological safety. The goal of the feedback is to help and enable the team, not to criticize and find fault. There must also be a common understanding of the engineering standards across the organization.

Cadence: The team peer review sessions mustn't be just a one-off activity. Experiment with the frequency: maybe they should be every week or every quarter. The whole team must participate with as much transparency as possible—without putting the team under pressure.

Metrics: If there is a predefined company engineering standard, metrics will be available in a dashboard or similar. What is the content under review? Ideally, every team will have access to a display of qualitative and quantitative metrics. Data collection for these metrics should be as automated as possible. Many software life cycle tools already have meaningful metrics built in. But as important as metrics are, you can have too much of a good thing. Which metrics matter and can you see them on demand? If the metrics are truly relevant to the team, then they'll watch them and use them to make decisions.

Formality: It's essential that the organization supports and acknowledges the team peer review. A common trap is that the reviews are too formal, so engineers don't feel like they can discuss issues openly. When senior management invites large crowds to the reviews or records them, then the level of interaction will suffer. In the other direction, the review might be so informal that it's thought of as optional. Try to find a balance between these extremes.

Momentum and Marginal Gains

The benefit of team peer reviews may seem limited, but picture this: Technical leaders review their teams and other teams. The reviews are scheduled and displayed on the company calendar. As the reviewers collect more information, they start to see patterns with some issues. This is a valuable signal that teams should refine and improve their standards and tools. It's also an invaluable way to share knowledge across the organization. Great technical leaders will spot friction points and start removing them.

First Principles for Engineers

For an effective software engineering team to function, everyone must have an engineering mindset. The department must be aligned on the problem they are solving. Any individual who over-indexes on their function needs to focus on the purpose. Notable warning signs include sentences like "I just test the system." "I only look after security." Or "I'm the manager and I'm not that technical." Or "I don't understand the solution." The whole engineering team should have an engineering mindset, even those who don't write code.

A frequent problem for organizations that hire programmers is that they end up with lots of code. This may seem like a great outcome, but remember *code is a liability*. Every line of code written comes with a cost. Always question and seek out the value.

Removing Friction with Automation

When organizations make it easy for engineers to change code quickly in a safe, secure manner, they can deliver value quicker and keep the flywheel moving. Automation is a key for enabling in reducing developer friction. An organization with a disciplined software development protocols likely relies on two principles:

1. **Infrastructure as code:** developers do not manually configure cloud infrastructure, e.g., you can't just open the AWS dashboard and change something.
2. **Delivery pipelines:** everything is changed in a controlled manner.

Both protocols are very sensible, but if the language used is just text configuration (YAML*), this will lead to frustration, slowness, and friction.

Let's describe this differently. You are a developer and have been asked to create a simple API service that returns five data fields. The code for the service is trivial. It has already been written and tested. All you need to do is create the cloud infrastructure and deploy it.

In 2010, pre-cloud, this was quite an ordeal. You had to write some code to create the API—it's easy but time consuming. You also had to secure a server to deploy

---

* For almost ten years, cloud engineers used YAML to create cloud infrastructure. (If you don't know what YAML is, great—move forward with profound relief. You are one of the lucky ones. If you must know, it stands for Yet Another Markup Language. Yes, it's awful, but it's just very loosely formatted text.)

to and engage a different team to configure everything. Configuration was out of your control and could take anywhere from days to months. With luck, you set up complex and costly automation for your product, but after that, you deployed your API easily. The whole process took weeks, at best.

In 2017, you were in the cloud! Using CloudFormation or Terraform, your API needed 1,500 lines of configuration code (which is text). This was great, as writing that code was a one-time effort, and you could do it yourself—no hand-offs. You copied an example from somewhere else; it was almost correct, about 98%. You changed the remaining few attributes, and the code broke. You spent the next day changing things and trying to work out why it was failing. You already had automation in place, so after two days, you had a fully automated cloud infrastructure-as-code created and deleted at will. Awesome, but trying to get the cloud configuration code correct was a little slow.

Fast forward to 2022. Now, you have an example of Cloud Development Kit (CDK) code that is fourteen lines long. It's typescript, so you can check it with your integrated developer environment (IDE). You can write a unit test to ensure that it works. And when you copied it from the code repository, it worked the first time. The deployment pipelines are set up already. You can activate your new API in an hour!

Let's back up a little. Previously, when a software engineer needed to create an API, they grabbed a trusted copy of Gregor Hohpe's *Enterprise Integration Patterns*, found the pattern, and coded it up using Java. This resulted in a decent API but took three weeks. What was once code in a book is now a piece of software. What's more, you can combine these software components—it's like applying the concepts of building blocks to cloud development.

Today, when we need to create that API as a cloud-native service, we can simply pull down a pattern from GitHub and execute it. You can have an API with the infrastructure to deploy it within thirty seconds. Now you can take the source code and add your logic.

This automation is key to removing developer friction. And when friction is low, when the developer isn't spending days or weeks writing an API, they can turn their attention to the next best action to bring value to their organization. They can keep the flywheel turning, moving their organization into the future instead of sitting at the starting gates. But how did we get here?

The Cloud Development Kit

Let's explore the origin of CDK (cloud development kit) and CDK Patterns. CDK is basically like a LEGO® kit for, say, a pirate ship. It contains all the interlocking and reusable pieces (cloud components) that a builder needs, plus blueprints, to build a pirate ship. In other words, an organization can use already tested and reliable code, combine it, customize it for their unique needs, and then deliver value via the cloud.

CDK has a strong link to serverless. It illustrates how developers create a higher-level abstraction to remove friction for other developers. This has been happening for decades and will continue to happen. The pace of change is increasing, and open-source practices further accelerate these higher-order patterns. In 2019, Liberty Mutual started to experiment with CDK as an acceleration approach.[*] After all, why write your own code from scratch when you could use expert written and tested code that was already created for you? In 2020, Matt Coulter, a senior architect at Liberty Mutual, created the CDK Patterns open-source project.[†]

CDK Patterns is an example of a higher-order construct. They take an architectural pattern (from someone like author Gregor Hohpe) and implement it using CDK. The pattern is now executable in a language that will work in your cloud environment. This is a striking improvement upon previous infrastructure as code approaches, which may have failed or required configuration changes. CDK Patterns lowered the barrier for entry to the cloud considerably, removing friction for developers and organizations looking to take the next best action.

It's important to note how different today's coding landscape is. Similar software development models as CDK existed in the past (e.g., Linux), but open-source projects seem more accessible now and are accepted more within large organizations. The community of developers is evolving and industrializing their tools. They are not evolving themselves out of existence; they are making their jobs easier. Removing friction. Why? So they can focus on business value more than keeping the lights on.

Achieving Speed and Reliability

The perennial question for any company with at least one software engineer on the payroll is a simple one: How can we make the engineers go faster? When viewed from the outside, software engineering looks like a prolonged activity that could easily be accelerated. Even though this isn't exactly true, leadership is right to be concerned over the cost of delay and the sheer burnout rate among engineers.

But for as long as companies have employed software engineers, there has been an alternate industry around "making them faster." Many will have heard someone say, "Can we get them to type the code in faster?" or "If they could copy and paste

---

[*] Part of this story is covered in the Liberty Mutual case study in the Introduction and in Chapter 16.
[†] For more, visit CDKPatterns.com.

code from another project, it would save time." Unfortunately, these time-savers were disproved many decades ago.

Like any problem-solving activity, creating software has an elegance about it, like an experienced gardener who seems to intrinsically know where things should go, when things should be done, and what not to do. It may seem like they are puttering around, but they are executing on years of experience. Like any mathematical formula, there are two overriding factors when it comes to code: Is it correct and is it efficient? The two are not always observed together.

The idea of a template or reference architecture was prevalent in the pre-cloud days. A reference architecture often explains a new way of solving a problem. In the early days, an engineer would read a page in a book with a diagram and then figure out how to create the suggestion from the book—often writing thousands of lines of code. The book was helpful, but there's a high chance that the engineer would miss a detail or introduce an error. The gap between reference and implementation was too large; there was not sufficient encapsulation in the process. It still required the engineer to write lots of extra code.

As we said, there has always been an industry of "software component creators" to help accelerate engineers. The rub has always been how flexible these components are. If the component is too rigid, then the overall solution will lack elegance (and therefore be inefficient).

In the first decade of cloud technology, some of the acceleration points lacked previous generations' maturity—often early solutions are immature and will require further refinement. It's ideal for functionality to be encapsulated behind an API. But how can a person programmatically define infrastructure in the cloud? Many engineers lost sleep while fighting with "infrastructure as YAML"—infrastructure as code has been crying out for someone to encapsulate it.

What has just been experienced with CDK and CDK Patterns is a building block. This is more powerful than a reference architecture as it gives you a working component to start with. It's even more powerful than an annotation, as you can change anything that you disagree with—the implementation does not constrain you.

As a foundational forcing function, infrastructure as code is necessary when moving at speed or working in the cloud. Some traditional infrastructure engineers will push back against this—"You're ignoring my specialty and trying to make me a software developer"—but this is missing the point. Code takes away the manual nature of configuration. No matter how good the process is, there is always the chance that someone will press the wrong button or click the wrong box. There are numerous examples of developers accidentally causing their companies to lose millions of dollars in an instant. The nature of the cloud is ephemeral; if something breaks, it's deleted instantly. This means it needs to be recreated instantly. So, you see, automation is the only way forward.

There is a very specific mindset at play here that is well covered by the DevOps movement. It's not enough to implement one or two of the pieces. The whole picture must be put together, as they all depend on each other.

- A deployment pipeline enables automation.
- The building block (i.e., cloud platform) comes with tests—you can execute these as part of your deployment.
- Create a single path to production.
- Include other processes or governance work. A serverless mindset enables service choice.
- Code is a liability, so steer away from creating a huge, custom solution. Less affinity to components.
- Well-architected enables improved quality.
- Include sensible defaults (well-architected settings and tags) as part of the pattern. For example, observability, security, and performance features could be activated by default.
- Cloud security policy enables automated security remediation.
- Employ a future-proof security policy that demands role-based separation for all assets, immutable infrastructure, and automation everywhere.
- A single platform enables speed.
- Consolidation enables resilience.
- Any changes or future versions can be incorporated with an automated redeploy.

All of this is also consistent with the "code is a liability" mindset. The less code your software engineers write, the less chance they have to introduce errors and the less you must manage. Many previous attempts to speed up software engineers have been constrained in the wrong areas. By limiting software engineers' choices, you restrict the creativity in what they can produce and introduce fear, uncertainty, and doubt. Software engineers need the option to look under the covers. Many mechanical engineers liked to take things apart when they were young. Software engineers are no different. We need to let people look under the covers, and CDK allows this in the cloud.

Reference architectures help engineers communicate new ideas, but they don't speed up software engineers' day-to-day work. Some off-the-shelf frameworks contain interesting concepts but require a considerable amount of effort to get right. Many frameworks end up being bloated, unsupported, or incomplete.

The only quick way to make software engineers go fast is to teach them quickly. Using building blocks (e.g., CDK Patterns, infrastructure as code) will help them understand what is happening under the hood. In time, they will create their own building blocks and use them to teach others. Remember, software engineers spend a lot of time teaching their peers—not all training happens in the training room.

The key inertia point to watch out for here is a culture of command and control. The engineering department is not a factory; we cannot make faster machines and expect productivity to increase. A better analogy for an engineering department is a school. Give the department the resources and space to innovate, create, and explore—then it is possible to achieve actual acceleration. Governance should never be combined with acceleration; they should always complement each other. Building blocks will help accelerate your engineer's journey into the cloud with the appropriate constraints.

The Map

Let's look at an example map of the developer experience at Laura and Clive's organization.

Laura: Let's draw out a simple value chain for an engineer. They need to solve a business problem, which is in Genesis by nature. The inertia blocker is poor alignment with the company's goals and lack of feedback from leadership—usually caused by politics and prioritization challenges. The poor engineer isn't quite sure what to build and why. After that, there will be market constraints—the inertia here is tribal rules; expectations aren't written down. There are ways to get around the market constraints, but the engineer might not know them. Next is the engineer's ability to build—i.e., deliver working software. The inertia point here is a lack of knowledge. And of course, to build, the engineer needs an excellent environment to work in.

Clive: Good, and we'll just start at the bottom (the component furthest removed from the user) and move them left across the x-axis. It's possible to start at the top, but avoiding the underlying issues may create more problems.

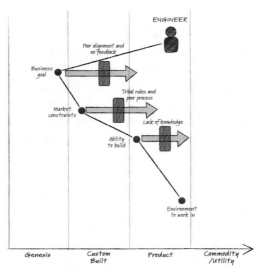

Figure 14.1: Mapping the Developer Experience

Laura: Let's create a new value chain of knowledge, which will act to pull ability to the right along the *x*-axis (away from Genesis or burgeoning knowledge and into a Commodity, which also represents subject matter expertise here). The knowledge value chain must contain a self-serve solution, and there needs to be a good team around the engineer to create a safe space to innovate.

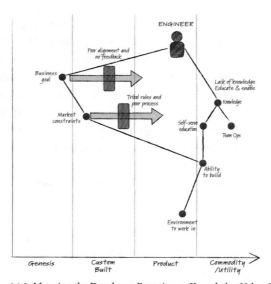

Figure 14.2: Mapping the Developer Experience: Knowledge Value Chain

Clive: Then, we can turn the market constraints (which are valid but often difficult to see) into enabling constraints (which need to be obvious).

Laura: What's the difference?

Clive: A market constraint could be security or a financial audit. That would connect to an enabling constraint like infrastructure as code (IaC)—in other words, the engineers don't have console access. Both are related, but the enabling constraint is easier to understand for the engineer.

Laura: Okay, so constraints rely on standards, architecture patterns, and IaC.

Clive: And there's also a link to the ability to build—these will make the software development process easier.

Laura: Now, let's unblock the business goal by aligning the engineer to it.

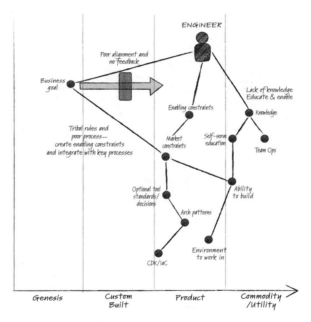

Figure 14.3: Mapping the Developer Experience: Constraints

Clive: The most critical need is a fast feedback loop, which you get from good DORA scores (throughput and stability in deployments) and observability data. To help get a high DORA score, we also need to minimize dependencies and handoffs. This helps ensure the environment is set up for good flow efficiency with minimal waiting around.

Laura: And combined with giving the engineer an obvious problem to solve, you start making progress.

Clive: The final piece is an expectation to share knowledge. This prevents silos in the org, which helps the business goal.

Laura: Another critical part of the developer experience is being satisfied with doing a good job. They need to know that their work has made an impact and not been completed in vain. And they should be happy with the environment. With all these elements in place, job satisfaction is easier to achieve . . . and this helps with productivity, retention, attracting good talent, etc.

Clive: I think this is all coming together well. Another key piece is alignment with the larger strategy—knowing that the business goal they're working toward and the tech choices and standards they adhere to align with the overall org/division/team strategies. Being able to link their daily work to the overall strategy is incredibly powerful.

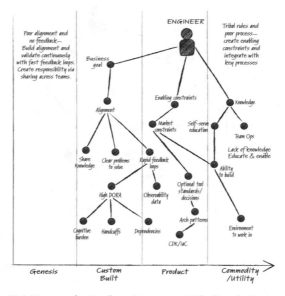

Figure 14.4: Mapping the Developer Experience: Unlocking the Business Goal

Takeaways

Having a frictionless developer experience is likely the number-one differentiator between high-performing and low-performing organizations. It would be incredible to see how many developers are working in companies with a bad developer experience and how much this costs the companies. When it comes to the third phase of the Value Flywheel Effect, a bad developer experience full of friction and obstacles will easily put a wrench in the gears and slow your momentum to a halt.

We need to celebrate engineering excellence and work hard to make the developer experience the best that we can. A great place to start is to focus on teams, motivation, and the four DORA metrics. It's also important to instill a "code is a liability" mindset among engineers.

At the same time, we need to inject some commercial thinking into engineering teams, and that's not as easy as it sounds. One of the major pain points for engineers is friction in the organization. We shared the story of CDK (Cloud Developer Kit) and CDK Patterns as a great example of removing friction and creating a fantastic developer experience through automation.

If you're still a bit fuzzy on where to start—or a bit fuzzy on what the developer experience looks like in your organization—sit down with a developer and map out their experience writing software. Take note of the things that frustrate them and the things that make their job easier. Creating a map like Laura and Clive's won't solve the engineer's problems (mapping solutions is explored in the next chapter), but it'll help get everyone on the same page and create a development process to aspire to.

CHAPTER 15
MAP YOUR SOLUTION
(AKA MAPPING THE STACK)

Mapping your solution is often referred to as mapping your tech stack. This activity can (and should) be done for new builds and existing builds. The most effective way to run this exercise is as a team exercise, either in person around a dry-erase board or virtually through services like Mural or Miro.

The next best action phase of the Value Flywheel Effect has two key goals. The first is to do whatever we can to create an immediate impact and reduce friction for the development team. The second is to introduce the team to the concept that there will be future changes that will not be attempted now—in essence, the next best action is the first of many next best actions to come. The next best action is not a "one and done" event. It's the first move in a game of chess. Like in chess, it's important to sequence out the steps that should lead to a checkmate. That's where mapping your tech stack or solution comes in. Of course, there may be pivots and obstacles along the way, but the map will help the team navigate those obstacles together and remain focused on the goal.

Setting Expectations and Preparing the Team

If the team hasn't heard of Wardley Mapping, share a one-pager on the key concepts and maybe share a video (check out LearnWardleyMapping.com from Ben Mosior). There is no prep the team must do apart from being familiar with the evolutionary axis (Genesis to Commodity) concept. Also make sure the team understands the goal of the map. You can set the stage by saying, for example, "Let's have a discovery mapping session to decide what we need to modernize to make our lives easier."

If you are new to mapping, resist the temptation to take up a whole morning or day with the exercise. Engineers are busy people, so book a sixty- to ninety-minute block of time and be prepared to create the map over several sessions.

A dry-erase board is important, either physical or virtual. Whatever you're creating your map on, it's important for the whole team to be able to see it while it's being created. While you're mapping, ensure that the whole team participates by adding components as sticky notes. It doesn't matter if they're placed correctly or not when they're first mapped. As the conversation matures, the team will adjust the position of the components together.

The most important thing to remember is that it does not work to create the map in advance of the meeting to save time. The action of the team creating the map together is what will help them own it and the chosen path forward.

Here are a few tips for your mapping the stack/solution session:

- Start off with a user persona to anchor the map.
- Resist the temptation to redraw your architecture diagram. It's useful to have a copy nearby for reference, but don't copy it onto the map.
- Simplify, simplify, simplify. If a UI has ten pages, just represent it all as a "UI" component. We won't execute the map, so it's okay to generalize.
- Some parts of the system may get left out if they aren't important for this conversation.
- Resist the temptation to add the whole company to one map; keep the scope to your app or subsystem.
- Keep it light-hearted and don't push for the finish.

An Application Evolution

Suppose you're a member of the leadership team at a large bank. The application you selected to map is a legacy system that creates a mortgage quote for a bank customer. The app is operated by bank staff and ties a few back-end systems together. The app is well designed, but some of the components are quite old and are slow to fix. They are expensive to run and difficult to extend for the "next generation" project next year. The team has support to start making improvements, but they're not sure where to start. They need to find the next best action to take.

Initial Scenario

Gather the team and try not to be too formal. Four or five engineers sitting in a shared space or on a call is perfect. Put the axes of the map up but start listing the value chain to the side—this gives the team a chance at a first pass and postpones the difficult decision of where to put things on the x-axis. Focus on the y-axis first.

We always start with the user need, so pop in a general persona for a user. There will likely be several personas you could choose from (e.g., online customer, branch staff, mortgage specialist). Select a general persona and resist the temptation to add three or four anchor users. Let's go with "bank customer" just to get people started.

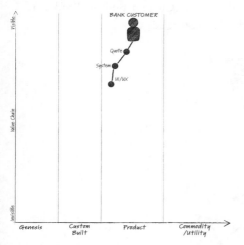

Figure 15.1: Bank Customer Value Chain (Part 1)

Now start flowing down the chain: the user gets a quote, the quote needs the system, the system needs a UI and UX (there will be badly named components; move beyond this). (See Figure 15.1.)

It turns out that the quote application system is served from two places (it has two dependencies). You didn't know that. We're learning already!

The UX is a modern rewrite and has a whole bunch of complicated network hops. The team is quite animated about it: they designed it but are not happy with it, which leads to a ten-minute sidebar. You sense the tension and generalize the component on the map as GW—gateway.

The component under the UI is a little more traditional and points to the old back end, the mainframe. Some of these components are owned by other teams, so your team only knows the basics. That's okay. You draw two separate value chains for the newer and older systems branching from the UX and UI. (See Figure 15.2.)

During this discussion, the team might mention pain points they encounter. Focus on the components for now, but to prevent losing track of the pain points, create an area to the side of the map called "climatic patterns." Add the pain points the team lists but that don't have an obvious home on the map yet here. You'll come back to them later.

The conversation has given you a good idea of the team's maturity. Once the value chains are complete, you simplify them, mapping the value chain with the newest components in Product along the x-axis and the chain

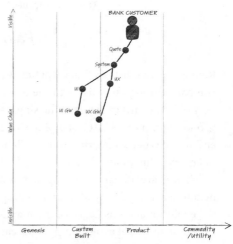

Figure 15.2: Bank Customer Value Chain (Part 2)

with older components in Custom Built along the *x*-axis. By guessing the starting position along the evolutionary axis (*x*-axis), you give the team a chance to tweak things if a component feels out of place. This stage is very important, as asking the team to place each component on the *x*-axis could take a long time. But remember that the exact position doesn't matter, only the phase (Custom Built or Product) they are in. You now have a map of the stack! (See Figure 15.3.)

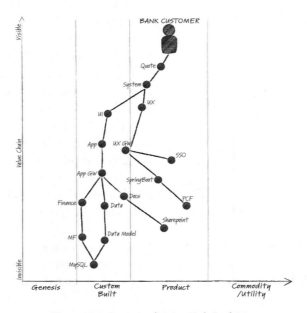

Figure 15.3: Quote Application Tech Stack Map

Pain Points

Remember that list of climatic patterns (pain points) you made? Now is the time to run back through that list with the team. The team is quick to tell you that the UI is very old and hard to change. The single sign-on (SSO) system is a pain to configure. Cloud Foundry was just a stepping stone. The docs are a pain to manage. The back-end services need a rewrite, and they'll have to start adding in new back-end services in around nine months' time!

These are all valuable insights that help show what the team could do as their next best action. But by identifying components that could move toward the right on the evolutionary axis (*x*-axis), the map is only an exercise in the art of the possible. Let's plot an actual evolution path for each of those components (see Figure 15.4).

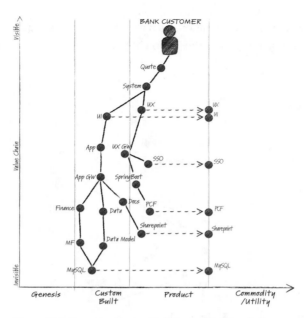

Figure 15.4: Quote Application Tech Stack with Climatic Patterns

Easy Moves

Let's now explore potential actual solutions to some of those pain points. We're one step closer to finding our next best action. The team is aware of several modern cloud architectural patterns that they have been keen to try. They discuss what they can offload to the cloud provider to reduce their operational burden.

Decisions made during a mapping session should be reversible. They are solutions the team knows they can back out of if they're not happy with the features, cost, performance, or any other nonfunctional requirement. Again, this is why we call it the next best action, not the right action. All the signs point to this being a good path forward to deliver business value aligned with our clarity of purpose. But we can pivot and change course (map again) if new knowledge presents new obstacles.

Now we have a map of our possible tech solution (Figure 15.5), with the components that we are going to offload to cloud providers shifted to the far right (Commodity) of the map. But bear in mind, this is still a conversation with a few engineers over a map. We are in a safe environment asking, "What if?" What may be a simple line on a board could be two years of work in reality. What is important at this stage is getting beyond the implementation and plotting a direction forward.

Once we get over the implementation, then we can assess the impact of the move and what else it enables. Mapping is the divergent part of the process. We will converge later.

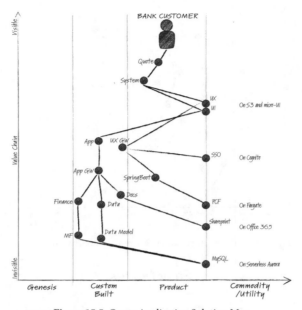

Figure 15.5: Quote Application Solution Map

Evolutionary Architecture

The exercise of moving the painful components across the map has entered the "what now" phase. When these components are moved into a commodity and no longer take up our developer's time, what can we do next? This is when we start talking about the valuable work that the team wants to get to.

The gateway components (labeled GW on the map) will require significant work to move the old services away from the mainframe. The engineers also need to modernize the data model, as it's required for a large future effort that hasn't started yet. You and the team label these with arrows showing how work should be invested to move them to the right along the evolutionary axis (*x*-axis).

It's taken you and the team some time to dig through these layers, but this is normal. The map (see Figure 15.6) has served its purpose in letting the team raise challenges and move through them systematically.

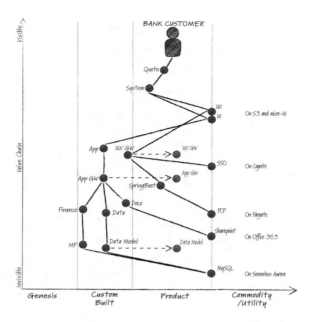

Figure 15.6: Quote Application Gateway Component Movements

Creating Major Impact

We are now starting to see the shape of a multi-year road map. What was a horrible old legacy system that was too complex to even comprehend where to start making improvements has now become a series of clear stepping stones.

The process of creating a map this detailed will take more than one sitting, think maybe three to four sessions. And when you're done, you might be able to extract the team's valuable observations and drop them into a road map visual for the executive team (like in Figure 15.7).

There are three simple ways to create this type of road map for modernization. First, map the stack with the team (as we've just illustrated). Second, ask an architect to do it (know that they will likely make some of it up). Third, ask a consultant to do it.

The first option takes days, the second will be incorrect, and the third will take months, be totally incorrect to the point of damaging, and cost a huge amount of money—but at least the slides will be awesome.

Mapping with a team might be challenging, but it's the most accurate and fastest way to understand the tech stack and map a solution forward.

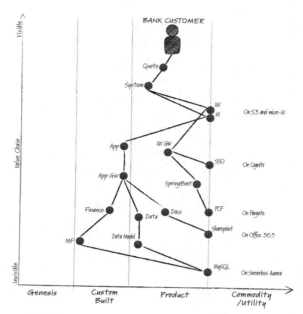

Figure 15.7: Quote Application Multiyear Solution Map

Takeaways

Mapping your solution or tech stack is critical to deciding what improvements you need to make and what gaps you have before you can take your next best action. Engineers will always have things they don't like and things they want to rewrite in an application. The mapping approach is a great way to identify the capability that the component provides, and once the engineers understand the approach of mapping, they'll start to ask the right questions: "Do we really need to build that? Or can we offload that to a vendor that uses a SaaS?" Often, teams need help putting potential changes into a language and narrative that leadership will understand.

This type of evolutionary architecture (looking ahead at how a software system must evolve over time), is an important approach that is becoming necessary when building in the modern cloud. And if your engineers have trouble with mapping the stack, you can use the Wardley Mapping Grid technique (see Chapter 3) to help them classify components and tap into a shared understanding of the map.

CHAPTER 16
CASE STUDY—LIBERTY MUTUAL INSURANCE

Our third case study is a continuation of the story we began in the introduction to this book and is an effective illustration of the third phase of the Value Flywheel Effect: Next Best Action. Liberty Mutual has demonstrated that building a best-in-class developer experience and adopting a serverless-first strategy has enabled a real Value Flywheel Effect that drives both business and technology strategies.

To recap, with more than $40 billion in annual revenue, Liberty Mutual is the world's sixth-largest property and casualty insurance company and an industry front-runner in technological innovation. To achieve its goal of becoming a global digital company, Liberty Mutual focused on three main areas of digital transformation: customer centricity, agility, and cloud-native development. To that end, the company made a strategic business decision to pursue a serverless-first approach—a move designed to give it an edge in a competitive, global, and increasingly digital market. We spoke to Justin Stone, Senior Director of Secure DevOps Platforms at Liberty Mutual, who shared some perspectives.

The Call to Action

At Liberty Mutual, knowledge about cloud engineering started to build before they explored the public cloud in 2013. They had already modernized many of their practices by that point. The "single path to production" principle, which meant they could automate many of their governance steps, helped lay the groundwork to change perceptions.

They started their DevOps journey early, with goals like "75% of technology staff writing code" and "same-day production deployments for new code" and included all the infrastructure improvements to make that happen. Once they explored public cloud providers AWS and Azure in 2013, their network, security, and operations capabilities began to improve even more. The concept of guardrails in software development was a key mindset change. They moved from centralized traffic control to a well-defined freeway—you can go as fast or slow as you like, but stay on the freeway!

With digital infrastructure in place, the next phase was even more significant. Modernizing systems—which includes the people, the process, the technology, and the solutions—is a challenge many enterprises face today. There's a delicate balance between the promise of a digital ecosystem and the ability to deliver true digital capability.

Serverless was never a goal for Liberty Mutual—the goal was to have teams that can provide capability quickly using the public cloud as a platform. Many different parts of Liberty Mutual realized that another way of working was required to achieve this goal. But there was no template from another company like Liberty Mutual. How could teams create cloud applications that deliver digital capability in a fast-moving world—all in an efficient, secure, stable, and effective manner? The most important principle of all was to put the user first—the user could be a policyholder, a claimant, an agent, a broker, an employee, or even a general member of the public—helping people live safer, more secure lives.

By 2016, the transformation was already well underway. Much of the ground-work was now in place. James McGlennon, CIO of Liberty Mutual, worked with his executive team to create a six-pager titled "Our Technology Manifesto—Accelerating Our IT Transformation." This document demonstrated the commitment and direction of the transformation and gave everyone permission to drive forward. It touched on the importance of Agile development, cross-functional teams, a product focus, cloud-native computing, data-driven methodologies, and technology leadership.

The impact of such a simple document was immense—it was like the start of a marathon. It started everyone moving in the same direction and at their own pace. As excitement and empowerment grew throughout the enterprise, different departments would build on various areas and break new ground. McGlennon created an environment of learning and experimentation.

The marathon analogy is a good one. Individuals don't start the race when the starting horn sounds; the work is started months or years before that—preparation, training, learning, refining, and building determination. The launch of the manifesto document was similar—there were years of work prior, but the publication of the document in 2016 was like a starting horn.

In the following years, other papers would build on the original vision—let's be responsive, let's focus on AI/machine learning, serverless-first, aggressive movement on retiring older systems, bold and audacious moves within the business. A wave of change moved across the enterprise, focusing on innovation, speed, value, and learning. All was made possible by a strong technology foundation—the guardrails kept teams on the right path; they were buffers, not blockers.

Some technology leaders started to explore the benefits of serverless and cloud application architecture during this time. Some early wins led to a new avenue and a new strategy: serverless-first.

With any change program, there is no large waterfall plan of change. There was an incremental movement that involved experimentation, learning, and sharing.

Between 2015 and 2017, some of the technical leaders in Liberty Mutual started to create solutions with a serverless architecture. Event-driven architecture was always an aspiration but was challenging with older technology. Serverless architecture made it possible to build different systems, either new or adjacent to older systems.

The run cost, scalability, and sheer potential of what could be achieved was eye opening. Some of the teams (like ours) used Wardley Mapping during these projects to predict movement in the technology, which enabled them to make effective technology choices and reduce the amount of technical debt. These pioneers coached many other teams in later years. Creating experts early in the change ensured some well-respected technology leaders had a clear strategic vision.

Key Enablers

During the early serverless implementation, some friction points had to be worked around. Using a single path to production for the deployment pipeline was crucial— it meant there was control and it required partnership, as newer services needed to be added quickly to the deployment architecture.

As infrastructure as code was a requirement from day one, it forced teams to use CloudFormation to create and configure infrastructure. This was a significant barrier early on, as CloudFormation has a steep learning curve. Liberty Mutual created a software accelerator to lower the barrier of entry, which provided a consistent experience from deployments and scaffolding. It also relied on CDK (the Cloud Developer Kit). Liberty Mutual Architect Matt Coulter created some CDK patterns to introduce repeatability to infrastructure as code and reduce friction for developers. Internally, Liberty Mutual had its own CDK patterns, including all the specific Liberty Mutual requirements and standards (e.g., tagging and security policies). Thousands of applications have used this approach, saving millions of dollars in developer time alone, not to mention reducing cognitive load.

Very early on, Liberty Mutual set the expectation for teams to shift left. They removed the silos that separated teams and reduced the number of handoffs needed during production. This meant that teams had more responsibility for their solutions. Significant investment in secure development (threat modeling by developers) and using Well-Architected Frameworks (self-auditing by developers) enabled teams to catch issues early and self-correct.

Guardrails and checks were still required by external specialist teams, but self-policing by teams helped raise the quality bar. In 2020, Liberty Mutual observed a 300% increase in deployments with only a 0.5% increase in failure rate. All applications using a CI/CD pipeline combined with tracking DORA metrics were furthering our business goals.

Upskilling Engineers

Liberty Mutual has always valued technology as a critical asset. Skills and training are crucial to ensure that employees can operate at a high level. For that reason, Liberty Mutual provided extensive training programs to help engineers learn cloud-native principles and put their skills to practice in real projects.

With any upskill effort, it's vital to invest in your people, create a sense of excitement, and empower teams. Some trainings took place in a traditional classroom environment and focused on team-based skills. The teams ran workshops, coding dojos, open-space events, Lean coffees, and internal conferences such as Dev Days. With an approach of "show don't tell" and by creating an attitude of "achieve the impossible," it was clear early on that many engineers become energized and committed by working together and showing off their progress.

Providing engineers with the time and space to learn was a significant move. Open-space and "unconference" events gave engineers time to learn from each other and helped build confidence. External conferences are important, but internal events give engineers from your company the chance to use new technology in the company environment, demonstrating what's possible.

Leadership

Any large project with financially significant systems will carry an element of risk when making substantial changes. Leadership must commit to a new way of doing things and have courage when there are bumps in the road. There are always teething problems with new technology, but Liberty Mutual had a technology manifesto and committed leadership, so the will to push through initial issues was there. A fundamental mindset with leadership is described in *Accelerate* by Dr. Nicole Forsgren, Jez

Humble, and Gene Kim. The book proves that high software delivery performance correlates with strong business performance. It's possible to be fast and safe. One imperative for the leadership at Liberty Mutual was to measure the speed of deployments, which in turn helps reduce risk.

Evangelize

As the speed of the Value Flywheel at Liberty Mutual increased, more teams started to get in on the serverless mindset and deliver extraordinary business outcomes. This led to even more internal sharing and peer validation, new techniques explored, and further success. The learning environment was already there, so internal platforms celebrated success and helped other teams along—engineers built a sense of pride, business owners realized critical outcomes, and technology leaders built momentum.

Success

There are many large portfolios of work that benefited from the transformation at Liberty Mutual. John Heveran, CIO of Global Risk Specialty, shared some benefits of the Excite program with us.

> As part of a Claims modernization program, a senior, cross-functional team assembled to continue the evolution of a core claims system. Before the transformation, these projects could have lasted ten years, with considerable effort, delays, and complexity. In the insurance industry, the service given to a policyholder making a claim is the highest priority. As part of the senior leadership team on the Excite program, John spoke of the feeling of "getting everyone in the room" and the potential of moving quickly, with agility and in a customer-centric way. . . .

The teams used design thinking and domain-driven design to run workshops to determine customer needs. It was decided early on that everything would be event-based, so that teams could move quickly. It's a complex system that is decades old, so Liberty Mutual had over two hundred integrations with various systems. In taking a serverless-first approach, the teams moved at an astonishing pace to deliver working software regularly. There was lots of reuse and orchestration—the amount of custom build was quite small.

The teams used CDK Patterns to accelerate development and had a swift feedback cycle. Automation was a core development principle, so the team created a minimum viable product and scaled incrementally. Teams had the autonomy to solve their problems and ensure the system worked for all stakeholders.

For quality control, the foundations put in place within Liberty Mutual helped the team move quickly. Serverless and well-architected principles were also used extensively across the program. This led to a focus on cost optimization, observability, and performance. Cross-functional teams could visualize the critical data points and make informed decisions while the system was being built.

With such an extensive, event-driven system, all the event support was offloaded to the public cloud with services like Amazon EventBridge, AWS AppSync, and AWS X-Ray. Offloading all that operational burden to the public cloud created a significant amount of capacity for the Liberty Mutual team. That extra capacity could then focus on the business problem, not the underlying infrastructure.

Moving Forward

As of 2021, Liberty Mutual has many serverless-first portfolios covering topics as wide as a global digital ecosystem, centralized financial services, virtual assistants using natural language processing, many AI solutions, and countless smaller programs. The positioning of a large company as a serverless-first enterprise is more than just technology. It's a combination of customer centricity, agility, employee engagement, team empowerment, and business focus. The executive team at Liberty Mutual knows that technology is a crucial enabler of business goals. This also travels to the external market, as presentations at technical events build a sense of pride in engineers and a desire for others to join the company and experience this journey. Werner Vogels, CTO of Amazon, described Liberty Mutual as "organizational nirvana" for the cloud infrastructure and cloud application architecture approach at the Serverless-First Function event in 2020.[1]

The Value Flywheel Effect continues. There will be more six-pagers and bold, audacious goals going forward. The focus on talented, technical rebels is still strong, and core engineering principles such as API first, digital products, and serverless-first remain front of mind. Liberty Mutual remains focused on AI and machine learning combined with underlying data engineering, as many large companies are.

With all of this said, Liberty Mutual believes progress happens when people feel secure. By providing protection for the unexpected and delivering it with care, they help people embrace today and confidently pursue tomorrow. Their people are the most important asset, so they have created an environment where creativity, inclusion, and innovation have a real impact. In attracting top talent and engaging and retaining their employees, they strive to be a global employer of choice. Serverless-first is not the goal; it's only a contributing factor.

Takeaways

This chapter illustrates the mindset and commitment required to make profound organizational change. Liberty Mutual started with some core guiding principles around modernization, standardization, and creating an excellent developer experience and then showed leadership by going on a journey. That journey ended up with a serverless-first strategy that was critical to the results and success of the transformation. There are enablers such as infrastructure as code, standard paths to production, creating a learning environment for engineers, and a committed leadership team. These all combined to create the Value Flywheel Effect.

The chapter also illustrates that you don't need to be a Silicon Valley blue-chip company to embrace modern technology. If anyone had suggested in 2011 that Liberty Mutual, the more than one-hundred-year-old insurance company, would be invited to keynote at the largest technology conference in the world (AWS re:Invent), there would have been a second look—maybe even a snigger. But that's what happened in 2021.

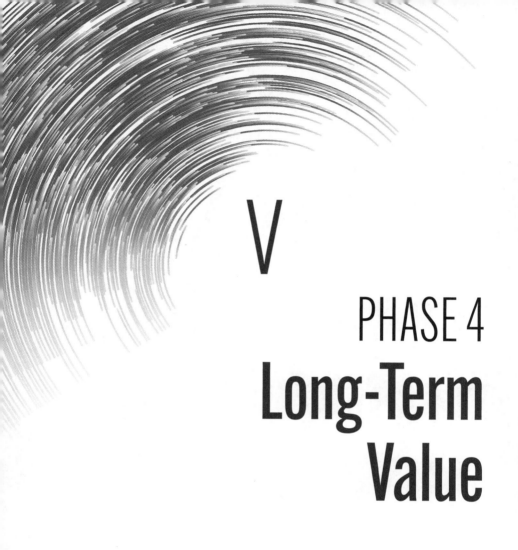

V

PHASE 4
Long-Term Value

PERSONA: CTO

KEY TENETS

A problem-prevention culture: Well-architected and engineered systems.

Keep a low carbon footprint: Sustainability.

Map the emerging value: Next-generation companies can see ahead.

CHAPTER 17

PROBLEM-PREVENTION CULTURE THROUGH THE WELL-ARCHITECTED FRAMEWORK

The last phase of the Value Flywheel Effect focuses on creating long-term value over short-term gains. Well-architected systems and sustainability combine in this phase to create a culture of problem prevention as opposed to incident management. Long-term value in a system is often hard to describe, but it's easy to recognize when a team focuses on problem prevention—both from the attitude of the team and the lack of outages.

In a similar way, architecture has always been a source of great confusion. Is it a role? A responsibility? An attribute of the system? Is it important? And do we need it anymore? Is it a picture? What does it even mean? But understanding and focusing on good architecture is key to preventing problems before they arise and even predicting and building to avoid possible future problems.

Putting a stop to endless arguments, all three leading cloud providers (AWS, Azure, Google Cloud Platform [GCP]) have produced well-architected frameworks and guidance for teams and organizations to guide good engineering and architecture approaches within their platforms. Thankfully, these three frameworks are nearly identical, so we don't need to go into each of them separately. Instead, we'll focus on the AWS Well-Architected Framework for the purposes of this book. We have previously discussed all the architectures extensively on The Serverless Edge website, and you can go there to learn even more.

What Is the AWS Well-Architected Framework?

The AWS Well-Architected Framework helps cloud architects build secure, high-performing, resilient, and efficient infrastructure for their applications and workloads. It provides a consistent approach for customers and partners to evaluate architectures and implement designs that can scale over time.

The AWS Well-Architected Framework started as a single white paper but has expanded to include domain-specific lenses, hands-on labs, and the AWS

Well-Architected Tool, which provides a mechanism for regularly evaluating your workloads, identifying high-risk issues, and recording your improvements.

Let's take a quick look at what the AWS Well-Architected Framework contains. It's built around six pillars:

1. operational excellence
2. security
3. reliability
4. performance efficiency
5. cost optimization
6. sustainability

The Framework provides detailed sections (usually three or four) for each pillar, with two or three questions in each. These open questions lead you to the solution in a white paper or best practice.

Since the Well-Architected Framework is a commoditized set of opinionated standards, architects don't have to invest a lot of time crafting and agreeing on standards before they are published. The subject matter experts from the cloud providers have already done that and will continue to evolve them with their platforms. And not all these standards apply all the time, but as a technical leader, it's essential to focus on the principles and guidance that do apply to your specific domain.*

The AWS Well-Architected Framework also supports portability: if a developer moves from one team to another, or indeed from one supporting organization to another separate organization, their experience and expectations remain consistent. In the past, a developer would become an expert at the specific architecture practices of their unique team or organization. But the AWS Well-Architected Framework is organization agnostic, making the developer's skills and experience much more transferable.

When the Framework is discussed as part of an architectural review, a spirit of learning and collaboration should be created in the teams. It's essential to make the reviews sustainable, low-friction experiences. Meet the teams where they are (experience- and capability-wise) and bring them together in the spirit of learning and collaboration, then celebrate small wins through deliberate, incremental improvement.

How organizations embrace the Framework's guidance is critical. Do you see it as a box that needs to be checked? A process? Or a differentiator? Encouraging teams

---

* You might find the Well-Architected Lenses helpful; they're essential subsets of the Well-Architected Framework tailored for specialized domains, like serverless, FinTech, machine learning, and Internet of Things.

to embrace the Well-Architected Framework in their architecture and engineering practices truly is an excellent step forward, and when the organization applies it at scale, the economies of scale are more significant and drive healthier development environments for their teams.

When an organization is in a state of maturity, the Well-Architected Framework should be treated like continuous improvement—an atomic habit that makes good teams great. Let's put a hypothesis out there: *If the organization invested in facilitating the integration of the Well-Architected Framework into their core ways of working, then we would quantifiably see organizational improvements in the quality of our team execution and the quality of our outcomes.*

The technical lead of the team should drive the use of the Framework. But they also have other responsibilities. Creating a well-architected infrastructure is more than the architecture; it's creating an environment of high performance. It's a good idea to do the following:

- Reduce the distance between the most effective teams and the least effective (emerging) teams—more commonly measured by the DORA metrics.
- Define and support the architectural enabling constraints to guide all teams, including consistency and benchmarking of engineering standards.
- Create efficacy (efficiency and effectiveness) by streamlining problem-solving methods and creating situational awareness between teams (including reuse).
- Highlight and celebrate good engineering rigor and expose shortcutting and technical debt.
- Establish general engineering proficiencies and the development of those proficiencies.

By helping to bring all teams up to the same standards, your organization is one step closer to creating a problem-prevention culture, which lowers your risk and increases your reliability.

Building on Well-Architected

Let's consider the idea of a typical well-architected review of a piece of code. We must start with a definition of what "good" software looks like. Next, we have an external body review the team. Most companies don't make it past this point.

Imagine what would happen if teams could review themselves! Imagine that the business's expectations are understood so well that you can trust the teams to meet the agreed quality standards without any further involvement from leadership. Once we get to this level of trust, we can move into a good cadence for the team, where reviews are just business as usual. The teams need to have this type of mechanism for continuous improvement so they can maintain their well-architected systems.

Software is evolving, messy, and complicated—a "one and done" review is not a long-term solution, it's a jumping-off point. The long-term solution is a continuous cycle of improvement. But what of the architect now?

What if we replace the architect with an "experienced technical expert"? The expert could be external to the team, external to the company, or within the team—it doesn't matter where they exist if they can support the team. We need a mechanism that enables the team to discuss challenges, successes, and experiences with the technical expert safely. Can we create some accountability?

It's important to ensure the teams don't fall into a build trap (see Melissa Perri's excellent book of the same name).[1] With the ability to move fast, teams typically focus on shipping to production and might not be as invested in engineering excellence around the six pillars of the Well-Architected Framework as they could be. The focus may not be on continuous improvement (that is, proactivity), but more on *reactive* corrections and rapid delivery. In other cases, teams start with small workloads, and the DevOps overhead is negligible. However, as time moves on, the team scales out the workload, and the DevOps overhead increases significantly. In these cases, the teams always end up needing to complete large projects to resolve tech debt or reliability issues.

These sorts of trends can't be corrected by directing technical leads to books or meeting them once a quarter for a technical review. The teams are typically succumbing to the everyday pressures of delivery. Reversing these trends requires leadership to engage in the delivery process itself; it requires clarity of direction and a way for teams to continuously introspect themselves, their performance, and their capacity to act. When continuous improvement is lost, it's hard to bring it back again—a mindset change is required, and it needs to be consistent for all teams regardless of how they were engaged.

The book *Atomic Habits* by James Clear promotes how the psychology in slow, deliberate, and sustainable incremental improvement is advantageous.[2] Can we use "well-architected" as an industry-recognized standard to guide teams on a journey of improvement?

We have found there is an approach that works based on the Well-Architected Framework, which we call the SCORPS process. SCORPS stands for security, cost, OpEx, reliability, and performance. We developed the SCORPS process in 2021 to address the need for a lightweight process to help drive improvements on teams. Remember, taking the time to instill this continual learning and quality is key in creating a culture of preventing problems before they ever occur.

What is the SCORPS Process?

The SCORPS Process (Figure 17.1) is based on two main cadences: Target a well-architected review benchmark each quarter. And target a group SCORPS team dashboard review each sprint.

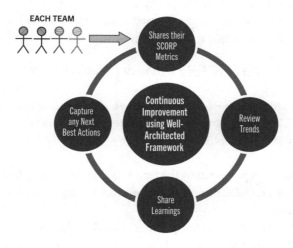

Figure 17.1: SCORPS Process

As you may discern, the quarterly well-architected review process is a standard review of the team's workload with a solutions architect (likely from outside the team). This is aimed to be a thorough deep dive into each of the six pillars of the Framework.

The SCORPS review process facilitates more frequent reviews of the team's operational metrics. The frequency is aimed at regular cross-team collaboration to share experiences, practices, approaches, and learnings about developer operations and production workload performance. In other words, the reviews let engineers learn from the mistakes of others. But the reviews are also about learning from their successes, of which there will be many.

We suggest conducting SCORPS reviews every two weeks. The rationale for this is the following:

- **Why solve the same problems in every team?** A problem shared is a problem halved, but creating situational awareness into engineering excellence across all teams is a potent force for good.
- **Connect developers and teams.** Ideally, we should be working together to improve and gain more economies of scale. Teams should be helping each other improve.
- **Maintain emphasis on the good fight.** Issues with the operation and performance need to be surfaced regularly. Sometimes, that means pushing back or creating space in the development backlog for improvement.
- **Build a passion for excellence.** Fuel curiosity, get ideas out into the open, celebrate the small wins, and generate pride in a good job.
- **Alignment.** The process can be used as an alignment tool for architecture to remain engaged at the team level.

The SCORPS Review Process Flow

With the solid rationale above for the two-week collaboration cycle, we must make the process work. This is a high-level description of the flow and how it currently works in organizations adopting it today:

- All teams are represented by the teams' lead engineer and Scrum master.
- The architect, senior principal, engineering director, or the like facilitates the session.
- If the dashboard isn't already fully automated, then before the session the lead engineer will prepare their team's SCORPS report/dashboard for review.
- The review lasts around one and a half to two hours (ideally about ten to fifteen minutes per team). Each team takes 10 minutes to talk through critical trends, typically focusing on previous reports' deltas.
- The facilitator will go through any high-level notices to all developers. These are things like enterprise impacts, security mandates, or changes to the pipelines.
- The group will review current DevOps actions for each team and get a quick summary of progress. If there are items that come up during the review that the team wants to research, they will follow up.
- Some deeper-dive topics will come up (e.g., testing methodology, review of analytics tool setup, and control flow graphs). These get added to the portfolio summary. The lead engineer will then typically set up a future tech share on the topic.

The Role of the Facilitator

The facilitator has an important role. On a mechanical level, they are responsible for keeping the process on track, which is no mean feat when you have ten squads. This requires discipline and using the process wisely, knowing what to pick and what to get into. As mentioned earlier, the facilitator, ideally, is a technical expert with plenty of experience in DevOps and the Well-Architected Framework. Still, they also need to be in a position of authority and be able to influence the team's ability to prioritize their work. Here's why:

- The facilitator must ask questions. They should be comfortable directing the team to look at an area that maybe isn't trending well (such as cost, performance, or response times) with continuous improvement in mind.
- The facilitator should always attempt to connect the engineers and teams. For example, if one team has a fantastic behavior-driven design technique and another could benefit from it, then the facilitator should suggest that they pair up.
- They should constantly be evolving the SCORPS process. Every aspect of the SCORPS review process must add value for all the engineers and teams. If a part of the process isn't working or adding value, then the facilitator must address it.
- The facilitator should always be interested in what the teams are trying to achieve, whether in the review or post review with product owners or management.
- They will celebrate the successes and wins of each team with the group, no matter how small. Progress is progress! If they're improving their skills, teams and engineers should leave the review feeling like a million bucks.
- They will facilitate a positive sharing environment where all voices get heard. Failures are never negative. They are opportunities to learn and become better at what we do!

It is a challenging role to fulfill, but it is important to ensure the success of the process.

SCORPS Process Day Zero

With any improvement effort, the most significant thing to keep in mind is, "You need to meet the teams where they're at." Some teams will have been together for an extended period and have great DevOps practices with high levels of automation and insight. Other teams will not. They may be newly formed or, for one reason or another, might not have had the time, expertise, or capacity to achieve the operational maturity of some of the more experienced teams around them.

You also need to make sure that management and the business know the initiative's aims and goals. This is because the process requires investment from the teams in terms of participation. Sometimes doing the right thing involves slowing down from time to time, which is not always a straightforward conversation when it comes to meeting delivery timelines.

It's critical that the lead engineers own the SCORPS process. They must buy in and feel like they have a stake in the process. They should agree on the following things:

- **Ways of working agreement:** The agreement should include a general timeline of the process, a safe space commitment, attendance guidelines, sample minutes, etc.—all the typical things you would tend to find in a working agreement.
- **The SCORPS report template:** The SCORPS report contains all the critical operational metrics relating to team and workload performance. This report collects insights that are influenceable and impactful to all teams and is structured around the six pillars of the Well-Architected Framework. Metrics should be automated, but don't wait for automation. It's a great start to use a wiki page and collect manually. If anything, this will encourage automation.

Becoming a high-performing team takes time and effort. It requires investment in your craft and learning from your successes and failures and also the successes and failures of others. The process is certainly not perfect and should evolve and change. When teams start to follow this process, it's likely that:

- The majority of teams will develop automated dashboards (e.g., Data-Dog, Splunk). An active set of data points will drive improvements, and ownership of those data points means teams should keep the dashboard lean.
- Teams will improve focus on performance improvements. Business-critical workloads sensitive to performance will be made front and center and subject to enhanced observability and monitoring.
- Test automation is always problematic, but testing techniques and quality is always improved through teams cross-collaborating.

- Security will become front and center. There will be increased investment in threat modeling and the facilitation of mitigations of identified threats.
- From an operational excellence perspective, an increased investment in release processes and support processes will improve team morale and customer satisfaction.
- Track teams' progress and celebrate success.

Looking Forward

We have talked about the next generation of engineering teams. In many ways, they will be high-performing teams. Technology is an integral part of the business, and we need to use it to drive the company forward and create an environment in which this can happen.

When we look ahead, we can see how future trends in the business world will force certain behaviors. The planned and predictable world of yesteryear is disappearing fast. We are already in a world of complexity, systems, and speed. We need to have a different mindset if we want to be strategic. We leave behind us the land of the plan and SWOT, entering a world of Wardley Mapping, probes, and experiments. The people needed for this world have always existed, but maybe not enough companies existed that encouraged learning, diversity, and challenge. We are entering a new era.

Before we finish up, let's take a peek into what a team might look like in 2040. This will certainly be wrong, but at least someone reading in 2040 will be amused at how wrong we got it. At most, it might encourage someone to think differently about their own preconceptions.

Problem Prevention: Our team in 2040 celebrates problem prevention over problem creation. It's easy to track systems, and the concept of a "black, magic box" is long behind us. We use resilience, data, and engineering to maintain the stability and throughput of our software systems. Teams are rewarded for avoiding failure, not fixing issues.

Technology Stack: The term "serverless" has long disappeared, and the idea of "public cloud provider" is niche—a term of old. The cloud is now ubiquitous and the operating model is the concern of a few specialists—much like electricity today. Cloud is the backbone of the industry. Of course, there will still be legacy software and "containers," but this is an area of specialist expertise. The consumption model of technology is vastly different, and companies have extreme creativity when creating software solutions. Teams don't talk about cloud providers and skills; they interact with systems and capabilities. Customer experience is still paramount and still requires significant investment.

Engineering and Architecture: We are still designing systems, and we have concerns like those of today—throughput, stability, security, cost, operations. The methods we use are different. We don't write as much code. The code we do write is at a higher abstraction. Testing is still a challenge and a much sought-after competency.

Sustainability: A key architectural quality is sustainability. Companies are willing to pay more for greater sustainability. It's possible to measure how much compute carbon a company is burning, and many consumers use this as part of their purchase process because it is published. The top architects can design sustainable architectures using event-driven techniques like the serverless approaches of old. The idea of running a datacenter with your own machines generates a huge carbon bill, but some companies are willing to take this risk for various reasons.

Service and Product: There is a clear drive toward companies that focus on the back office of the industry and consumer-facing product companies, creating services for other companies to use and creating new capabilities versus building experiences for consumers.

Takeaways

We've introduced the Well-Architected Framework to instill good behavior into your teams and start creating a problem-prevention culture. An industry-standard opinion on good architecture will help teams understand what they need to do. It's important that quiet success is celebrated, and noisy success is analyzed. Look at your cloud provider and align with their version of well-architected—all the major cloud providers have one and they are all excellent.

Create a process of continuous improvement, not a one-off audit. The SCORPS process is something that we have had success with, so either use it as is or adapt it to your own needs. The big takeaway is using it to empower the team; don't beat them up with it.

Sustainable processes and a sustainability-focused architecture will pay back in dividends if you address it now. This is key to solving problems before they arise instead of being stuck in a cycle of incident management. We'll dive into sustainability and looking ahead to future trends more in the next chapter.

CHAPTER 18
SUSTAINABILITY AND SPACE FOR INNOVATION

Mariana Mazzucato puts forward an interesting question in the book *Mission Economy*: Is capitalism in crisis? Mazzucato presents an argument that short-term thinking by businesses—e.g., running from quarter to quarter—results in a lack of leadership and strategic thinking.[1] This type of short-term thinking means we're only tinkering around the edges of our potential instead of creating sustainable, long-term value.

Businesses need a robust mission or north star to make any real change and to innovate. To truly innovate, the mission must be more than just "hitting our goals this quarter" or "increasing our stock price by one point." Consider: Are we at an inflection point? Will more employees demand a long-term view or a compelling mission?

The trouble with software—with technology—is that it's only a part of the company. Here in the IT department, we could be serverless, domain-driven, hyper-convergent, responsive ninjas—but it doesn't matter if the executive team is asleep at the wheel.

The phrase *internal efficiency* does not mean what it once did. The age of the CFO squeezing every budget is long gone. It's time for frugality to be the focus over cost-cutting. Be strategic and long-term in your behavior, but don't waste money. We (in technology) are often so fixated on saving money that we forget that we also need to generate income. When generating revenue, a certain amount of gameplay is required. What is the more significant play? What can make a big impact? Can we spot the emerging trends, the emerging practice, and the emerging value?

Long-term, sustainable value and innovation can be achieved when there is a clear, compelling vision in play and teams are aligned with a healthy environment to complete their missions. A serverless organization can reduce overhead and accelerate this momentum. This is the goal and final phase of the Value Flywheel Effect. The goal here is an aligned organization, determinedly working toward a goal using the most effective and appropriate technology.

This feels like a great place to be. It's the ideal space for innovation to develop. Indeed, if an organization has made it this far, then our work is done here, right? We've spun our flywheel, made it to the fourth phase. We've reached our goal and can sit back and enjoy the ride.

Unfortunately, no, far from it. The external market is an altogether different proposition. Anything that we would describe as an industry is competitive, volatile, and evolving quickly. Our ship may be first in class, but even the best ship can't still the rough waters we're sailing in. Of course, technology is critical for every company. If that's the case, you don't want to be dragging internal technical baggage into the rough seas of market competition with you. But don't worry, your CEO doesn't have to be a Python coder to sail ahead.

As a company, we need to understand the components and capabilities in the value chain and get good at those that are core to the company's value proposition. Internal inefficiencies, or inertia, will cause drag. The executive team needs to be aware of both growth and efficiency—top line and bottom line. They need to be proactive and watch actual data—they need to "see into the organization" and steer the ship effectively. They need to understand leading as well as lagging metrics. It's better to have expert navigators at the executive table, not talented sailors—we don't need a bunch of drill sergeants. Navigators need a north star; let's walk through some areas that will help put a fair wind in your sail.

Create Space for Innovation and Long-Term Value

Innovate Using ILC Cycle

Any growth story of a company starts with an idea, an innovation—the spark that starts the endeavor. If successful, the company will scale their innovation and leverage the asset. The next stage is critical but doesn't always happen: the asset is commoditized to create space for the second wave of innovation. This process is called the innovate/leverage/commoditize (ILC) cycle. It's not new, but many companies fail to recognize the cycle to create a second significant impact.

It's like the famous "difficult second album" in music or "second season syndrome" in European Soccer. When a team moves up a division, they can survive the first season, but are often relegated and drop back down again in the second season. The ability to work the ILC cycle and take advantage of "systems behavior" is often the mark of success for companies and is key to creating sustainable, long-term value over short-term gains. Amazon repeatedly demonstrates this technique, for example.

As we can see in Figure 18.1, over the span of fifteen years, Amazon went through the innovate/leverage/commoditize cycle several times with books alone. They not only created a brand-new ecosystem around ordering books online but also commoditized that ecosystem and effectively attacked their own capability by introducing the Kindle and a marketplace for digital books. Soon after launching Kindle, Audible was acquired, which innovated the audiobook market. There are many more nuances in this story, but at a high level, it's an excellent illustration of not sitting on your laurels and disrupting yourself.

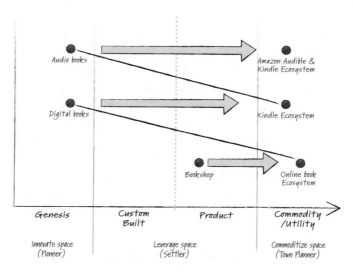

Figure 18.1: Amazon Books Example Map

Business Domain Discovery

The area of domain-driven design[2] has been around for twenty years. According to Martin Fowler it is "an approach to software development that centers the development on programming a domain model that has a rich understanding of the processes and rules of a domain."[3] Systems thinking has been around an awful lot longer, which is defined as "a holistic approach to analysis that focuses on the way that a system's constituent parts interrelate and how systems work over time and within the context of larger systems."[4] As our organizations become more complicated, we need a different approach to creating software.

People like Nick Tune champion techniques like outside-in business domain landscape discovery. In his words, "An outside-in approach starts with the business model, the user needs, and step-by-step zooms into the inner-workings of domains. I like this approach because it's value-driven."[5]

No matter which you choose, the point is that there are many techniques that offer a more mature approach than the traditional departmentalized approach to software and people.

Why is this important? Today, business is changing rapidly. We are all aware of this. And in this environment of rapid change, it's not practical to create a structure and then force every opportunity into that structure. Change happens too quickly, and your organization will end up one of two ways: either you miss the opportunity, or you must reorganize on the fly and find yourself constantly on the back foot, trying to define and perfect your precious structure. The worst-case scenario is the scaling phase runs out of control, and commoditization of your production is near impossible, as the business domains and software have created a sprawling mess of dependencies and inefficiencies that are very hard to package up and commoditize.

Domain-driven design allows you to talk about your systems as they are linked to your problem domain. The idea of a bounded context—a subsection of a business domain that has clear boundaries—is essential. There may be an opportunity in the future to replace this with a SaaS (software as a service) solution or outsource. We often must build capability that supports the primary goal. The option to offload that capability in the future is key to creating space for future growth or innovation.

Observability & Metrics

In yesterday's systems, creating a dashboard with all the frequently updated KPIs (key performance indicators) was the stuff of dreams, even if updated once a week. There's a different problem with modern cloud systems—it's easy to build dashboards and metrics are everywhere. The risk is dashboard overload: there can be too many competing dashboards, making it hard to get a consistent, high-quality view of the important metrics. Without a clear view, it's hard to see where an organization is creating long-term value versus short-term gains.

Let's look at a hypothetical team that has been working closely with their business partners. The business value is well understood. The team has a good environment, so they don't have to waste weeks setting things up or doing foundational work. As the work starts, a cross-functional team takes an "outside-in" approach and travels on a joint discovery journey. There is a good flow of information—many questions are asked and issues explored. The problem definition is cocreated, and the technical approach reflects the business domain.

When the team starts to build something, there is no question of how value is defined. There are even some metrics highlighted that will be important. The natural first step for a good engineering team is to create a dashboard (with the business stakeholders) and visualize critical metrics. A mature approach to observability will combine business, operational, and application metrics into a single view. The business can see how the system evolves in real-time and learn how to operate it before it is finished.

Thankfully, all the cloud providers have robust telemetry or observability solutions in place. The question is no longer "Can we do this?" but "How do you want it to look?" It's not a matter of capturing the data; it's a matter of deciding what not to report on. You should have already agreed on your leading and lagging KPIs, so they should easily translate into specific actions or events. Dashboarding should not be an afterthought; it's a first-class activity that should be designed alongside the software.

In years past, different departments used different tools. Hence, Sales, Engineering, and Ops had different dashboards and tools, which often led to inconsistent reports—not good. Who can find out if we're achieving our desired long-term value in that mess?

A better approach is high- and low-level dashboards. If there is a dashboard for customer experience/system availability/service performance, everyone looks at the same dashboard. There is a single view, so all groups are on the same page if things start to drop. Lower-level dashboards could be database infrastructure, dependencies, and network performance—meaningful but likely to only be used by teams working on that specific component.

There are two critical points to note here. The dashboards are not unique to each department; they are shared. This implies a common language and shared understanding of what is important. This common language and shared understanding come about not because of the dashboard; it's because work has been done up front (clarity of purpose has already been established in the first phase of the flywheel). The dashboard simply reflects the alignment. We know what good (and bad) should look like.

Second is the acceptance that our system is evolving, and we will continue to observe it. We will set KPIs (key performance indicators) and evolve KPIs. A metric is not a directive; it's a signal that requires investigation. The evolving nature of metrics helps us to continually refine our evolving system, so the goal remains focused on long-term value not short-term gains.

A focus on leading metrics enables a more effective feedback loop. Companies like Amazon obsess on key input metrics. The number of Amazon Prime subscribers is one of the most incredible leading metrics available to Amazon. While customers pay for a Prime membership, the real value to Amazon is those customers' future purchases and interactions with other Amazon services. The very fact that delivery is now free (and fast) means the customer is more likely to order from Amazon.

Evolve with Your System and People

Undoubtedly, any business's top priority is reading the market and predicting what will happen next. It's easy to focus on the new and obsess with what might happen next. If a leadership team adopts Wardley Mapping, they will begin to see emerging trends or practices in the market. Often a practice on its own will not change the industry; the game changer usually appears when a new product is built on top of an existing practice. There are many well-documented cases:

- In music, the digital music MP3 format predated the Apple iPod.
- In mobile phones, the touchscreen device predated Apple iPhones.
- In media, the idea of video streaming predated Netflix.
- In user interface, voice recognition technology predated Alexa by decades.
- In knowledge, both the internet and *Encyclopedia Britannica* predated Wikipedia.

You don't want to spot a future trend but not have the people or system to execute on it. Luckily, we're here to help put you in a position where that won't happen. Two great attributes to capture the evolution of systems and people are resilience and psychological safety.

Resilience

We know from biology that resilience means the ability to adapt to change. If an organization is not set up to adapt to change, well, we all know what happened to businesses like Blockbuster and Blackberry. Let's view our technology systems from this perspective.

A system should have space to grow and evolve. When an event damages part of a resilient system, it can recover or rebuild. Often, architects may tightly constrain a system to protect it. But the alternate effect happens—once the damage is absorbed, the constraints prevent healing.

Let's think about a system (i.e., the thing you're building in your company) that combines engineering, business, and technology. There is constant growth as the system evolves and is extended.

Organizations that fear systems really fear the idea of not being in control of the system. *What if this system that drives my business evolves into something I don't want?* The system should evolve in line with the customer need. Careful attention to the input metrics will ensure evolution, not sprawl.

A fundamental cloud principle that you get for free with serverless is the ephemeral behavior of computing capacity. Services only run when called and then disappear. This makes your services more resilient, because you repeatedly test their ability to start up and shut down. Compare this to the old days, when companies would boast that a server ran for 637 days without a restart. It sounds great, but it might not switch on so easily when it eventually switches off (e.g., after a power outage).

A secondary fear is system failure. A system that's designed to "never fail" is complete bogus. Everything fails all the time. The aviation industry doesn't design planes that never crash; they build resilience and safety into their systems and handle failures as they occur. Chaos testing (injecting faults into the live system) is an excellent approach for testing resilience—but the process, unfortunately, makes some stakeholders very nervous! The primary goal is to practice continuous resilience; it's not a once-a-year activity or something to be afraid of.

Stability and Security

Any organization in the cloud must create software that's secure by design. Public cloud providers have very mature and advanced principles for companies building in the cloud. You can be sure that security is the absolute top priority for these platforms, but how high is it on your list?

It's no surprise that stability and security are linked to resilience. True stability is not just a property of the software; it also includes the people, the culture, the processes, and the infrastructure. What about the output and performance of your Agile teams? Do your teams deliver at a nice, regular cadence, or is there inconsistent delivery? Inconsistent delivery is an early signal of poor stability, low quality, technical debt, problem creation, and burnout.

Adaptation

Like resilience, but bringing in the idea of emergence, adaptation is a critical practice. Giving a system the space to repair is essential; the room to change behavior and adapt is equally as important. In the world of business, this could be described as "being agile." Unfortunately, that well-intentioned term has somewhat lost its meaning. Most agile systems today are very constrained and may prevent adaptation.

How the organization views technology is critical here. If the organization views technology as a cost center, then the company will focus on "improving the bottom line"—let's tighten up costs and save money through standardization, risk reduction, automation, operational excellence, and repeatability. All of this sounds very appealing, but if the system has not been designed to adapt, it will resist attempts to update it. Any changes may be blocked or significantly slowed by standards and poor automation.

In contrast, when technology is used to increase the top line to drive growth, there is more appetite for adaptation. Serverless can allow engineering to move quickly in lockstep with the business. For this to work, engineers need to have a serverless mindset and move swiftly in combination with a business team that is strategic and empowered to move with the market.

Situational Awareness

As we move forward, there's a different style of leadership required. Clearly, it must be people centric. (We saw this in the first two phases of the Value Flywheel.) The core principle of Wardley Mapping is to build situational awareness—and to discuss it with your team out in the open. The old practice of performing a SWOT analysis focused on what had already happened, with little regard to how the future would change. It was a retrospective practice.

Let's revisit the key tenets of our Value Flywheel with a future-facing, proactive lens, as opposed to a backward-looking, reactive lens in Table 18.1.

Table 18.1: Key Tenets of Value Flywheel Effect: Reactive vs. Proactive Thinking

	Tenet	Reactive Thinking	Proactive Thinking
Phase 1	Clarity of purpose	Each department has its own metrics and targets (sales, security, hosting, operations). Competition is healthy.	Agree on the right KPIs ahead of time for the organization as a whole.
	Obsess over your time to value	If we can deliver all our features by the end of the quarter, it will be great.	Promote effective execution.
	Map the market	We need to build this because our competitor just announced it.	Team spots a market opportunity and are the first movers, taking the market by surprise.
Phase 2	Psychological safety	Hasn't been an issue yet.	Create a good environment for future work.
	Sociotechnical systems view	Let's review the headcount and hire more people to meet our targets.	Let's review our team goals and ensure our strategy aligns; then, we can adapt based on gaps.
	Map the org for enablement	The team gut-feels estimates and reacts to problems as they arise.	Team uses mapping to find blind spots and areas to evolve.

Phase 3	Serverless-first mindset	We're within budget.	Work to lower future operations and cost.
	Frictionless developer experience	We are still making our release. Developers are always complaining. It's what they do.	Remove friction and cognitive load that is unseen.
	Map your solution	We don't measure technical debt.	Plan ahead to avoid unnecessary work.
Phase 4	Problem-prevention culture	We don't have time for gold-plating. We're busy building features.	Celebrate by testing with chaos.
	Sustainability	Our system is complex, but there's one person who knows the whole thing. He's like the Oracle. We can't ever lose him...	Allow all to be informed and invested. Teams operate at a sustainable pace on a sustainable system.
	Map the emerging value	Every month we have a presentation with all the results. Some of the graphs are very rich and detailed. We are awash with vanity metrics, but the executives believe a data-driven organization is essential.	Ensure that gut feel and emotion don't drive the business. We have actionable metrics.

You might recognize some of the reactive statements in your old (or perhaps current) beliefs. They may feel normal to you. The problem is that they focus on individuals, organizational structure (i.e., not the business need), or flying blind (i.e., the problem has not happened yet).

In the future, the pace of change will continue to increase—companies cannot afford to be rigid and have blind spots. With good situational awareness, you'll see a steady flow of information, and then the organization can act on those insights. Another phrase for this is sensemaking. Many of the data (or signals) you see will be unclear or weak. It is the team's responsibility to listen, learn, and spot patterns.

Sustainability in Software

The concept of inefficiency or degradation in software has always been very difficult to explain to nonprogrammers. All systems have issues, and some are caused by mistakes, others by the simple march of time. Well-written software might exist in a system that is now changing, and the software might not be performing as originally intended.

Over thirty years ago, Ward Cunningham (pioneer of extreme programming and Agile Software Development, among many other things) used the term "debt" to explain inefficiencies that appear over time. The term evolved into technical debt, which is now often used to describe older software that requires some type of maintenance. Of course, like a financial loan, the longer you wait to address this required maintenance, the higher the price to pay—as interest is always accumulating. In the software world, the interest is more complexity to untangle as engineers build on top of the older software.

Technical debt was a strong concept, but the financial impact on the business was hard to describe. When security became more prevalent as the internet evolved, older software ran the risk of exposure via an attack. When data privacy laws were passed, like GDPR, older software with complex data had a higher risk of exposure than newer, compliant software. When we moved to the cloud and started to pay for consumption, older software had a higher cost due to its inefficiencies. Even with all these commercial reasons, we still find ways to tolerate inefficient software. Too many of today's systems are inefficient, over-complex, not fit for purpose, or outdated.

What if we had a metric for inefficient software? Cost was almost that metric, but the software was so bad that the cloud providers started to offer savings and cost reduction plans to sweeten the deal. It's not a smart commercial move to penalize a multibillion-dollar customer for having poor software; they'll just move to a competitor.

Some cloud providers are starting to measure how much carbon their datacenters produce. They can invest in designing an energy-efficient, sustainably powered datacenter that we can feel better about using. In this way, cloud providers can improve the sustainability of the cloud. But what about sustainability in the cloud? We, the customers, can still forget to switch off servers and implement poor, inefficient architectures.

Cloud providers are constantly improving how they report the carbon usage of your cloud workload. Your bill will include services used, price, and carbon usage. What happens when companies are asked to report on their carbon usage from travel, buildings, physical products, virtual products—including applications in the cloud? Some digital companies may have to optimize their software systems to meet sustainability goals.

More to the point, software teams will become aware of how much carbon their software uses and will likely feel bad about an inefficient system with a high carbon burn. What if the carbon usage is reported at the end of quarterly earnings calls? It's already a buzzword in earnings calls, as reported in the *Financial Times* in May 2021.[6] Let's fast forward: if your company has a very poor sustainability score due to inefficient software and this fact is reported, how would this affect your attempts to recruit the software engineers of the future at graduate fairs?

Carbon usage could become a leading metric for modern cloud efficiency. Despite all the fancy presentations, the slick marketing, the stories, and the cool developer advocates, a single metric at the end-of-quarter call would cut through everything. There are many stories of engineers joining a company only to realize that the tech stack is not what was promised. This isn't happening so much now, but every job-seeking engineer will spend considerable time assessing the amount of technical debt they'll need to deal with in a new job and will not join if the picture looks ugly.

A well-architected, serverless system will score very well in sustainability. The compute is very efficient, managed services (run by the cloud provider) will typically be more efficient than normal companies can achieve, and the portability requirements of a Well-Architected Framework mean it may be possible to run in a low-carbon region (i.e., you are not tied to one region, like US East). Further, it's possible to reduce the size of payloads, compress more, use a slightly smaller machine, or run a batch job in an off-peak window. There are practices that we used decades ago when compute, storage, and network were in short supply that we could resurface.

Takeaways

A well-architected system is sustainable, resilient, and easy to commoditize, and your people will be part of the evolutionary approach. Now you can create space for innovation and future value.

Once you have the right environment in place, you must interact deliberately and strategically with that system. In short, you are applying changes to the system. The fact that you are also in this system is challenging—good leaders will separate these two roles.

Your next tasks will be to develop serverless systems, create mission-focused teams, embrace a strong product mindset so you can meet your long-term goals, and invest in sustainable operations. These endeavors will help prepare you to seize new opportunities rapidly—especially when combined with pragmatic domain-driven design. You'll need to bring business, operational, application, and development metrics together to improve visibility into your organization's performance. Additionally, a serverless mindset will drive business growth and internal efficiency. The twelve tenets of the Value Flywheel Effect will make sure you are not flying blind.

Your software developers are the backbone of your company's adaptability. Encourage constant evolution and practice continuous resiliency and make sure that security is everyone's top priority. Your whole organization must practice radical transparency and welcome challenge. Align incentives and objectives for a fast-learning environment and examine how your business's people, technology, business domain, and customers interact. Finally, consider sustainability in your software and think about how a carbon usage measurement can be used as an indicator of technical debt and thus motivate you to reduce your organization's carbon usage.

CHAPTER 19
MAP THE EMERGING VALUE

There is a specific pattern to some maps. Moving components creates space for innovation or emerging value in your organization. Sometimes the value is new (not yet identified) and the map can help you see that, and sometimes the value is latent (you know it's there) and the map can help create space for it. In fact, the entire Value Flywheel Effect can also be modeled in a single map, as shown in Figure 19.1.

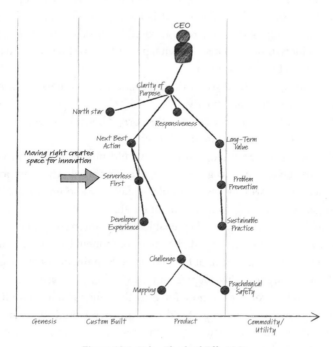

Figure 19.1: Value Flywheel Effect Map

Mapping for Emerging Value

Let's take this concept of moving components on a map to create space for innovation in your organization and work it into a conversation. We'll revisit Laura and Clive for this scenario.

Laura: If we take everything we have been talking about, how would we create a single map? Who is the user—the anchor for the map?

Clive: It must be the CEO. The CEO of a business in the future.

Laura: This is a CEO of a business, say, ten years from now? It's a non-traditional business, and let's not get into what type of company it is or the size—it shouldn't matter.

Clive: Yes. What's their key, foundational need? Is it growth?

Laura: It could be, but it might also be good results.

Clive: And growth means so many things. How can we capture that need?

Laura: How about "convergent expansion"? I've been waiting for ages to use that phrase.

Clive: Come again? You aren't using that—how about "sustainable operations"?

Laura: Okay, plain English! Their goal is an aligned organization, growing against the annual goals, or OKRs. It could be more people, better results, more products, more regions—the vital part is the togetherness and growth. It's more than business as usual.

Clive: Yes, you cannot stand still. I think situational awareness is critical. You need to be proactive, not reactive.

Laura: Good. That really drives a lot of the correct behaviors. Does situational awareness need a foundation of stability?

Clive: Yes, but you are missing growth. I would put adaptation in between those. That gives scope to grow, but it needs stability. And stability needs resilience—there will always be problems, failures, and unexpected events. The organization needs to take a hit and maintain stability.

Laura: I like how resilience is a key enabler—that doesn't seem evident. Let's draw it out. The CEO has a need, then that component has a need, and so on.

Laura: The CEO needs sustainable operations. Sustainable operations equal situational awareness plus adaptation plus stability plus resilience.

Clive: Great. What would be a more forward-thinking need for our CEO?

Laura: You want to be looking ahead. I think they would like their people looking ahead and—not sure what's the best way to put it—getting out of the weeds. Maybe long-term thinking?

Clive: How about long-term goals? And I would say you could bring in the Dr. Westrum model here around organization types. Pathological for power-oriented, bureaucratic for process-oriented, and generative for performance-oriented. Our CEO wants to run a generative organization.

Laura: And the best way to be a generative, learning org is to be a diverse org. Strong diversity is an excellent sign of a healthy organization.

Clive: I think ethics is a crucial need for diversity as well. There must be a shared understanding of what we need to do and what we will not tolerate.

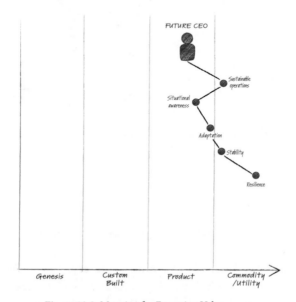

Figure 19.2: Mapping for Emerging Value

Laura: Exactly. I think this is why many companies can't get "fail fast" working; they don't build this line properly—experimentation on its own feels like "just making stuff up." I think we can bring in experimentation next.

Clive: That's nice. Also, it's good that experimentation is coming in. You need a safe-to-fail culture, which links to the psychological safety stuff we talked about. Let me draw that up. Let's not get over-concerned about how far we place them along the evolutionary axis—aim for "good enough."

Laura: That's healthy. I'm sure any company would welcome an underlying practice built on psychological safety and resilience. Let's add in some pipelines showing the evolution of components. What do you think we can add?

Clive: Pipelines for what?

Laura: A pipeline showing the evolution of a technology or practice that is currently evolving. Something that's not ubiquitous yet, that's currently in flight. Only a few people are doing it now, but it'll be more widespread in ten years' time.

Clive: Well, software systems is an obvious one. Serverless.

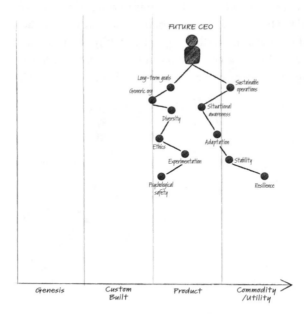

Figure 19.3: Mapping the Emerging Value (Part 2)

Laura: Remember, most will just think about serverless compute, so let's put down serverless architecture. How would you work it back?

Clive: One step back would be IaaS (infrastructure as a service)—software hosted on the cloud but not using all the higher-level services.

Laura: Then stepping back, it would be just technology—I'm thinking technology as part of the business.

Clive: What would you call that? They are more like systems than architectures.

Laura: Okay. And before that, we just have "IT as a cost center." Not really part of the business, just used by the company. Phones, email, a vendor product—using IT, but not really thinking about changing it as part of product development. Good. Let's start with IT systems and evolve to serverless systems. And which component needs that?

Clive: Definitely resilience.

Laura: Any other pipelines?

Clive: What about mindset? You want people who are aligned to the north star, not just putting a shift in.

Laura: Yes, how about Mik Kersten's *Project to Product*—that fits in well there. That's a massive journey, but what would the in-between steps be?

Clive: So, we start doing projects with little acknowledgment of much outside the plan. Maybe then we start to really focus on the task, the autonomy to perform that one thing well.

Laura: And then we start to fixate on the results. We might still be in a project structure, but the outputs or results become more important than the project plan.

Clive: And then you progress to a product mindset—100% outcome-focused.

Laura: Never mind the plan! Feels like this one is linked to the psychological safety stream.

Clive: And for a third pipeline, what about people? There's a transformation journey for people as well. The destination is that "mission-based" idea— like Mariana Mazzucato's book *Mission Economy.*

Laura: Working backward from that, the polar opposite is a person being focused on their job, their role. Working in a medical company—are you a programmer or are you helping cure patients? I suppose in between that we must identify with your company or your skills.

Clive: Yes, input focus, to output focus, to outcome focus again. I think this also links to psychological safety.

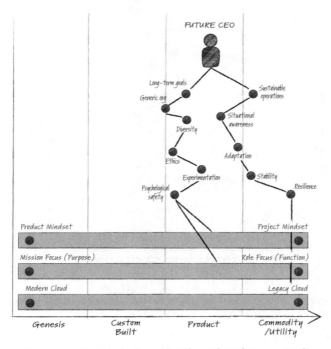

Figure 19.4: Mapping the Emerging Value with Evolutionary Pipelines

Laura: Hmm, that's a good shape.

Clive: So, what patterns do we see?

Laura: Is there a pioneer/settler/town planner picture in here?

Clive: I can't see it. We already have the movement in the pipelines. There are also two value chains—sustainable operations (an existing need) should be to the right of long-term goals (a forcing need), but in a healthy, future company, they're all over to the right. What about the advanced practice lens? If we highlight these? And have them drive something that's a new need?

Laura: Yes, like an emerging practice that you can only really leverage once the two value chains are healthy? What would that be?

Clive: Something around speed. Companies that have this sorted can move quickly.

Laura: Yes, how about "rapid progress"?

Clive: And the emerging practice is "high velocity." When you have the three pipelines evolved, you can move really quickly.

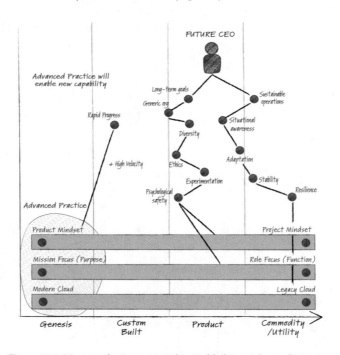

Figure 19.5: Mapping the Emerging Value Highlighting Advanced Practices

Laura: Good, but what's the benefit for the CEO? They'll be thinking, "Okay, but what does the org get out of this?"—and rightly so.

Clive: We also forgot about inertia. There's an inertia point blocking those pipelines; many companies will struggle to make it to the far right.

Laura: I'm going to be blunt and say traditional leadership. Suppose leaders are empire-building—getting into power-plays and putting themselves before the company. In that case, they will remain traditional and not make it to serverless tech, a product mindset, or a mission focus. Traditional leadership will not be comfortable with the perceived loss of control.

Clive: If you can make it past that inertia, these emerging practices will create new value, allowing the business to spot and capture a future market space. I think those combine to give you that ability.

Laura: Yes, I was thinking "first mover," but that's not right. After all, many companies have moved first but failed to capture.

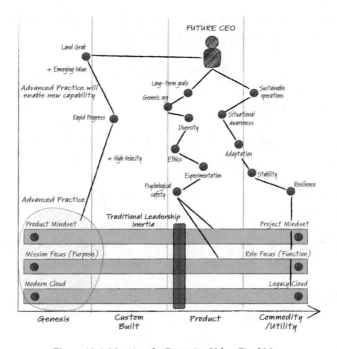

Figure 19.6: Mapping the Emerging Value: Final Map

Analyzing the Map

For this map, we can sense-check the value chains. This is an alternate way to challenge the map.

Value Chain One

Our first value chain looks like this:

Sustainable operations = situational awareness + adaptation + stability + resilience.

We can also see that it depends on the organization's mindset, focus, and cloud technology (the three evolving pipelines).

Project mindset + role focus + legacy cloud implies sustainable operations will require more effort and budget to achieve.

Product mindset + mission focus + modern cloud implies sustainable operations will be more achievable.

Value Chain Two

Here's our second value chain:

Long-term goals = generative organization + diversity + ethics + experimentation + psychological safety.

Like our first value chain, this one also depends on the company's mindset, focus, and cloud systems.

Project mindset + role focus + legacy cloud implies long-term goals will require more planning, budget, and skill to achieve.

Product mindset + mission focus + modern cloud implies long-term goals will seem more realistic due to a lighter footprint.

Emerging Value

Product mindset + mission focus + modern cloud will lead to rapid progress.

Rapid progress will enable a "land grab" or other required gameplay patterns. The gameplay patterns (including land grab and first-mover advantage) are listed in Wardley's Gameplay Patterns and in Table 19.1.

Wardley's Gameplay (context specific patterns that user can apply)			
User Perception	Education	Bundling	Creating Artificial Needs	Confusion of Choice
	Brand and Marketing	Fear, uncertainty, and doubt	Artificial competition	Lobbying/counterplay
Accelerators	Market enablement	Open approaches	Exploiting network effects	Co-operation
	Industrial policy			
De-accelerators	Exploiting constraint	IPR	Creating constraint	
Dealing with toxicity	Pig in a poke	Disposal of liability	Sweat and dump	Refactoring
Market	Differentiation	Pricing policy	Buyer/supplier power	Harvesting
	Standards game	Last man standing	Signal distortion	Trading
Defensive	Threat acquisition	Raising barriers to entry	Procrastination	Defensive regulation
	Limitation of competition	Managing inertia		
Attacking	Directed investment	Experimentation	Center of gravity	Undermining barriers to entry
	Fool's mate	Press release process	Playing both sides	
Ecosystem	Alliances	Cocreation	Sensing Engines (ILC)	Tower and moat
	Two factor markets	Co-opting and intercession	Embrace and extend	Channel conflicts & disintermediation
Competitor	Ambush	Fragmentation play	Reinforcing competitor inertia	Sapping
	Misdirection	Restriction of movement	Talent raid	Circling and Probing
Positional	Land grab	First mover	Fast follower	Weak signal/horizon
Poison	Licensing play	Insertion	Designed to fail	

Takeaways

As maps get more advanced, they do not need to be more complex. You could spend a lifetime learning the ins and outs of mapping, but the shape discussed in this chapter is a good one to learn early. The Value Flywheel Effect will introduce momentum, which will enable some components to move into the Commodity section of the map. The fact that you can map them and predict their movement, sometimes years before it happens, is invaluable. Some of the techniques and areas of emerging value that you can then explore may be very important for your team, department, or company. Don't wait until the change happens to you; map it out and make it happen.

CHAPTER 20
CASE STUDY—BBC

Our fourth and final case study features the BBC Online team and illustrates a culture of problem prevention, one of the key tenets of the fourth phase of the Value Flywheel Effect. The BBC Online website is complex and requires the highest standards of architecture. The team has balanced business needs with a best-in-class technology approach to create a well-architected solution and deliver valuable service to readers all over the world in times of need.

Every software project is complex. Even moderate-sized software systems can have hundreds of features and interaction points, making them behave in hard-to-predict ways. We're all used to our computers doing random things—such as crashing applications or forgetting printers. And we're all used to news reports of massive IT failures, which are commonplace, because the systems we build are so complex that we're unable to fully understand them.

It is sensible, therefore, to strive for *simplicity* in our software systems. The simpler something is, the more it can be understood, and the easier it is to support it, improve it, and adapt it (again, key for achieving sustainable, long-term value versus short-term gains). It's an obvious argument but goes against the natural entropy that software projects experience as new requirements appear. To quote Steve Jobs, "Simple can be harder than complex."[1] Fortunately, serverless architecture offers an approach that can help create simpler software.

We were lucky enough to have Matthew Clark, Head of Architecture for BBC's Digital Products, provide this important case study and intimate look inside their process.

Over the past few years, the BBC has successfully moved much of its web and back-end infrastructure to a serverless design. In doing so, it has shown how serverless computing can make a significant difference in delivering a complex project. By allowing teams to focus on what's most valuable, serverless has allowed the BBC to create a modern, scalable service they can build and maintain efficiently. This case study shows how the BBC used serverless to bring the simplicity needed to deliver software at scale.

The Road to Serverless

BBC Online is a set of websites and apps that offers news, sports, TV, radio, and much more. Their goal is to offer simple, world-class experiences that are useful to everyone. They offer millions of pieces of content in forty-three different languages to over a hundred million users a week. The most significant part, BBC News, is the most popular news website in the world. Altogether, it includes over two hundred different page types, each with its own features and behaviors, which come together to make a service for everyone.

As with most technology projects, the BBC's challenge is keeping on top of the complexity of running such an extensive service. From weather forecasts to educational games, a broad range of content means a wide range of capabilities is required. There are also key nonfunctional requirements, such as reliability, security, and performance. During major moments such as the Olympic Games, millions of users can be watching and reading content at once. Ensuring a high-quality experience at that kind of scale is challenging. Combined with other essential features—such as SEO, accessibility, and personalization—the BBC's sites and apps may feel simple, but under the hood they are anything but.

The other challenge the BBC has is that its sites must be ruthlessly efficient. As a publicly owned organization with a fixed income, it must spend its time and money wisely. There is also intense competition, such as Apple News and Netflix, that have significantly more resources. To succeed, the BBC needs a technology strategy that lets them move quickly and efficiently, focusing only on what matters.

Overall, BBC Online is large, complex, and popular, and it must be efficient and competitive. That's a significant engineering challenge, however you cut it, but serverless architecture provides at least a partial approach to make it achievable. As of 2021, half of the BBC's web pages are rendered using serverless technology. They are reliable, fast, and perhaps most importantly, simple to maintain and extend.

Focusing on the Differentiator

By replacing physical machines in datacenters with virtual machines (VMs) in the cloud, we reduce the amount of maintenance we need to do. But some maintenance remains. For example, the cloud removes the worry about a disk failing but not a disk running out of space. VMs—and to a lesser extent, containers—still require a sizable amount of upkeep. Some BBC teams have found that up to 50% of their time could be spent supporting their virtual infrastructure. The fallacy of DevOps is that while it has given teams control over how their service will operate, it has also introduced a significant maintenance overhead. And that's an overhead we'd instead do without.

Serverless removes the overhead of configuring and maintaining VMs (or other server-based solutions). Issues such as patching operating systems or managing log files either go away or become simpler. That frees up time, and perhaps just as importantly, removes the number of distractions that a team may face. Any opportunity to simplify a project is a welcome one. The more a team can focus on what's most valuable—their product differentiator—the more successful they'll be.

Today, around half of BBC Online's systems use serverless cloud capabilities, such as functions, queues, and databases. The other half use VMs, containers, and other server-based cloud tools. There is a clear pattern: teams that have been able to adopt serverless deliver features faster than those that do not.

Take, for example, the challenge of scaling to large numbers of users. The BBC regularly experiences high and sudden traffic levels, such as during a breaking news event. VM-based services require substantial work to scale for such variable traffic. Multiple techniques support high traffic levels (such as auto-scaling, which deploys additional VMs automatically), but all require a significant amount of configuration and testing. A new website feature may often be blocked due to high load concerns, often resulting in new projects to extend systems so that they can handle the load. On the other hand, serverless systems can usually handle scale much better, as near-infinite compute is available immediately. BBC Online has shown this to be the case.

BBC development teams have repeatedly found that serverless solutions simplify challenges (such as scaling) and remove maintenance overhead (such as managing disk usage). Why do something that others can do for you? Serverless architecture epitomizes the philosophy that teams should do all they can not to reinvent (or reimplement) the wheel. Leave the servers to the cloud providers; focus on the desired behavior instead.

Moving Faster

With serverless handling many of the challenges of hosting, teams can focus on innovating their products instead. Take, for example, the BBC website's home page. This high-profile page was developed and launched using a serverless approach in under two months—quite an achievement given its significance. Once launched, its small development team could innovate the page further, adding regional variation, performance improvements, and new designs. Serverless functions and databases meant there was little infrastructure to support—so the team could concentrate on enhancements instead. Overall, the BBC releases an update to its website every twenty minutes on average. The release train of updates never ends.

Continual efficient updates are a crucial part of modern software development. By launching a *minimal viable product* early, then iterating improvements based on user feedback, teams are more likely to create successful products that the customer wants. This is particularly true given how hard it is to predict what success looks like. After all, no one knows what the next killer mobile app will be. With technology and society evolving faster than ever before, successful organizations are the ones who respond to new opportunities and innovate quickly. The low start-up overhead of serverless makes it the perfect place to experiment with new ideas and see what works. The best way to understand what the future holds is to get there faster. Serverless and fast-moving iteration go hand in hand.

Moving faster brought another unexpected benefit to the BBC: an ability to remain on the cutting edge of technology. Take, for example, their preferred development language, Node.js. Every year, a version of Node reaches the end of its supported life, so the systems using that version must be upgraded. With server-based applications, this is a significant challenge, requiring substantial testing. With serverless architecture, this upgrade still needs to happen, but it becomes much more manageable. The fast-moving teams can apply the upgrade sooner. The smaller serverless functions are also easier to upgrade—and easy to test in parallel with the existing version. As a result, the BBC's serverless website was upgraded to the latest version of Node within two weeks of it being available. This, in turn, provided a significant speed improvement, resulting in a noticeable reduction in cloud costs.

Team Ownership

BBC Online is such an extensive service that no one can realistically understand how it all works. The team handling weather forecasts, for example, cannot and should not know the intricacies of creating podcasts. Teams need as few dependencies and distractions as possible if they are to focus on their responsibilities efficiently. Yet this independence is sometimes at odds with ensuring that no problem is solved twice. The weather and podcast teams may have different content, but much should be shared when they create their web pages.

BBC Online teams follow the DevOps model. They take responsibility for what they own, from development to operation. They use serverless where possible to reduce their operational overhead. And by the same philosophy, they use infrastructure and services made by other BBC teams to ensure they are not solving a problem that has already been addressed elsewhere. This takes investment. The BBC had to create multiple new teams to provide standard platforms and tools. Done right, a "golden path" can be created—a standard way to do everyday tasks so that product teams don't have to reinvent things. In keeping with the DevOps approach, each team decides which shared solutions they use. No solution works for everything, and there are sometimes valid reasons to pick a different approach. Done right, the 80:20 rule should apply—a common service will work for 80% of projects. We're making the common things easy and the specialist things possible.

For example, take continuous delivery (CD) pipelines, which most teams need to efficiently test and release their product. In the past, it was typical for each BBC team to create its own CD pipeline, which would often take weeks and have a significant maintenance overhead. So, a new team was formed, called "Developer Experience," to create a common approach to CD pipelines (among other things). Their solution worked for all teams creating websites, APIs, and data services—roughly 80% of the wider department's needs. Some specialist teams, such as those maintaining the BBC's search engine, needed something more bespoke and maintained their own solution. Altogether, duplication was minimized without restricting ownership or what any one team could achieve.

Production Ready

Since moving to serverless, the number of incidents affecting the BBC website has significantly reduced. A challenge for some teams is working out how they can justify offering 24/7 support given how infrequently issues occur. Failure is inevitable, no matter what technology is used. But with serverless, teams are owning less, which means there is less to go wrong.

A serverless approach also encourages simpler software designs that are easier to understand. A serverless function is typically smaller than a server-based application (whether monolith or microservice). Smaller, simpler parts are less likely to fail—and if they do, they are easier to fix or replace. Of course, if parts are smaller, more are needed to create a fully working system. This results in an extensive, distributed system that's inherently tricky to understand and manage. To mitigate this, the BBC has introduced consistent monitoring, logging, and tracing. Tooling like this helps determine where a failure is occurring, and once found, the fix is usually quick and easy.

Infrastructure as Code

As serverless architectures typically have more parts, we need to ensure the parts are correctly configured. BBC teams achieve this by always defining their infrastructure using code with tools such as Terraform or Cloud Development Kit. This is tracked using source control to clarify what has been configured, by whom, and why.

Infrastructure as code brings another advantage: the ability to standardize across accounts. The BBC has dozens of DevOps teams, each with their own cloud accounts. Many of these teams need the same infrastructure setup based on organizational best practices. By sharing infrastructure using code, one team can own a configuration (such as how a virtual network should be configured), and others can use it in their own accounts.

It's another example of ensuring that no problem is solved twice. When multiple teams have the same challenge—such as managing secure user access—the ideal is for one team to take ownership and create a solution for everyone. That way not only is there a more efficient outcome, but the one shared solution is likely to get more investment and thus be of higher quality. This ability to quickly "organize around the problems" as they appear is tricky for teams to adapt to but unquestionably produces a faster and higher quality result.

Serverless Cloud Costs

A common concern with serverless computing is cost. For all the major cloud providers, the billable rate to access a unit of compute is considerably more through serverless than it is through a VM. (The BBC researched cloud providers and calculated that based purely on CPU and memory usage, a serverless function is two to five times more expensive than an equivalent VM.) Serverless is a convenience that comes at a price.

Despite this theoretical price difference, there are two practical reasons why the actual cloud cost of a serverless application will not be any higher than a server-based equivalent—and may be far cheaper. First, serverless costs are usually proportional to how much resource is used. Consider the BBC website again: the more users it has, the more serverless functions will be invoked, and the higher the cloud cost. (This is a simple correlation that the BBC's finance team appreciates!) On the other hand, server-based websites have a more complex price model in practice, because one web server handles many users. During quiet times, a web server will be accruing costs even though it's underutilized. And because you never know when more users will turn up, a server must continually have some capacity on hand. Most production servers run at 10–20% CPU utilization—or to put it another way, over 80% of procured VM capacity is often unused. The serverless "pay only for what you use" pricing model can make more sense and offer better value when put like this.

Second, there is the "total cost of ownership" argument. As discussed in the previous chapters, serverless architecture lets teams focus more on what's important and less on the infrastructure. The single biggest expense most organizations pay is employees. Even when serverless does cost more, it's probably a better value overall when we factor in the time it saves.

Making New Features Possible

The BBC website sometimes shows a real-time count of how many people are currently accessing a particular piece of content. It's not uncommon for over a million users to be simultaneously reading or watching the same thing. Showing this user count is a great feature of the page, but calculating it in real-time is an engineering challenge. The BBC could not justify a large project just to show this number. But with serverless, a low-cost solution became available.

This "counting service" required the ability to analyze user events to create a summary of how many users were accessing each piece of content. The number of users varies considerably, so compute and storage needed to be available at different rates. That, of course, is perfect serverless territory. Using a range of tools (in this case, AWS Kinesis, Lambda, and DynamoDB), a small BBC engineering team managed to create and deploy a 100% serverless service to count real-time viewers in under two months. It has now been running for four years, with minimal maintenance and predictable costs. It's been so successful that multiple other systems now also use its capabilities. It is, in some ways, the perfect example of a serverless project—turning a complex problem into a simple, scalable, reliable, and affordable solution.

Limitations

About a third of BBC Online's systems could never become serverless, at least not with today's cloud technology. The web traffic management service, for example, handles large numbers of open network connections—a tricky and potentially expensive thing to do with a serverless function. And the BBC's specialized video transcoding requires specific VM hardware. Serverless is too new a paradigm to work for all use-cases. (Though that will change with time.)

Serverless means giving up control. The cloud provider ultimately decides what features to offer and how many things are configured. That immediately rules out some projects that have specialized requirements. It may also mean projects have to compromise; for example, a project might have to use a specific development language. Whether that's the right compromise will vary depending on the requirements.

So serverless isn't a panacea. It is one of many approaches to designing software and, like everything, should be considered alongside other options. But to gain all the benefits we've discussed, a "serverless-first" approach makes sense. Consider serverless as the default option until you've seen otherwise. Even if it only works for some projects, the opportunity benefits are worth it.

Takeaways

Software systems will always be complex. As the examples from the BBC in this chapter have shown, serverless infrastructure can help reduce this complexity. Simpler, smaller components usually result in faster development, easier deployments, new product opportunities, and lower overall costs. This in turn creates space for innovation and sustainable, long-term value.

When things do go wrong, out-of-the-box integration with monitoring and logging solutions enables you to fix issues quicker. And the serverless capabilities created are easier to share between teams, encouraging consistency and optimizing projects even further.

To quote Gall's Law, "A complex system that works is invariably found to have evolved from a simple system that worked."[2] Serverless can be the simple foundation from which teams collectively create rich, fast-moving, and cutting-edge products.

CONCLUSION
GETTING STARTED

M any readers of technology and business books are looking for a quick fix, a model that can be quickly applied and that promises instant success. In the early days of Agile Software Development, the Scrum methodology advised readers to follow the steps to the letter. If they did, the prescribed outcome was guaranteed.

I'm not sure I have ever observed Scrum working perfectly. Scrum is based on the understanding that the process needs to be changed to suit the people and the company, but it rarely is. Human beings are messy and complicated; that is why what we do is so challenging and rewarding. Every company is different, and software is written to solve new problems—problems that are unique to your company.

The Value Flywheel Effects exists in your company, but don't expect to find it locked in a back storeroom. You must work to merge the competing concerns of technology and the business and make those concerns one. Don't focus only on the technology; it's essential, but your people are more important. Therefore, the sociotechnical concept will make a comeback—remember, it was originally created during WWII (and it will likely get a shorter name in the future). As tech in companies matures, more leaders will understand that an equal and aligned focus on both the socio (culture and people) and technical aspects is crucial for delivering long-term value.

When driving change, whether it's a new company or your current company, focusing on the Value Flywheel Effect and getting it running smoothly is paramount. Focus on techniques like mapping, finding your north star, and open space events as a form of discovery.

Finally, you must move through the Value Flywheel quickly. Often, clarity of purpose either doesn't exist or is not written down. It could even differ between members of the executive team. Don't be afraid to approximate something and move on. Focus on momentum over perfection. Progress will be disjointed at first, but keep moving forward. The importance of a quick win cannot be understated.

Collaboration, Not Conflict

There are thousands of books written about teamwork, leadership, and collaboration, yet we still struggle. The culture of "one-up-manship" and "the brogrammer" in the technology industry is toxic, damaging, and unhelpful. We can only succeed through collaboration (not conflict) and through diversity, inclusiveness, and accessibility. Hopefully, that message is coming through in this book loud and clear.

If you're from the business, try to build empathy for your engineers and understand their challenges. Many engineers will try and solve everything. Coach them to solve the correct problems.

But we must also look beyond engineering to drive change and build trust with the entire leadership community—don't be a threat. Take the product organization. It's important to make strong connections and help product leaders achieve their goals.

If you're in IT, look outside the IT department. What challenges are the traditional departments having? You might be surprised to discover the pain points in sales, procurement, logistics, etc. Finally, educate yourself about security and compliance functions. Help remove friction; don't fight against it. Enable and empower, don't command and control.

Let's move through the four phases of the Value Flywheel and offer some quick hints to get started.

Clarity of Purpose (Phase 1)

The worst thing you can do is assume you know the problem. Gerald Weinberg wrote one of the great books on software development in 1985—*The Secrets of Consulting.* The absolute joke is that you don't need to be a consultant—the advice applies to anyone giving advice, which is all of us. There are two interesting pieces:

> "In spite of what your client may tell you, there's always a problem."[1]

And the law of the hammer:

> "The child that receives a hammer for Christmas will discover that everything needs pounding."[2]

This advice is decades old but still rings true. Problems should not be concerns; they require exploration and attention. Once the problem is identified, it would be straightforward to declare serverless as the solution. But serverless will not solve your problems.

There are four activities worth consideration when building focus: finding your north star, mapping the market, obsessing over time to value, and achieving alignment.

Clarity of Purpose: Finding the North Star

Discovering the purpose can be as easy as talking to a few people and reading the website or it could be many months of soul-searching and shoe-gazing. Agree on a foundational purpose to act upon—there will be refinement later.

The North Star Framework from Amplitude is very revealing. It can expose a well-understood strategy or the complete lack of one—prepare for both outcomes. A north star should represent a metric or suite of metrics; the teams must understand it and be of value.

Mapping the Market

A high-level map of the market or domain is a beneficial exercise at this point. Capturing the climatic patterns is critical to success, as it indicates the teams' concerns. There may be underlying issues that are not immediately obvious. This map should be broad but not very deep—stay out of the weeds.

There are two advantages to running this session early. First, it's possible to identify what the team is passionate about and their emotional responses to different areas Some helpful indicators include frustration at slow progress, anger at the loss of opportunity, disappointment with poor execution, and worry about the potential risk. Ask how these issues are impacting the business. Second, harmony in the room is essential. Is there good alignment regarding the map? Do people agree on the analysis? Is there a healthy challenge? And are people up to speed on the business?

The market map is a thirty-thousand-foot view of the territory. It will indicate an approach and possible hazards!

Time to Value

One of the most significant indicators of the Value Flywheel Effect is time to value. How long does it take from the moment a product manager starts to shape a new feature before it is in the hands of users? This metric captures the alignment in the business unit to effectively prioritize and consider impacts. It also captures the engineering maturity of the organization to assess, build, and release the feature. Technical and business debt can impact time to value just like poor alignment. A measure in days or weeks is good; a measure in months or years is an issue.

Can you start to measure and track this metric? Is there an event that you can capture upon feature creation? Story written, press release written, or product specification started? Then, what is the event when the customer can access and use this feature? The feature should be something of value to the customer, not minor configuration changes or hidden updates.

Alignment

Ideally, there is alignment around the potential avenues of pursuit, and there is a means to measure progress. The worst-case scenario is a lack of alignment, and the map should have highlighted that. Once alignment is achieved, it's important to plot a path immediately. You'll repeat this process many times. As we've said, the Value Flywheel should turn many times, so you'll continue to revisit this initial phase. The progress we make now may help ease concerns that affect alignment. Don't fall at the first fence!

Challenge & Landscape (Phase 2)

A quick win is always important. There must be value identified, and it is realized relatively quickly. We've all been involved in big projects driven by consultants. The burn rate is eye-watering, and the project has been running so long that no one can remember what it was for. Maybe a slight exaggeration, but the cost model is not. Vast amounts of money are sunk into the project before any material value is created—let's avoid that.

Psychological Safety

At this stage, it's vital to assess if there is an atmosphere of safety in the organization. Is there a sense of participation? Do team members have a voice? Have there been means to explore areas?

Sociotechnical View

The interaction between people and the technology system should be clear. Is there a healthy understanding of the "business of work" between people and architecture? Potential signs to look out for here are "black box" or "ball of mud" components—no one knows what goes on there. The imbalance may come with a lack of transparency or silo-building.

Mapping the Org

There should be suggestions of things we can do to remove blockers or create value. Let's map out the organization's capability and see how things might move. The exercise will serve two different purposes. First, it will help test the change ahead of time and predict what may happen next. Second, it will unearth any resistance to the change or lack of alignment. Prepare for a relatively simple map; an overly complex map at this point may indicate unnecessary complexity.

Potential skills or knowledge gaps may present themselves at this point. Providing some training, workshops, or sessions to upskill and bring people along is essential. A sense of urgency is also critical—a lot of training is online and can be acquired quickly. Don't let training acquisition slow down progress.

Challenge

It's imperative that a challenge is present at this stage. People will have questions, so it's crucial to surface them and factor concerns into the work. The problems will be valid, so don't ignore the challenge or stop it. A map invites challenge, so an environment of inquiry should exist around the map. It's better to uncover an issue early and be aware of it.

Next Best Action (Phase 3)

We should have several maps at this stage, and we should have alignment. It's unlikely that all problems have surfaced, but there should be enough to make progress. Speed is an essential element here. Software development and change should be incremental. It's better to flush a difference through the system and observe what happens. The best-case scenario is we all learn and build confidence. The worst-case scenario is that a huge problem is unearthed. Either way, we are learning quickly, and we will fail fast.

Code is a Liability

It's essential for software teams to understand that code is a liability. It requires extra effort to solve a problem, and code should be the last option. There has been so much hype about software that "let's just build it" is an acceptable approach for many problems. But this is a surefire way to create technical debt. What checks and balances are in place to ensure teams do not write unnecessary code?

Serverless-First

The team should be building in the cloud, but are they leveraging the cloud? A serverless-first approach will ensure the operational burden is low and feedback loops should be fast. It may take several iterations of the Value Flywheel to lock in a solid technology strategy properly, but start early. A serverless-first approach is not a big bang. Start looking at managed services or ways to offload complexity to the cloud vendor.

Developer Experience/Friction Points

During the delivery of your first change, observe friction points that slow down or impact the developer experience. Developer experience is a crucial component of the time to value metric.

The first challenge is to ensure that data is available that can report on the developer experience. Have you measured the DORA metrics? Can you monitor the flow of the engineering teams? Have you minimized the handoffs and dependencies on other teams? Other common areas of friction are security and deployment pipelines. All are critical to get right but are often victims of poor communication or under-investment.

Mapping the Stack

Working in partnership with the areas above, the next activity is to map the tech stack. What tools, components, and platforms are the engineers using? What do they need to move away from, and what is the target state? What are the inertia points? The map of your tech stack session with the team may be challenging at first, as the value is not clear. Toward the end of the session, there should be a wealth of input on the challenges for the engineers.

Long-Term Value (Phase 4)

Now that you have proved you can push a change to production using this new approach, you can start to move quickly. The velocity needs to stay high. As the team gains more confidence, you should observe an increase in throughput.

A Culture of Problem Prevention

With a view to long-term value, it's essential to position a mindset shift to problem prevention. Techniques like AWS Well-Architected Framework and having a high regard for engineering excellence are critical. More so is how we reward the activity. Adopting pre- and postmortems for engineering problems will create an environment of psychological safety, challenge, and learning. Teams must be rewarded for systems that quietly run. Problem prevention must be prioritized over problem creation. Don't praise the fixers of problems; praise the prevention of problems.

Sustainability

Every company that uses technology consumes compute resources; for some, this consumption is significant. Start to position a green engineering approach with the executive as part of the sustainability program. Serverless on the public cloud has a lower carbon burn than virtual images on the public cloud. Buying your server for your office or datacenter is the highest carbon burn. An effective, cost-optimized system design will also result in a more sustainable system.

Emerging Value

A critical difference between traditional and next-generation companies is the ability to recognize and realize emerging value. Once the team grasps the basics of mapping, it's possible to cover a wide range of elements in your market. It's easier to hide complexity and predict movement. This clarity on the current state will enable the team to indicate what else is possible. There are specific patterns during mapping that uncover emerging value.

Serverless-First as a Strategy

Now that the pathway has been tested, help tell the narrative and shape a dialogue around serverless-first. Maybe write a six-pager or think up a way to communicate, implement, and celebrate this approach. Do you need to set up any checks and balances? Do not declare Lambda as the only compute method; instead, encourage a "best fit" culture. Teams should discuss the best solution. This includes giving them the time and space to do so and having the psychological safety to disagree and challenge without making enemies.

Rubber Stamp the Cultural Changes

Fight against "quick hit" innovation. Measure your time to value in a dashboard and ensure it's part of the executive narrative. Track your outages and stability—and be transparent about them. Celebrate problem prevention, not problem creation.

The Importance of Mapping

Wardley Mapping has been ever-present across this book. We talk about it as a technique that can be used to explore an area with a group and create a shared understanding. Mapping is also a very specific way of thinking that is hugely beneficial for you as an individual. It takes some time to be confident with the technique, but eventually the idea of an anchor (or a customer), visibility, evolution, movement, and inertia will become ever-present as you think about scenarios. As you map, remember to ask the following questions:

- Who is this for?
- Do they really care about this detail?
- This thing we are building, how will it evolve, will it get replaced?

- How can I speed up that replacement?
- What's stopping that acceleration?

It's almost like a mental checklist that helps separate the transient value from the permanent value. Mapping is a superpower. We often joke that you can predict the future with maps. I believe you can, but the maps don't tell you when things will happen.

Business, Not Technology

As a technologist, we all want to open things up and tinker. But we are no longer hobbyists. As a technologist who is paid by a company, the business of that company is my number one priority. Unfortunately, this is rarely covered in computer science classes. Many university graduates will need a few years to figure this out; some will never figure it out.

Some of the most successful business leaders in the world started as engineers. So why do so few "normal companies" have technologists as senior executives or CEOs? Why is it acceptable for large companies to waste billions of dollars on poor technology choices, often the result of a CEO who doesn't have a handle on technology? What would happen if some of these companies applied the Value Flywheel Effect and used Wardley Mapping?

Final Word

As you have seen through this book, the shift to move to the cloud is a clear next best action for many organizations. But many are so eager to move and reap the benefits that are being promised that they aren't entirely sure what to do when they get there or even how best to travel.

A key reason for this is simply a misalignment in the organization itself. Typically, the business owner expects moving to the cloud or going serverless will reduce costs. The engineer assumes it means "to use Kubernetes."

Imagine if, instead of this misalignment, your organization had a combined strategy and vision, where it was clear that the use of the cloud would not only try to fix the bottom line but also improve the top line (or growth profit) of your business. Cost-cutting and optimization are critical, but the real prize hidden in the modern cloud is driving growth and value (the key tenets of the fourth phase of the Value

Flywheel Effect). And isn't this the goal or definition of success for an organization? To deliver value to the user and grow to adapt to that user's changing needs.

The most pertinent question that we must ask of any transformation effort is quite simple: "What are we going to do when we get there?" If the answer is "We're agile; we'll figure it out when we get there," then you have an alignment problem. And if you have an alignment problem, then no transformation, no cloud, no Power-Point strategy is going to fix that for you. You will continue to struggle in the future as much as you have in the past.

Things like Dev versus Ops silos, tech versus product silos, unclear reasoning behind technical decisions, and short-term thinking all build business, technical, and organizational debt. It clogs up your flywheel. Like gears grinding together, you'll struggle to build momentum.

But technology leaders cannot drive the business forward in isolation. We cannot do it *to* the business. Instead, the business and technology must combine their thinking and align their efforts to achieve *sustainable, long-term* success.

Every organization needs to navigate through the minefield that is the modern-day technology business. To do so, you will first need to build the energy necessary to propel this move, and you will need to distribute this energy, or power, to every part of the organization. This is your Value Flywheel Effect.

You will also need a map to help you navigate the rough waters ahead. But remember that the path isn't always the same; it is ever-changing. Every part of the organization must be able to see this map at all times to navigate change, and you must constantly adjust course based on challenges and opportunities that arise. Keep adjusting the map together to get where you want to go.

No one outside your business can create this energy or draw this map for you. This power, sense of direction, and ability to adapt must come from within. And they must come from the whole organization, not from the business or from IT, but cocreated together. Think of this as an expedition. There are specific patterns and beliefs that you should agree on for any quest—almost like a doctrine—that will enable you to move fast, move in the same direction, and avoid obstacles.

Over the last nearly three centuries, there have been three industrial revolutions that have significantly altered the shape of how we do business and live our lives. But the frequency and intensity of these transformations have only been accelerating. In just the last twenty years, software delivery methods have shifted from Lean to Agile to DevOps, legacy to digital to the cloud and serverless.

We are witnessing a paradigm shift in how we use technology and how we write software. Everything is possible, but the number of people who can unlock that potential is limited. We could instill fifty years of software experience into a single book; instead, we hope we have taught you a sensemaking system that will help you ask the right questions and focus on the right problems, so you don't waste time and effort solving problems that have already been solved.

Focus your energy on creating space for innovation instead of keeping the lights on. On joining forces between the business and technology instead of being adversaries. We hope this book has taught you a better way to integrate technology throughout your company and teams to create a competitive advantage, both in the modern cloud and for whatever transformation will come next.

AFTERWORD
HISTORY OF THE AUTHORS AND MAPPING

I never set out to write a book. I have Adrian Cockcroft to thank for pointing out to me that this book needed to be written. When we had that first conversation, I went for a few walks, had a think, and then broke my own rule and mapped by myself.

Once you learn Wardley Mapping, you see things in a way that you can never unsee. It's like you have a new subconscious that will instantly see through things and spot different patterns. I'm sure Simon Wardley is delighted that he has taught so many people how to see things that they can never unsee.

The original map of this book (in Figure A1) is untouched from March 2021. It was the obvious place to start. I often map to make sense of things, and this pattern just jumped out.

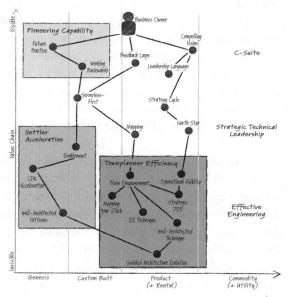

Figure A1: Wardley Map of The Value Flywheel Effect Book Concept

In the next six months, that map evolved into the map in Figure 19.1, which we call the "Space for Innovation" map. The four constituent parts of the Value Flywheel are there. The Town Planner Efficiency area in the original map evolved into Long-Term Value. We don't reinvent architecture rules; we refine them and commoditize them. The Settler Acceleration area became Next Best Action. Serverless and bias for action gel together. The industry is slowly realizing that good engineering teams can build very quickly, but we need to spend time figuring out the right thing to build (the product and engineering partnership is critical). The Pioneer Capability area became Clarity of Purpose—the differentiator. Only *you* know what this is, as it's your business, so you will benefit or suffer from the quality of decision-making.

Finally, mapping brings it all together—both the technique and the mindset (open to challenge). I would argue that the mindset and the willingness to accept challenge is more important than the mapping, but the Wardley Mapping technique is the best way that I have found to open up the conversation.

On reflection, I hope that you don't follow this book to the letter. Mark, Michael, and I (Dave) have spent decades figuring out a better way to write software. We don't build physical things, so we don't need precision plans. We build virtual capabilities on virtual infrastructure, so we iterate, evolve, learn, fail, and pivot. There is no best way, but there are better ways.

I hope you take away the mindset that we have created. It still blows my mind that many don't think like this. For me, serverless is the purest distillation of this mindset that we can use today—yet people still talk about functions versus containers and miss the point. I think serverless-first will change the industry, but it will take time. It may get a rebrand and mindsets will change. We need to leave the bravado of tech bros behind us and embrace a future of humanity, empathy, and curiosity.

Sustainability as a concept works on so many layers across this thinking, but I wanted to be respectful of the term as the environmental impact must be top of mind. There is also sustainability in how we run our teams (prevent burnout and reduce cognitive load) and sustainability in the business model—the Value Flywheel itself.

In 2022, it feels like we are entering another "dot com bubble burst" cycle of correction. Venture capitalists have been handing out funding like crazy, but more often than not, I see companies who do not have their flywheel turning. They have an imbalance in their technology strategy or their business model. It's not hard to spot. I have found that you can very quickly sketch out the Value Flywheel for a company based on their website. What skills are they hiring for? Can you map their market? Are they doing anything different? What's their quality of leadership? Sustainability approach? The weak signals are plain to see if you know how to look.

And never forget that code is liability—such a simple phrase with so much depth behind it. Are you building software applications or a system? Many engineers don't think in systems, and many leaders don't think of the sociotechnical system that contains their teams, their software, their customers, and their business. I hope that this book will change how you think about what you are building.

When I first spoke to IT Revolution, they said, "We don't work with authors. We work with practitioners." For a split second, I think they thought they had offended me. "No, no," was my reply."I'm happy to be a practitioner!"

Today, my current role is as a technical fellow with Bazaarvoice, a global commerce platform that supplies authentic user-generated content (UGC) to all manner of brands and consumers. We have all parts of the Value Flywheel, and it's interesting to apply the same thinking to increase momentum.

Mark and Michael are both architects with Globalization Partners, a service that enables companies to hire people anywhere in the world. Interestingly, both companies have a "multisided platform business model." The value proposition is making connections between two or more customer groups, which is enabled by software, or software as a service. The idea of a "multisided platform" is relatively new and is perfectly illustrated by the Value Flywheel Effect.

In short, we continue to test and prove our thinking in the wild, learn new things, and give back to the community. We are very aware that we are only at the beginning of this huge paradigm shift. For years I used the painting *The Great Wave at Kanagawa* by Hokusai to visualize the change that modern cloud or serverless and new business models are bringing. Guess what—the wave has broken, but waves are not singular. There are more coming, and I hope this book will help you ride these waves.

We are always interested in stories and learnings. Please reach out and say hello on Twitter @ServerlessEdge or online at TheServerlessEdge.com.

Thank you for reading. Onward and upward!

—David

USING THE VALUE FLYWHEEL EFFECT TO MOVE AN ORGANIZATION SERVERLESS

The following is a fictionalized representation of how an organization might use the Value Flywheel Effect to shift to a serverless-first strategy.

The Outage

Laura was under severe pressure. The app server had crashed again, right in the middle of the sales promotion. She had begun to hate Thanksgiving, the feeling of dread in the weeks before. Laura is the lead engineer, but this is too much even for her.

It's happened now . . .

As she grabbed a coffee on the way into the office, she knew what lay in store for the day ahead. Susan would be pragmatic, as always, but she would need to justify the crash—the VP of Sales would be giving her a hard time about. . . .

Of course, Rob would be delighted. He'd stayed up all night on Saturday and "saved the day." She still can't believe he deployed that fix—untested. It was pure cowboy stuff.

She had been on the phone with about twenty-five people for hours yesterday. It was so unnecessary. Any decent engineer knew this was a preventable problem. Rob hadn't been so active when they spent two months trying to get the new architecture approved.

Rob "The Glory" frustrated her to no end. Good engineers should *prevent* crashes from happening, not just react to them. Laura was still angry that the team had decided to take the safe option and patch up the old server. "It's never let us down before," they'd all said.

Well, there's a first for everything. It'll be a $1 million lesson.

The system had been down for twenty hours. They say a one-hour outage leads to $50,000 in lost sales. With their global audience and promotion in play, that figure was probably conservative. The first rule of software development was reliability. The system must be available and processing sales. We can't lose customers due to tech faults.

As Laura came out of the elevator, she overheard a few people talking.

"Rob is on fire. That guy is a genius," a voice said.

"I heard he stayed up all night!" another said.

Ugh. It was going to be a long day. How could the team unlearn this behavior? Something Laura had read about last week came back to her: a blameless postmortem. This article had said that an organization should create an environment of psychological safety and use data to learn why an error occurred and prevent it from happening again. It sounded great—but there was no chance of that happening in Laura's company, surely.

The "lessons learned" meeting was starting in ten minutes. Laura was sure it would be more like *Game of Thrones*. At least Susan would be there. Laura thought Susan was a brilliant leader and a great CTO.

As Laura predicted, the meeting ended up being ugly. At one point, the eye of Sauron (Rob) turned to poor Clive. Rob had been on a roll and started to imply that Clive, one of the strongest cloud engineers they had, hadn't tested the database load correctly. No one had the data at hand, and for around five minutes the meeting had turned into "I told you so." and "What are you implying by that?" Playground stuff. Thank goodness Susan stepped in and parked that topic.

The Way Forward

Later that afternoon, Laura and Clive sat down to look at the data. In addition to being a great cloud engineer, he was super disciplined.

"Why do we even do architecture spikes?" asked Laura.

"I know, that last one was a disaster," sighed Clive. "We are so locked into SAFe, and this idea of an architectural runway is killing us."

"Totally. I feel like it takes me six weeks to justify a two-week effort. If you gave me eight weeks, this outage would never have happened. I spend so much time in stupid meetings and 'updating the board' that I can't get to my actual work. It's a circus," said Laura as she scrolled through the data.

They all disliked the "Agile Theater" that was going on. But with one hundred people on the SAFe train, they both knew nothing was happening fast.

Laura turned to Clive. "Listen, we mapped this out last month. We need to take the observations from that map and execute. This wouldn't have happened if we'd done this a month ago."

"You have a point. But the SAFe train will never prioritize this work. Well, they might now, after the outage—but can we wait another six weeks until the next planning session?"

"Nope!" replied Laura.

"We're not working at a sustainable pace. It's all gut feel and chest-beating. I sense a window of opportunity." Clive scratched his head, thinking. He scrunched his face up for a minute and said, "Shall we go talk to Susan?"

Laura said, "You took your time. Let's go."

Two days later, Laura wandered over to Clive, who was sitting deep in thought at his desk, staring into space. "Ground control to Major Tom," sang Laura.

"What! Sorry, I zoned out," said Clive, snapping back to attention. He started laughing. "I still can't believe what you said to Susan the other day!"

Laura smiled. "Well, Susan, being the CTO, is the smartest person I've ever met. No point in sugar-coating any of this. She already knows. We've mapped it out. We know what needs to be done."

Clive rolled his eyes. "I know, but I thought she was going to throw us out. I've never heard anyone talk to an exec like that before."

"Really?" Laura replied. "I was just being honest. We lost about a million dollars last weekend; I didn't think she'd be in the mood for a load of PowerPoint slides. I just said we need to dump this useless platform ASAP and go serverless. It's a dead dog."

"But she designed the whole thing. It's her pride and joy!" exclaimed Clive.

"The architectural approach is still solid, but the platform is letting us down. We're just evolving the system to a serverless solution. It's saving the day," Laura said. She tried to sound confident, but in truth, she was starting to get a little nervous.

The only thing more nerve-racking than making a big pitch was having that pitch accepted. They had spent a long time talking about this new approach months back, but they only had a short time to try it. They had made mistakes, and it made people nervous. Everyone reverted to a safe place. Laura had been nervous at the time, but everyone agreed that they didn't have time to replace the old system.

Looking back, she knew she should have argued her case harder. Well, it was a different ball game now. The system had crashed during Thanksgiving, and they had, at most, three weeks before the big sales season ramped up again. At least they had completed all the preparation work back then; it's just a matter of dusting it off and making it happen. On the plus side, she had the full backing of the CTO and leadership; on the flip side—the engineers were a little nervous.

The Meeting

The meeting to kick off the work started at 2:00 that afternoon. Laura decided to go to lunch with Clive and Rob before the meeting. They laughed at the phrase "go to lunch."

"You mean, don't eat lunch at your desk," said Rob. It had been so crazy these past six months, even sitting in the office kitchen felt different. Laura couldn't remember the last time they went out of the office for lunch. The group disagreed about minor technical details almost daily, but they had been friends for many years and usually looked out for each other. They felt bad that things had gotten so bad on Monday, so they decided to sync up. It must have looked like they couldn't stand each other from outside engineering, but they all loved the to and fro of a technical discussion. To the uninitiated, it sounded like they were arguing—they viewed it as violent disagreement!

After some chit-chat, Laura cleared the air. "Listen, folks, I know we like to sweat the small stuff, but this is serious now. We have one shot at this. I've been through this before. If we can get started, we can stabilize this mess and get back to normal. We're all sick of the constant patching and firefighting."

"One hundred percent agree," said Rob, "I'm sorry for throwing you under the bus on Monday; I was exhausted after the weekend. Small kids and staying up all night are a bad combination. Clive, I just wasn't thinking."

"No problem, man. I trust Laura. She's the lead engineer, and I'm glad we can finally move on this serverless approach," said Clive.

Laura was strangely calm at the start of the meeting. Susan had decided to join, along with a few other engineering leaders and the engineers that would work on this project. There was an air of anticipation in the room. Monday's frustrations had died down a little.

Laura opened the call to welcome their remote engineers. "Can everyone on the call hear me? We have a mixed audience today, so let's keep it remote first. Speak into a mic and please be respectful of the person talking," Laura started. "Oh, sorry, Susan—would you like to kick off?" Laura offered.

"Oh! Please, Laura—you've got this. I'm happy to listen in," Susan responded. "I'm fully behind the plan. I'm keen to listen in, support, and don't be afraid to assign me some work! This is important."

"Great," replied Laura. "I doubt we'll need you to write any code, but we will need some air cover. And you might have to help us bump a few things up on the priority list."

Laura leaned in toward the microphone. "I know we had this conversation a few months back, and it wasn't the right time. Since last weekend's outage, we need to do something. There's no point going over old ground, but we need to move quickly. You all know that my last company had a mature serverless stack. I've worked out a robust plan for us. We have all been working in the cloud for a few years now, so we have the skills despite what you might feel. This is not an overly aggressive plan, but we need to execute and move quickly." Laura paused, took a breath, and scanned the room and remote attendees.

"The goal for the last six months was to get a 50% increase on last year's sales. We're getting the traffic, but the system is letting us down. I think we have all been having informal conversations about adding a stability metric to that. I suggest 50% increase with three nines availability, that's 99.9%, and a goal for every checkout to complete within three seconds.

"We know that the problem area in the site is the catalog, so we can quickly replatform that and hopefully hit our targets at the same time. I calculate this replatform will give us enough extra capacity to get through the holiday season. We have two immediate tasks.

"One, we need to turn that goal into an SLO, that's a service-level objective—including the infrastructure and dashboards needed to make it real. Two, we need to start the replatform today. We've already done the groundwork, so we just need to pull the trigger. I know that was a lot of information, so any questions before we get into the details?"

Laura stopped for a breath and looked over at Susan. She was nodding. A good sign!

Clive cleared his throat and looked around the room. "Well, I've already started some of the SLO work, so I'd be happy to take a small team and flesh that out. It needs to happen anyway, so what you've suggested is perfect. We just need to double-check it, as we'll have everyone watching that number now."

"Thanks, Clive," Susan said.

"What about the deployment pipeline?" Rob asked. "I like the plan, but that thing is way too complex for what it's doing. I'm worried about adding in extra."

"Yes," replied Laura, "we're going to get to that, and you are correct. I think we can look at CodeDeploy. Susan has offered to help get that pushed through, as it will simplify deployment. It might even be the start of general simplification of our deployment pipelines."

Susan nodded her head. "Yes, I'll help the team get that put in place quickly. We'll have to prioritize the security checks, but the CISO is aware of this. Laura will take the lead on this, but I think it's the right time to modernize."

"Okay, now down to details…." Laura started to sketch out the design they had created a few months back. She was relieved. It was a good design, and it would take some load off the old system.

The Quick Part

The next day, Laura came in a little early, grabbed a coffee as usual, and was happy to have a little space to think things out. She had been at the company a year now, and it certainly was a case of much done, much to do. In her last role, they had a very mature serverless approach. Her current company had mature cloud practices, but they had held back pushing toward serverless. It was the one thing Susan had warned her about when she first joined. Those words certainly rang true now.

"We have a big opportunity here, but it's a matter of timing."

Migrations like this are never about technology; it's about the will of the people to change. Susan was super smart. She knew they had to prepare for a full push on serverless, but she also knew she needed a flag to rally everyone. Laura sighed. They certainly had a rallying cry, but an outage on Thanksgiving weekend is probably the most stressful rallying cry possible.

Laura grabbed a pencil. She knew what needed to happen but felt the need to draw it properly. It would be easier to visualize it.

She sketched up the topology in AWS. At least everything was in a right-sized account, and the security model was good—that was a big help. That piece of the migration was tough, but it's done now. The application is split up into microservices, which is also good, but they don't have the database designs correct. That was the choke point. The system was fine, but they'd overloaded the database with reading catalog information while writing sales orders. She relaxed as she sketched out the different components. This wasn't complicated at all.

Then she added a new deployment pipeline. They'll create a low-friction pipeline so engineers can deploy instantly. The catalog is constantly changing, so the team could be super responsive here. They'll grab a few CDK Patterns for APIs, observability, and a simple GraphQL service. They could plug these together today, automate the deployment via CodeDeploy, and create a basic dashboard. This will all be serverless, so it'll scale as needed. She had insisted they use metadata in the user interface to make this replacement easy. A quick calculation predicted that this would take 42% of the load away from the database. But that would need to be measured.

The next part would be a little trickier. They would wrap a step function flow around the ordering mechanism. This would closely track orders and ensure they could recover if the system failed. There was talk of writing this in a custom state machine. Crazy talk. Serverless-managed services was the way to go—she could wire this up in fifteen minutes and there'd be nothing more to be said on the matter. . . .

Laura sat back and admired her diagram. Yes, this made the endeavor much clearer. She grabbed the paper and her laptop to show Susan.

The Slow Part

Three weeks later, Laura and Susan went out for lunch. "It's nice to be out of the office," Laura said.

"Headspace!" joked Susan.

They both knew that the serverless effort had gone well. As predicted, it had been quick to implement and worked like a dream. Performance and stability were even better than expected.

Susan started talking about the next phase. "Let's wait until the new year, but I'm going to bring in the Well-Architected Frameworks and start building a sense of pride back into the engineering teams. As we start to move the rest of the architecture to serverless, I want teams to measure their efforts and celebrate the gains they're making. I'm not going to beat teams up, but they will gain a lot of confidence as they realize these improvements. Now that we have proved it in one place, it'll spread like wildfire."

"Yes, and it's critical that we enable the teams. They know this works, so we need to get out of the way and into the background, ensure they have everything they need," replied Laura.

A year later, no one was worried about Thanksgiving. The sales figures had increased by a further 62%, and the system's stability was incredible. The sales team decided to reduce the price of the bestseller on Black Friday, so they did it during the sale! This was unheard of. Improve time to value, they kept saying. Let's not quit while we're ahead. It's the Value Flywheel Effect.

BIBLIOGRAPHY

Amazon. "Press Release: Announcing Amazon Kindle." Amazon (November 19, 2007). https://press.aboutamazon.com/news-releases/news-release-details/introducing-amazon-kindle.

"AWS Serverless-First Function | Day 1 | Dr. Werner Vogels." Video, 14:18. Posted by AWS. https://www.twitch.tv/videos/639294277.

Bryar, Colin, and Bill Carr. *Working Backwards: Insights, Stories, and Secrets from Inside Amazon.* New York: St Martin's Press, 2021.

Christensen, Clayton M., Scott Cook, and Taddy Hall. "What Customers Want from Your Products," Harvard Business School (January 16, 2006). https://hbswk.hbs.edu/item/5170.html.

"Clay Christensen: The Jobs to be Done Theory." YouTube video, 7:09. Posted by HubSpot Marketing, November 8, 2009. https://www.youtube.com/watch?v=StcObeAxavY.

Clear, James. *Atomic Habits: An Easy and Proven Way to Build Good Habits and Break Bad Ones.* New York: Avery, 2018.

Collins, Jim. "The Flywheel Effect." JimCollins.com. Accessed May 23, 2022. https://www.jimcollins.com/concepts/the-flywheel.html.

"Complex Adaptive Systems." Human Systems Dynamics Institute. Accessed May 23, 2022. https://www.hsdinstitute.org/resources/complex-adaptive-system.html.

Cutler, John, and Jason Scherschligt. *North Star Playbook: The Guide to Discovering Your Product's North Star.* Amplitude. Accessed May 23, 2022. https://amplitude.com/north-star.

Doshi, Shreyas (@shreyas). "There are 3 levels to product work (1) The Execution level (2) The Impact level (3) The Optics level When an individual & their team are fixated on different levels, often there is conflict . . ." Twitter post, March 11, 2021. https://twitter.com/shreyas/status/1370248637842812936?lang=en.

Edmonson, Amy C. *The Fearless Organization: Creating Psychological Safety in the Workplace for Learning, Innovation, and Growth*. Hoboken, NJ: Wiley, 2019.

Emery, F. E., and E. L. Trist. "The Causal Texture of Organizational Environments." *Human Relations* 18, no.1 (February 1965): 21–32.

Forsgren, Nicole, Jez Humble, Gene Kim. *Accelerate: The Science of Lean Software and DevOps: Building and Scaling High Performing Technology Organizations*. Portland, OR: IT Revolution, 2018.

Fowler, Martin. "DomainDrivenDesign." MartinFowler.com. April 22, 2020. https:// martinfowler.com/bliki/DomainDrivenDesign.html#:~:text=Domain%2D Driven%20Design%20is%20an,through%20a%20catalog%20of%20patterns.

Gall, John. *Systemantics: How Systems Really Work and How They Fail*. Quadrangle, 1977.

Gothelf, Jeff. *Sense and Respond: How Successful Organizations Listen to Customers and Create New Products Continuously*. Boston, MA: Harvard Business Review Press, 2017.

Grasso, Cattie. "The Amazon Flywheel Explained: Learn From Bezos' Business Strategy." Feedvisor.com. January 15, 2020. https://feedvisor.com/resources /amazon-trends/amazon-flywheel-explained/.

Hohpe, Gregor. *The Software Architect Elevator: Redefining the Architect's Role in the Digital Enterprise*. Boston, MA: O'Reilly, 2020.

"Impact Mapping." ImpactMapping.org. Accessed May 23, 2022. https://www.impact mapping.org/.

"In Quotes: Apple's Steve Jobs." *BBC News*. October 6, 2011. https://www.bbc.com /news/world-us-canada-15195448.

Jacobs, Justin. "Carbon Is Now a Buzzword on Corporate Earnings Calls." *Financial Times*. May 16, 2021. https://www.ft.com/content/88e9e51d-b9c7 -4f0e-873f-6fa06afc13f3.

Kehoe, Ben. "Serverless Is a State of Mind." Medium.com. March 17, 2019. https:// ben11kehoe.medium.com/.

Kersten, Mik. *Project to Product: How to Survive and Thrive in the Age of Digital Disruption with the Flow Framework*. Portland, OR: IT Revolution Press, 2018.

Kroonenburg, Sam. "Back from the Future: Learnings from Three Years of Serverless." A Cloud Guru. Posted September 12, 2018. https://learn.acloud.guru /series/serverlessconf-sf-2018/view/6c7c00f8-3183-db34-83fc-f8931e070da5.

Lutkevich, Ben. "System Thinking." TechTarget.com. August 2020. https://www .techtarget.com/searchcio/definition/systems-thinking#:~:text=Systems%20 thinking%20is%20a%20holistic,the%20context%20of%20larger%20systems.

"Leadership." LearnWardleyMapping.com. Accessed May 24, 2022. https://learn wardleymapping.com/leadership/.

Mazzucato, Mariana. *Mission Economy: A Moonshot Guide to Changing Capitalism*. New York: Harper Collins, 2021.

McChesney, Chris, Sean Covey, and Jim Huling. *The 4 Disciplines of Execution: Revised and Updated: Achieving Your Wildly Important Goals*. New York: Simon & Schuster, 2012.

"Microsoft Security Development Lifecycle." Microsoft.com. Accessed May 23, 2022. https://www.microsoft.com/en-us/securityengineering/sdl/.

North, Dan. "Software That Fits in Your Head." Presentation at the GoTo Conference 2016. https://www.programmingtalks.org/talk/software-that-fits-in-your-head.

O'Hanlon, Charlene. "A Conversation with Werner Vogels: Learning from the Amazon Technology Platform." *acmqueue* 4, no. 4. May 2006. https://dl.acm.org/doi/10.1145/1142055.1142065.

"Opportunity Solution Tree." ProductPlan.com. Accessed May 23, 2022. https://www.productplan.com/glossary/opportunity-solution-tree/.

Pierri, Melissa. *Escaping the Build Trap: How Effective Product Management Creates Real Value*. Boston, MA: O'Reilly, 2019.

Pink, Daniel H. *Drive: The Surprising Truth about What Motivates Us*. New York: Penguin, 2009.

Rocco, John. *How We Got to the Moon: The People, Technology, and Daring Feats of Science Behind Humanity's Greatest Adventure*. New York: Crown Books for Young Readers, 2020.

Schwab, Klaus. "The Fourth Industrial Revolution: What It Means, How to Respond." World Economic Forum. January 14, 2016. https://www.weforum.org/agenda/2016/01/the-fourth-industrial-revolution-what-it-means-and-how-to-respond/.

Sinek, Simon. *Start with Why: How Great Leaders Inspire Everyone to Take Action*. New York: Portfolio Books, 2009.

Skelton, Matthew, and Manuel Pais. *Team Topologies: Organizing Business and Technology Teams for Fast Flow*. Portland, OR: IT Revolution Press, 2019.

Smallwood, Norm, and Dave Ulrich. "Capitalizing on Capabilities." *Harvard Business Review*. June 2004. https://hbr.org/2004/06/capitalizing-on-capabilities.

Smart, Jonathan, Zsolt Berend, Myles Ogilvie, and Simon Rohrer. *Sooner Safer Happier: Antipatterns and Patterns for Business Agility*. Portland, OR: IT Revolution Press, 2020.

Snowden, David. "The Cynefin Framework." TheCynefin.com. Accessed May 2022. https://thecynefin.co/about-us/about-cynefin-framework/.

Swan, Chris. "Simon Wardley on the Cloud Landscape." *InfoQ*. Full transcript from the 2014 QCon interview with Simon Wardley. 2014. https://www.infoq.com/interviews/Cloud-Landscape-Simon-Wardley/.

Tune, Nick. "Outside-In Domain Landscape." Medium.com. May 3, 2021. https://medium.com/nick-tune-tech-strategy-blog/outside-in-domain-landscape-discovery-3ec88aeb70db.

Vettor, Robert, and Steve "Ardalis" Smith. *Architecting Cloud-Native .NET Apps for Azure*. Redmond, WA: Microsoft, 2022. https://docs.microsoft.com/en-us/dotnet/architecture/cloud-native/definition.

Wardley, Simon (@swardley). "The proverbial shit will hit the fan however when a two-person company that produces a single function that everyone uses gets acquired for $1Bn. It's only a matter of years." Twitter post. February 16, 2018. https://twitter.com/swardley/status/964650519431172098.

Weiss, Todd R. "How Liberty Mutual Is Transforming Its IT Using Serverless Computing." TechRepublic. July 14, 2020. https://www.techrepublic.com/article/how-liberty-mutual-is-transforming-its-it-using-serverless-computing/

Weinberg, Gerald M. *The Secrets of Consulting: A Guide to Giving and Getting Advice Successfully*. Gerald M. Weinberg, 2011.

"Welcome to Domain-Driven Design." GitHub.com. Accessed May 24, 2022. https://github.com/ddd-crew/welcome-to-ddd.

Willink, Jocko, and Leif Babin. *Extreme Ownership: How US Navy Seals Lead & Win*. New York: St. Martin's Press, 2015.

NOTES

Foreword: Adrian Cockcroft

1. O'Hanlon, "A Converstion with Werner Vogels."

Introduction

1. Rocco, *How We Got to the Moon*, 113.
2. Sinek, *Start with Why*.
3. Weiss, "How Liberty Mutual Is Transforming."
4. "AWS Serverless-First Function | Day 1 | Dr. Werner Vogels."
5. Forsgren, Humble, and Kim, *Accelerate*.
6. North, "Software That Fits in Your Head."
7. Schwab, "The Fourth Industrial Revolution."
8. Schwab, "The Fourth Industrial Revolution."
9. Schwab, "The Fourth Industrial Revolution."
10. Schwab, "The Fourth Industrial Revolution."
11. Schwab, "The Fourth Industrial Revolution."

Chapter 1

1. Clear, *Atomic Habits*.
2. Grasso, "The Amazon Flywheel Explained."
3. Collins, "The Flywheel Effect."

Chapter 5

1. Cutler and Scherschligt, *North Star Playbook*, Chapter 2.

2. Cutler and Scherschligt, *North Star Playbook*, Chapter 3.

3. Impact Mapping, ImpactMapping.org.

4. "Opportunity Solution Tree," ProductPlan.com.

5. "Opportunity Solution Tree," ProductPlan.com.

6. McChesney, Covey, and Huling, *The 4 Disciplines of Execution*.

7. Swan, "Simon Wardley on the Cloud Landscape."

8. Willink and Babin, *Extreme Ownership*, 183–184.

9. Bryar and Carr, *Working Backwards*.

10. Amazon, "Press Release: Announcing Amazon Kindle."

Chapter 7

1. Christensen, Cook, and Hall, "What Customers Want from Your Products."

2. "Clay Christensen: The Jobs to be Done Theory."

Chapter 8

1. Wardley (@swardley), "The proverbial shit will hit the fan . . ."

2. Kroonenburg, "Back from the Future."

3. Personal correspondence with the authors, June 2021.

4. Personal correspondence with the authors, 2022.

Chapter 9

1. Skelton and Pais, *Team Topologies*.

2. Doshi (@shreyas), "There are 3 levels to product work . . ."

3. Kersten, *Project to Product*.

4. Edmonson, *The Fearless Organization*.

5. Forsgren, Humble, and Kim, *Accelerate*, 32.

Chapter 10

1. Hohpe, *The Software Architect Elevator*, xiii.

2. Gothelf, *Sense and Respond*.

3. Smart, Berend, Ogilvie, and Rohrer, *Sooner Safer Happier*.

4. Emery and Trist, "The Causal Texture of Organizational Environments."

5. Pink, *Drive*, Chapter 1.

6. Snowden, "The Cynefin Framework."

7. "Complex Adaptive Systems," Human Systems Dynamics Institute.

8. Snowden, "The Cynefin Framework."

Chapter 11

1. Smallwood and Ulrich, "Capitalizing on Capabilities."

2. "Microsoft Security Development Lifecycle," Microsoft.com.

3. Vettor and Smith, *Architecting Cloud-Native .NET Apps for Azure.*

Chapter 13

1. Kehoe, "Serverless Is a State of Mind."

Chapter 14

1. Skelton and Pais, *Team Topologies*, Chapter 5.

2. Pink, *Drive*, Part 2.

3. Forsgren, Humble, and Kim, *Accelerate*, Chapter 2.

Chapter 16

1. "AWS Serverless-First Function | Day 1 | Dr. Werner Vogels."

Chapter 17

1. Pierri, *Escaping the Build Trap*, Introduction.

2. Clear, *Atomic Habits*, Chapter 1.

Chapter 18

1. Mazzucato, *Mission Economy*, Chapter 1.

2. "Welcome to Domain-Driven Design," GitHub.com.

3. Fowler, "DomainDrivenDesign."

4. Lutkevich, "System Thinking."

5. Tune, "Outside-In Domain Landscape."

6. Jacobs, "Carbon Is Now a Buzzword . . ."

Chapter 20

1. "In Quotes: Apple's Steve Jobs," BBC News.
2. Gall, *Systemantics*, 71.

Conclusion

1. Weinberg, *The Secrets of Consulting*, Chapter 1.
2. Weinberg, *The Secrets of Consulting*, Chapter 4.

INDEX

ACKNOWLEDGMENTS

I remember writing an "art of the possible" document in 2015 and finishing it with a cheeky one-liner: "...and then I'll write the book." I'm so thankful to everyone for being part of this journey.

Treasa (my partner) and I have had countless discussions about the worlds of business and technology over more than twenty years. We have observed the opportunities and challenges of business and technology moving closer and merging. Mark, Michael, Treasa, and I decided to create The Serverless Edge (TheServerlessEdge.com) to capture our thoughts and ideas. It became a blog, a podcast, this book, and a meeting of minds. I am incredibly grateful for our partnership. They are the most insightful people I have ever worked with.

I would also like to thank Adrian Cockcroft for his support, his belief, and for politely telling me that this book needed to be written and that now was the time. Simon Wardley has also been generous with his time, advice, and friendship. Two people who are so brilliant and modest—true visionaries.

I would also like to thank those who helped with peer review, reviewing early concepts and providing fantastic feedback, including Adrian, Simon, Treasa, Seamus Cushley, Ajay Nair, Gregor Hohpe, Manuel Pais, Sam Dengler, and Gene Kim.

I think case studies are so important, and I'm so happy for the ones we included in this book. Thanks to Matthew Clark (BBC), Gillian McCann, Brett Caldon, and Troy Campano (Workgrid), Pete Sbarski, Drew Firment, Ryan Kroonenburg, and Sam Kroonenburg (A Cloud Guru), John Heveran, Justin Strone, and Liz Pollock (Liberty Mutual). I'd like to give credit to Liz Pollock for taking a bet on a bunch of crazy ideas a few years ago. A bold move for a visionary PR team!

The work that the authors and I did spanned many years with many teams. I'd like to thank all the teams that "came with us" on our tech strategies. Sometimes it's a pain to take that leap, and it seems like extra work, but I hope many engineers have grown from it. Specifically, I'd like to thank "the Belfast Mappers Meetup": Mark, Mike, Ben Steele, Keith Annette, and Matt Coulter. Gillian McCann requires special mention as she has always been three steps ahead of everyone else and will always have total clarity on "what's next." And a warm and heartfelt thank you to some of the Liberty Mutual leaders who helped and supported me personally, including John McKenna, Ed Carmody, Steve Brand, Gary DeGrutola, John Heveran, Justin Stone, Brenda Campbell, and Kostas Kouiroukidis (he was the AWS Account Exec and moved mountains for the team and I).

I have been part of the DevOps Enterprise Summit community and, before that, a reader of IT Revolution books long before I started this project. I can't describe how happy I was after that first call with Gene Kim and Anna Noak. I was already a superfan, but working with Gene Kim, Margueritte Kim, Anna Noak, and Leah Brown has been incredible. Both Anna and Leah are such talented editors. Along with the extended IT Revolution team, they are a joy to work with.

I'd like to thank Jim Collins, author of *Good to Great* (among many other books), for creating "the flywheel effect" concept that was part of the inspiration for this book. There are a small number of visionary thinkers who are laying the foundation for the next generation. Jim is one of them. I would highly recommend his site as a starting point (JimCollins.com).

As with any work, we stand on the shoulders of giants. There are too many to name, but here are a few of our inspirations. Thank you for all that you do: Amy C. Edmondson, Barry O'Reilly, Ben Mosior, Dr. Carlota Perez, Carol Dweck, Dan North, Dan Pink, Dan Ward, Diana Larsen, Ed Catmull, Gerald Weinberg, Grady Booch, Gregor Hohpe, Henrik Kniberg, Jim Collins, Jocko Willink, John Cutler, Jonathan Allen, L. David Marquet, Linda Rising, Mariana Mazzucato, Martin Fowler, Marty Cagan, Matt Wynne, Melissa Perri, Nick Tune, Ray Dalio, Scott Ambler, Seth Godin, Stephen Orban, Simon Sinek, Teresa Torres, and Thomas Blood. Also, all the IT Revolution authors and the DevOps Enterprise Summit community, specifically Dr. Nicole Forsgren, Matthew Skelton and Manuel Pais from *Team Topologies*, Jez Humble, Mark Schwartz, Dr. Mik Kersten, and Gene Kim.

In closing, I'd like to thank two very special people. First, my computer science teacher, Mr (Norman) Downey, who told me (and the class) when I was sixteen, "Show me the person who knows everything, and I'll show you the fool." His brilliance for computer science, his stubborn declarations that CS hasn't changed since the 1960s, and his intolerance for stupidity have never left me.

Second, my Dad, Gerry, who recognized a spark in me and bought me my first computer (ZX Spectrum 48K) in 1982. He shared his thirst for knowledge and constant curious mindset (before it was a thing) with me. Plus, he spoke to all the computer science teachers when I was in primary school and advised me which teacher was the best option. When I was eleven he said, "I don't know anything about computers, but that guy is the smartest, so I'd learn from him. So, what do you want to do?" My dad always took the time to "see what you think".

ABOUT THE AUTHORS

David Anderson has been at the leading edge of the technology industry for twenty-five years. Starting as a software engineer in leading telecom companies (including Three, Nokia, and Ericsson), David moved to Liberty Mutual in 2007 and continued to drive technology change and raise engineering standards. As Director of Technology, David had exposure to a wide range of technologies and techniques covering Architecture, Software Development, Leadership, AI/Analytics, and Cybersecurity. David was involved in the early phases of public-cloud adoption at Liberty Mutual in 2013 and continued to drive the change. Creating the Serverless-First Strategy in 2016, he was able to achieve significant, multimillion-dollar business results, create a new, industry-leading engineering standard within Liberty Mutual, and lead a generation of architects to become cloud leaders. David is also a member of the Wardley Mapping community and has been involved in many efforts, discussions, and sessions/research groups to further this strategic approach.

In 2021, David parted from Liberty Mutual to explore the serverless-first journey across the industry and joined Bazaarvoice as Technical Fellow. The Serverless Edge was formed to collate some of this thinking, and he continues to work with clients and partners to prove out the thinking in this book. The Serverless Edge team are on Twitter @serverlessedge and LinkedIn @the-serverless-edge. David can be found on Twitter @davidand393 and LinkedIn @david-anderson-belfast.

Mark McCann is a cloud architect and leader focused on enabling organizations and their teams to rapidly deliver business value through well-architected, sustainable, serverless-first solutions. Mark joined Liberty Mutual as a graduate in 2000, enjoying a twenty-one-year career rising to senior architect. Mark was heavily involved with Liberty Mutual's journey to the cloud, with a strong focus on adoption of serverless-first, the Well-Architected Framework, engineering excellence, and enabling teams to improve their time to value. Mark leverages Wardley Mapping to bring situational awareness to people, teams, and organizations, and to help them evolve and deliver sustainable, long-term value. Mark lives in Belfast, Ireland, works as a software architect with Globalization Partners, and writes for The Serverless Edge. Mark can be found on Twitter @MarkMcCann and LinkedIn @markedwardmccann.

Michael O'Reilly is a software architect who specializes in arming organizations with the ability to develop ideas into world-class products by leveraging the capabilities of the modern cloud. Since 2005, Michael has devoted his career to enterprise application and service development. He was part of the team that led Liberty Mutual's foray into the world of eCommerce, building out their main online insurance product set. Being a progressive thinker, Michael became an active leader in Liberty Mutual's transition to the cloud. He has become specialized in leading teams and the C-suite into modern cloud product development through sustainable approaches and practices guided by serverless-first and the Well-Architected Framework. Michael continues to help organizations embrace the modern cloud as a software architect with Globalization Partners and as a contributor to The Serverless Edge. Michael can be found on Twitter @bigheadoreilly and LinkedIn @michael-o-reilly.